# STALIN'S LIEUTENANTS

# STALIN'S LIEUTENANTS

A STUDY OF COMMAND UNDER DURESS

## WILLIAM J. SPAHR

★

PRESIDIO

Published by Presidio Press
505 B San Marin Drive, Suite 300
Novato, CA 94945-1340

**Library of Congress Cataloging-in-Publication Data**

Spahr's, William J., 1921–
    Stalin's lieutenants : a study of command under duress / William
J. Spahr.
        p.   cm.
    Includes bibliographical references.
    ISBN 0-89141-564-5 (hardcover)
    1. Stalin, Joseph, 1879–1953—Military leadership.  2. Soviet
Union—History, Military.  3. Soviet Union—Armed Forces—
Officers. I. title.
DK34.S67   1997
947.084'2—dc21                              97-12329
                                            CIP

Printed in the United States of America

*In memory of Nikolai Nikolaevich Iakovlev
and a friendship that ended too soon.*

*There never were such men in an Army before. They will go anywhere and do anything if properly led. But there is the difficulty—proper commanders—where can they be obtained?*

—Robert E. Lee, letter to John B. Hood 21 May
1863, cited in Lee's Lieutenants vol. 1, p. xvii


*Bonaparte always chose his marshals on the eclectic principle. Whenever he found one great quality he laid it under contribution. The great error, even with sensible men is, they bring everyone to a single standard and judge him by a simple rule.*

—Napoleon and His Marshals, J. T.
Headly, New York: Baker and Scribner, 1846, p. 177

# CONTENTS

# ACKNOWLEDGMENTS

An unfortunate accident (a fractured left hip) occurred as the last pages of this book were being written. The event placed an extra burden on my family and friends, causing me to call on them for even more help than usual. And they all came through, in some cases meeting my almost impossible requests. My wife, Barbara, in addition to serving as chief practical nurse on twenty-four hour, seven days a week duty, proofread and improved the text. My son David assisted me in countless ways. William Bryson was always available to solve problems for a computer illiterate. Bob Tarleton provided invaluable bibliographic help and source material. Bill and Harriet Scott were always ready to look into their unequaled library of Soviet reference materials to answer questions and furnish citations. David Murphy was vigilant for pertinent information uncovered in the course of his own research.

The photographs were supplied by Era and Ella Zhukova and through the courtesy of Counselor Natalia P. Semenikhina of the Russian Embassy in Washington, DC. The maps on pages 221 and 235 are based on maps found on pages 115 and 116 of Martin Gilbert, Atlas of Russian History, second edition, New York: Oxford University Press, 1993.

# INTRODUCTION

This work patterns a study of the Soviet high command under Stalin on Douglas Southall Freeman's monumental study of the leadership of the Confederate Army of Northern Virginia during the American Civil War. Freeman's *Lee's Lieutenants: A Study in Command* was published in three volumes in 1942–44. His purpose was to ensure that at least a score of able officers, who had fought under the command of Robert E. Lee and added to his fame, would not be forgotten. After Freeman completed his biography of Lee in 1934, he spent two years considering writing a biography of a soldier of "an earlier period." In the end he decided that he could not leave the period about which he had been writing for more than twenty years. As if to reinforce his decision to continue to write about the Civil War, Freeman observed that so modest a man as Lee would have lamented any presentation of his own services that might depreciate, even by silence, those of his comrades in arms.

Similarly, after completing a biography of Marshal Zhukov, Stalin's ablest military lieutenant, and after considering other projects, I concluded that there were commanders other than Zhukov whose service to the Soviet Army in World War II should be reexamined, especially under the light of glasnost (openness). Unlike Lee, Stalin was never seen on the front lines during the war, but it is safe to say that every Soviet soldier and officer knew who was in overall command of the Soviet Army. Stalin also differed from Lee in that he was not afflicted with the character trait of true modesty. It would not have bothered Stalin if his subordinates were forgotten. In his dress and public conduct, he made a pretense of being a simple man of the people, but he seldom discouraged his sycophants from lauding his military genius, and he considered the attention given Zhukov a personal affront. Of course, Stalin employed the traditional incentives to successful military performance: promotions, decorations, pay differentials, and perquisites. But whatever the awards and however they were given, they had to be somehow acknowledged by the recipient as being due to Stalin's inspiring leadership. Those who did not understand that unvoiced proviso became the targets of those around Stalin whose position and existence depended on their ability to appease the dictator's megalomania.

Freeman, searching for an organizing principle for his work, looked for alternatives to writing a series of separate articles on selected individual officers that would merely duplicate existing studies. He chose to focus on Lee's search for proper commanders. Taking a hint from a letter of Lee's (dated 21 May 1863), a portion of which is in the epigraph, Freeman decided to review the command of the Army of Northern Virginia rather than write a history of the army itself.

Stalin, for completely different reasons, was also searching for commanders; his purges of 1937 and 1938 had decimated the Soviet high command. The military actions that the Soviet Army had undertaken in the interval between 1938 and 1941 had produced two promising leaders: Georgii Konstantinovich Zhukov had demonstrated his fitness for high command in expelling the Japanese from Mongolia at Halhin Gol; Semen Konstantinovich Timoshenko had turned the disastrous start of the Winter War with Finland into a victory. But the leaders needed to defend the long western front were largely untried. The troops, if properly led, would go anywhere and do anything. Who would lead them?

Douglas Southall Freeman subtitled his work *A Study in Command.* For those serving under Stalin, the words "under duress" had to be added. Stalin's lieutenants knew that their performance was under continuous observation not only by their commander in chief but also by the political representatives of the Communist Party of the Soviet Union who were present at all command echelons. In the large units—the *fronts* and armies—these political officers were afforded communications that enabled them to report through the next higher levels of command to the main political directorate in Moscow, which had easy access to the paranoid dictator. The generals and the marshals were also under the watchful eyes of the People's Commissariat of Internal Affairs (NKVD), who were represented at all levels of command ostensibly to guard against espionage, sabotage, and treason. In the Soviet system under Stalin, failure was often synonymous with treason.

Freeman, writing some seventy-five years after the end of the Civil War and working in Richmond, had access to letters and manuscripts that enriched the official reports of the battles and often provided alternative versions of the bloody encounters. I, on the other hand, am forced to rely on the numerous memoirs that Stalin's lieutenants wrote after his death in 1953. Prior to that time, the dictator let it be known that the writing of history should be left to historians. The memoirs that have appeared since then were not immune from censorship as the internal politics of the Party and its "line" changed, according to the purposes of the current Party chieftain, from de-Stalinization to stagnation to glasnost. These sources, as they are compared one with another and with official histories published under one regime and another, provide a reasonable approximation of what actually happened. The memoirs themselves when so processed provide sometimes glaring exposures of the extent to which the memoirist compromised himself to support this or that political line.

Finally, there is a vast difference in the scale of the operations with which Lee and Stalin were concerned. *Lee's Lieutenants* is about the commanders of brigades, divisions, and corps. This study is concerned primarily with the commanders of *fronts,* large combined arms formations similar to the army groups employed by the Western Allies during World War II.

These men—their background, the way they were selected (and the way they were relieved), their successes (and failures), and their subsequent fate—is the subject of this book. It is about the way men commanded under duress.

# 1
# FORMING AN ARMY OF A NEW TYPE

The Soviet Army that reeled back from the German onslaught in the early morning hours of 22 June 1941 was the product of almost twenty-four years of political, economic, and social change that transformed the Russian Empire from an underachieving Eurasian colossus into a premodern industrial state. These changes afforded free reign to the Four Horsemen of the Apocalypse. The cost of what its advocates called the Great October Socialist Revolution and the upheavals that followed has never been calculated reliably in terms of human lives. Military losses in the various conflicts in which the Soviet state was involved from 1917 until 1940 have been calculated at 8,015,692* (Krivosheev 1993, 407). If and when the noncombat losses due to famine, forced collectivization of agriculture, and political and military purges are added to the acknowledged military losses, they may total tens of millions.

## THE GENERAL SECRETARY
The man whose policies were responsible for the major portion of these casualties, Iosef Vissarionovich Stalin, emerged as the sole leader of the Soviet state in the late 1920s and as its absolute dictator in the early 1930s. He rose to his dominating position while serving as general secretary of the Communist Party of the Soviet Union, the political party that, under the leadership of Vladimir Il'ich

---

*This number includes the wounded, burned, and frozen who were medically evacuated from the combat area to army, *front,* and rear area hospitals.

Lenin, had seized state power in the name of the workers and peasants in November 1917. By 1922, having emerged victorious in a civil war and stalemated foreign intervention, the new rulers sought to rationalize the complex administrative problems of governing the sprawling former empire struggling to recover from almost eight years of conflict. The Party was governed, in theory at least, by a Central Committee. A seven-man Politburo was chosen to prepare and direct the November seizure of power. Subsequently, the Politburo was continued as the Central Committee's executive agency. The committee assembled periodically in plenary sessions to confirm the Politburo's actions and guide its future course.

While Lenin was alive, he was the unquestioned leader of the Party. He had created it in the early years of the twentieth century under political conditions in Russia that often forced him to lead the Party from exile abroad using conspiratorial methods to communicate with the Party's underground cells within the homeland. The discipline required of an illegal, underground party struggling to survive under the surveillance and censorship of an oppressive regime was to remain characteristic of the Party even after it came into power in 1917 and remained so until its demise in 1991.

At the Eleventh Party Congress in April 1922, it was decided to strengthen the existing Secretariat by appointing a Politburo member as general secretary to supervise the preparation of materials for the weekly sessions of the Politburo, to ensure that the Politburo's decisions were delivered to the appropriate agency for implementation, and to perform other tasks for its members. Stalin was chosen for this position almost by default; none of the other leading figures in the Party leadership wanted the post. Stalin accepted it because he seemed to have a talent for administration and because he may have realized its potential to enhance his personal power. Stalin was proposed for the post by Lev Borisovich Kamenev, a Politburo member who considered Stalin a potential ally in the ongoing policy debates. The possibility of a power struggle to succeed Lenin was hardly in anyone's mind at that time, although Lenin was beginning to experience the headaches and fatigue that were the early symptoms of his terminal illness. The initial medical prescription was for Lenin to take a long vacation away from the capital, giving the new general secretary opportunities to deploy Party cadres, control the bureaucracy, and influence policy.

Stalin was initially noticed by Lenin because of his ideas on the nationality question in the Russian Empire. Stalin was an experienced revolutionary, and he had engaged in various illegal activities in his native Georgia, including "expropriations"—robberies to obtain funds to finance Party activities. He participated in several of the Party congresses, which had to be held abroad. He had been arrested seven times and had escaped five times. In 1913, he was arrested in St. Petersburg and exiled to Turukhansk, on the Enisei just below the Arctic Circle, a place to which the Russian secret police exiled those they considered the most dangerous revolutionary leaders (Lincoln 1994, 60, 61).

Exempted from wartime military service because of a withered left arm, Stalin did not return to the capital until March 1917 after the overthrow of the tsar. He became a member of the Party's first Politburo. After the November seizure of power, he was appointed to two posts in the new Soviet government—commissar for nationalities matters and commissar for the workers and peasants inspection. His role in the overthrow of the provisional government was a modest one, but in the civil war that followed soon after, his role was more noteworthy. Even so, the man who was to become his archrival, Lev Davidovich Trotsky, emerged from those conflicts with much greater fame and esteem than did Stalin.

Given Stalin's bent for administrative work, and his many and varied experiences in the revolutionary movement and the Party, his assignment to the post of general secretary appeared to be a logical one (Volkogonov 1989, book 1, part 1:136, 137). What could not have been anticipated was the proximity of Lenin's disability and death. Lenin suffered his first stroke in May 1922, soon after the Eleventh Party Congress. His right leg and arm were partially paralyzed and his speech was impaired. For treatment he was moved to Gorki, a village ten kilometers southeast of Moscow, where he remained until early October. Stalin, as general secretary, was his principal liaison with the Party and the government's business during the summer. Stalin had control over Lenin's visitors and generally ensured that the regimen the doctors prescribed for his recovery was followed. Lenin appeared to recover, and he came back to Moscow in October. But in early December he returned to Gorki, where he suffered a second stroke that paralyzed his right arm and leg. His doctors limited his activity to four minutes of dictation a day. On 9 March 1923, he was again stricken and suffered almost complete loss of speech. He died on 21 January 1924 in a nursing home in Gorki.

During the long bouts with his infirmity, Lenin attempted to remain in contact with state and Party affairs through visitors, notes, and letters to those who were involved in implementing or attempting to form the policies of the government. Lenin's determination to keep abreast of ongoing business was in direct conflict with the recommendations of his doctors. Stalin, in charge of the practical aspects of Lenin's recovery and sometimes at cross purposes with Lenin on policy matters, seemed to relish his role as Lenin's guardian. Lenin, for his part, became convinced that Stalin's restrictions on his activities were designed to keep him in ignorance of the true state of affairs in the Party and the country. Lenin observed that, as general secretary, Stalin had arrogated to himself "boundless power," and Lenin was not certain that Stalin would use it with care. A major element of that power was Stalin's decisive voice in the selection and assignment of Party cadres to positions in Moscow and the hinterland. Lenin also became convinced that Stalin, in his dealings with people as general secretary, was too crude and abrasive. The latter faults became particularly evident in Stalin's relations with Lenin's wife, Nadezhda Krupskaia.

On 4 January 1923, Lenin's conclusion that Stalin was unfit for the position of general secretary was added to a letter "to the Congress" that he had dictated on 24 and 25 December 1922. The letter was sealed in an envelope that was to be opened only after his death. Considering Lenin's concerns about the growth of Stalin's political power, it would have been logical to assume that Lenin intended his letter for the next Party congress, the twelfth, which was held in April 1923. Because Lenin was still alive, although barely functioning, the letter was not delivered to the congress. In May 1923, after the congress had adjourned, Lenin suffered his third stroke, which left him in no condition to wage the political battle needed to remove Stalin from office and achieve the other reforms that Lenin advocated in his last testament.

In May 1924, four months after his death, the letter was delivered to the Thirteenth Party Congress. By that time the "last testament" was fifteen months old. The letter was shown to selected delegates, but it was not discussed by the congress as a whole. A commission appointed to receive Lenin's documents recommended that Stalin consider Lenin's criticisms in conducting the practical work of his office. The matter ended with this slight slap on the wrist. Stalin offered to resign his post, but the offer was not accepted. He remained as general secretary and continued to expand his power base. Two members of the Politburo who strongly supported Stalin at this time were L. B. Kamenev and G. E. Zinoviev. They considered that by supporting Stalin they were blocking the access of Lev Davidovich Trotsky to leadership of the Party (Volkogonov 1989, book 1, part 1:131–76).

## STALIN'S PRINCIPAL OPPONENT—TROTSKY

In addition to his warning about Stalin and his growing power, Lenin was concerned about the potential for a split in the Party caused by the increasing hostility between Stalin and Trotsky. Trotsky had split with Lenin at the Second Congress of the Russian Socialist Democratic Revolutionary Party, held in Brussels and London in 1903, over the issue of whether the Party would be "hard" or "soft." Lenin wanted an active, militant, and disciplined membership controlled by a small, central apparatus that could be ruled with a firm hand— if necessary with a fist. In the votes on these issues that followed, Lenin's positions managed to win a narrow majority. Lenin and his supporters subsequently called themselves *Bol'sheviki,* derived from the Russian word for majority. The losers became known as *Men'-sheviki,* from the Russian word for minority.

Trotsky joined the Mensheviks, played a prominent role in the 1905 Revolution in St. Petersburg, and brilliantly defended himself in the court-martial that followed the suppression of the revolt. In 1906 he was sentenced to lifelong exile in Obdorsk, far up in the Arctic Circle. He escaped before he reached his destination and managed to reach Finland and eventually Vienna via Stockholm. He did not return to Russia until 1917. In Vienna he remained aloof from the political quarrels of the émigré groups, served as a war correspondent in the Balkans, and visited Spain and New York (Wolfe 1948, 231–48, 311–36). While attempting to return to Russia in 1917, he was briefly interned in Canada.

Trotsky returned to Petrograd (the city's name was changed in 1914 because of the Germanic derivation of Petersburg) in May 1917, a month after Lenin. In July he rejoined Lenin and the Bolsheviks. He soon resumed the position he had occupied in 1905—chairman of the Petrograd Soviet, which almost immediately became a center of political power in competition with the provisional government. He was appointed people's commissar for foreign affairs in the first Soviet government. It was in this position that he became the principal Soviet negotiator at the Brest Litovsk peace talks with the Germans and their allies, which began in January 1918.

At Brest Litovsk, it soon became apparent that the Germans were expecting to sign a peace treaty that would exact considerable concessions from the Soviets in terms of reparations and territory. Trotsky's response on 10 February 1918 was to declare that the Soviets considered the state of war between them and the Central Powers to be ended. Three hours later, Trotsky wired the commander in chief (CINC) of the Russian Army, the Bolshevik Nikolai Vasilevich Krylenko, that he should immediately announce that the state of war had ended and order demobilization on all fronts. The CINC, assuming that a peace treaty had been signed, issued the necessary orders. They had the effect of accelerating the deterioration of the combat effectiveness of an already demoralized and defeated army.

Lenin ordered the CINC to countermand his order, but the damage had already been done. He also had to convince his skeptical colleagues that the Soviet government had no choice but to accept the Austro-German terms. While the Soviet high command considered that the state of war with the Central Powers had ended and that it was unlikely that hostilities would be renewed, the German high command concentrated some fifty divisions to force the Soviets to accept their conditions. Eight days after Trotsky had attempted to end the war unilaterally, the Central Powers took the offensive on the entire front. The remnants of the old Russian Army

were incapable of halting them, nor were they capable of an organized retreat. Lenin attempted to inform the German negotiators
of Soviet acceptance of their peace terms on the evening of 18 February, but the German forces continued to advance until the German delegation at Brest Litovsk agreed to cease hostilities on 3
March 1918. When the treaty was signed, the Germans were in occupation of Poland, Lithuania, Latvia, Belorussia, and a large section of Russia. Pskov was in their hands. The Ukraine became an
Austro-German colony. On 10 March, Lenin and the Bolsheviks,
fearing the proximity of the Germans to Petrograd, moved the capital to Moscow.

During the two weeks of the German 1918 offensive, the Soviets
offered resistance with hastily assembled detachments and with partisans in the area of the front and in the rear areas of the advancing
German troops. Actions such as these in the vicinity of Pskov were
celebrated later as the first combat actions of the Red Army, and 23
February subsequently became Red Army Day (Korablev 1970,
200–212).

The problem of developing armed forces capable of defending
the infant Soviet state from internal and external enemies was one
that the Bolshevik regime had grappled with from its inception.
Power had been seized in the midst of a disastrous war by a force of
armed workers and dissident members of the tsarist army and navy.
Power was retained initially because the Bolsheviks promised land,
bread, and peace—promises that in themselves were enough to ensure the gradual dissolution of an army made up primarily of peasant conscripts who were weary of four years of bloody fighting and
eager to return home to participate in the anticipated distribution
of land.

## AN ARMY OF A NEW TYPE

By early January 1918, Lenin was calling for the formation of an army
of a "new type" to defend the gains of the revolution. Initially Lenin,
as did many of the leaders of the pre–World War I Socialist parties,
leaned to the creation of a militia type of army of workers and peasants. To create such an army, he hoped that, after an armistice and
the conclusion of peace with Germany and Austria, the Soviet state

would have a breathing spell. When it became clear that Soviet military weakness would leave the state powerless to resist the demands of the Central Powers and would also encourage foreign support for counterrevolution, the need to replace the old army became urgent. A decree announcing the formation of a Workers and Peasants Red Army *(Raboche-Krestianskaia Krasnaia Armiia,* or *RKKA)* from volunteers was issued late in the month. The influx of volunteers was disappointingly small—less than 50,000 by mid-February (Korablev 1970, 196).

The new state thus found itself virtually defenseless when the peace negotiations broke down at Brest Litovsk. The Soviet response consisted of a series of frantic messages from Lenin and the Council of People's Commissars to local Soviets urging them to resist. These were followed by public appeals to the working population to fight the Germans. Lenin also turned for advice to some of the former tsarist generals who had been serving in the now defunct field headquarters of the old army, the Stavka. According to one of them, this was the de facto beginning of what was to become the Supreme Military Council *(Vysshyi voennyi sovet)* (Bonch-Bruevich 1966, 205). On 3 March, Trotsky was named the overall chief of the council; Mikhail Dmitrievich Bonch-Bruevich, a general in the old army, was named its military chief. On 13 March, it was announced that Trotsky had resigned as commissar for foreign affairs after the conclusion of peace at Brest Litovsk and would become the commissar for war. According to Trotsky, he took the new post at the request of Lenin (Trotsky 1960, 348).

The use of the former tsarist generals to staff the Supreme Military Council brought to the surface a strong dissent from within the upper ranks of the Bolshevik Party. Nikolai V. Krylenko, who had been appointed commander in chief of the old army immediately after the October Revolution, resigned in protest and could not be persuaded by Lenin to change his mind. Krylenko felt that the old military professionals, particularly the old generals, could not be trusted to participate in the building of the new army because they could not understand and accept its radical differences from the old one. They would operate according to the old canons and could only harm and not help in the areas of organization and command of the new Red Army (Korablev 1970, 235). Krylenko's objections to the use of the "military specialists," as they were called, were for him a matter of strong principle, and he resigned rather than serve under them. Opposition to the use of the former officers was strong throughout the army, but many opponents continued to serve, suspiciously anticipating treachery from their hated former oppressors. Stalin accepted the military specialists reluctantly, looked on them with deep suspicion, and did what he could to hinder their success.

Trotsky, on the other hand, as the operating head of the defense establishment, realized that the enrollment of the military specialists was absolutely necessary to build "an army of a new type." To obtain the numbers of trained, experienced officers that the new army required, he was prepared to take the risk that some, driven by their loyalty to the old order, would betray the Soviet cause. To limit the opportunities for treachery, Trotsky installed trusted commissars to monitor the actions and orders of the specialists.

These handicaps notwithstanding, during the Supreme Military Council's relatively short life it reorganized and realigned the existing military districts in accordance with the new territorial realities. A system of military commissariats was organized to perform the function of personnel accounting, mobilization, and supply at the local level. In May 1918, the All Russian Main Staff was formed to assume the functions of several institutions of the old army that were still around, including the main directorate of the old General Staff (Korablev 1970, 249).

These organizational measures took place in the short breathing space provided by the conclusion of peace with the Central Powers. Early in April, the Japanese landed troops at Vladivostok. In May, the Czechoslovak Corps revolted. The corps—consisting of Czech prisoners taken by the Russian Army on the Eastern *Front* between 1914 and 1918 and Czechs and Slovaks working in Russian industrial plants with some former tsarist officers—was being transported on the Trans-Siberian Railroad to Vladivostok for eventual shipment to, and service on, the Western *Front*, where the war with the Germans was still raging. By 26 May, hostilities between the Czechs and the Soviets had broken out along the railroad in Central and Western Siberia (Kennan 1967, II:136–53). The Czech revolt encouraged Russian opposition groups to join in fighting the Bolsheviks, causing the almost instantaneous formation of a broad, hostile Eastern *Front*. These forces plus those in the Crimea and North Caucasus, and along the Don, supported by various foreign governments, created a serious and complicated military situation for the new government.

To meet the crisis, on 29 May the Council of People's Commissars authorized conscription as a first step. By 12 June, the first workers and peasants were being drafted, based on plans drawn by the Supreme Military Council and the All Russian Main Staff. On 26 June, conscription for rear area labor was decreed for the corresponding age groups of the sons of the bourgeoisie (Korablev 1970, 272–79). The RKKA expanded slowly. There was a critical shortage of commanders, and the idea of a mass army was anathema to many in the population—the Bolsheviks and their temporary political allies, the Socialist Revolutionaries, alike.

The situation in the east deteriorated rapidly. Although the Czech Corps was numerically small, it was far better trained, equipped, and led than the local Bolshevik detachments it encountered initially. Also there was no overall military command in the east. In early June, a former tsarist lieutenant colonel who had declared himself a Left Socialist Revolutionary (SR), Mikhail Artem'evich Murav'ev, and who had commanded the Petrograd Military District under the Bolsheviks in 1917, took command of the Eastern *Front*.* On 10 July, Murav'ev denounced Bolshevik policies and called on the Czechs to join him and his Left SR comrades in reopening the war against the Central Powers. Murav'ev's treachery confirmed the deepest fears of those opposed to employing the former officers. Four days earlier, fellow Left SRs had assassinated the German ambassador in Moscow in an effort to cause a break in German-Soviet diplomatic relations.

---

*In Russian and Soviet military usage, a *front* is a military formation consisting of two or more armies plus supporting troops. During World War II, *fronts* often included air armies. Because the transliteration of the Russian word is spelled same as the English word front which can often have a nonspecific connotation, the word will be italicized when it is used, as in this case, to designate a specific military unit.

## THE INTERVENTION OF THE NOBLE REVOLUTIONARY

Mikhail Nikolaevich Tukhachevsky, a former *podporuchik* (second lieutenant) in the tsar's army and a recently accepted recruit in the Bolshevik Party, was one of those Communists sent to the east to help Murav'ev restore the situation. Retrospectively, Tukhachevsky evaluated Murav'ev as being "almost illiterate" in his knowledge of military affairs, unable to direct military operations, one who pandered to his troops and an adventurer who used his proclaimed membership in the Left Socialist Revolutionary Party as a protective label (V. M. Ivanov 1990, 32, 33). When Murav'ev announced his intention to resume the war against the Germans and attempted to recruit Tukhachevsky to the enterprise on the basis of his noble heritage, Tukhachevsky declared him a traitor, and Murav'ev had him arrested and ordered him shot. When Tukhachevsky's Red Army guards discovered that he, like they, was a Bolshevik, they freed him and sent a delegation to warn other units of Murav'ev's betrayal (Tukhachevsky 1964, I:79). Later that same day, 11 July, Murav'ev was shot and killed in a cross fire by Bolsheviks who had become aware of his intentions.

To replace Murav'ev, Latvian colonel Vatsetis had been named commander in chief of the Eastern *Front* on 18 July. Vatsetis had been in command of the Latvian Rifle Division, which had played an important role in suppressing the Left SR revolt in Moscow early in the month. As the Soviet Military Encyclopedia (SVE) notes, Vatsetis ". . . literally created a *front* from separate detachments" (SVE 2, 34), aided by army commanders such as Tukhachevsky. The detachments were recruited from all over Soviet-controlled Russia in response to the calls for help from the Eastern *Front*.

In a short period of time, propaganda, revolutionary example, and coercion produced remarkable change. The Red detachments became regular units, the Party's influence was restored by the infusion of Party members from the industrial urban centers of Moscow and Petrograd, and the commissars were encouraged to play their role as revolutionary leaders. Military tribunals were established to demonstrate to all that revolution demanded the highest sacrifice and that unauthorized retreats would be punished severely.

## TROTSKY'S TRAIN

The Germans had warned Trotsky that if the White and Czech forces approached Moscow from the east, the Germans would come from the west to prevent the formation of a new eastern front. As Trotsky described it, the Soviets were between a hammer and an anvil (Trotsky 1960, 395). After the Whites took Simbirsk on the Volga, Trotsky was sent to the east to organize and rally the Soviet defenses. He decided to travel to the *front* by means of a special train that would serve him as a command post, communications center, printing press, electric power station, garage, and living quarters. When the train, which required two engines to pull it, was stationary for a period of time, one of the engines was always under steam to be used as a courier, if necessary. Trotsky was to occupy this train for the greater part of the next two and a half years. It was to become an important part of the Trotsky civil war legend as he moved with it from *front* to *front* rallying the troops, propagandizing the population, and conferring with the military specialists and other commanders. Assembling the train took some time because of the chaotic situation of the Russian rail system after four years of war and revolution (Trotsky 1960, 411–22).

When Trotsky left Moscow on 7 August, he planned to go to Kazan, not knowing that the city had already fallen to the Whites. He was forced to stop at Sviyazhsk, the nearest sizable railroad station to Kazan, where he found that the soil itself seemed to be infected with panic (Trotsky 1960, 396).

Trotsky and his train remained at Sviyazhsk for a month. When Kazan was retaken on 10 September and Simbirsk on the twelfth, he and his entourage had completed their first mission successfully. In the next two and a half years the train with the war commissar aboard would appear at critical areas on the broad battlefield that was the Russian Civil War. The train's record of success would make it an object of demand for those localities that considered their situation critical and in urgent need of help. Trotsky's performance, as a civilian minister of defense at the *front* during the civil war, is almost unprecedented in the annals of warfare. For Stalin and his adherents, Trotsky's fame and the accolades he was accorded must have been a bitter dose, particularly when the men's paths and ideas crossed during the course of the war.

Although Trotsky was to profess that he was not aware of it at the time, the titanic struggle between him and Stalin had begun. It was not to end until Trotsky was murdered in Mexico in 1940. Many supporting players in this tragedy, including two of Stalin's most capable commanders, were to become the innocent victims of the suspicious hatred that the struggle was to engender in the mind of the future dictator. The wave of "repressions" among the senior Red Army cadres, generated by what became known as the "military-Trotsky plot," would eventually swell to 40,000 between 1937 and 1940. The damage to the combat effectiveness of the Red Army could not be corrected by the time of the German onslaught. New commanders had to be found under the trying conditions of an all-out attack by what at the time was one of the world's most efficient fighting machines.

# 2
# STALIN AND VOROSHILOV GAIN MILITARY EXPERIENCE

## TSARITSYN

Stalin was halfway to his thirty-ninth birthday when, in late May 1918, he and A. G. Shliapnikov, a fellow old Bolshevik and member of the Central Committee, were given the assignment and plenipotentiary powers to go to the city of Tsaritsyn on the Volga to ensure that food supplies accumulating there would be sent to Moscow. Tsaritsyn, an important intersection of rail and Volga River transport routes on the right flank of what was to become the Southern *Front*, was at that time being defended from the attacks of the White Don Cossacks of Gen. Petr Nikolaiovich Krasnov supported by the Austro-German occupiers of the Ukraine. At Lenin's insistence, the two emissaries were accompanied by a detachment of 400 troops, including 100 Latvian riflemen (Volkogonov 1989, book 1, part 1:90).

On arrival, Stalin immediately became involved with the military defense of the city, which was in danger of being cut off from Moscow by Krasnov's troops. Stalin interfered with the operations of the military staffs, removed officers he considered incompetent, and began to use "repressive measures" to enforce his edicts. He also used members of his group who were in Tsaritsyn on food supply matters and members of his Commissariat of Nationalities for inspections of military activities. After a month in the city he demanded military powers, complaining that the "military specialists" had slept and been idle while the Whites were threatening to prevent food from reaching Moscow. When these powers were not granted immediately, Stalin warned that he would proceed to dismiss the offending officers and commissars without authorization (Volkogonov 1992, book 2:36). On 19 July he received the authorization and was announced as the chairman of the Military Council* of the North Caucasus Military District. Kliment (Klim) Efremovich Voroshilov, who had arrived in the city on 22 June and was designated as the commander of troops in the Tsaritsyn area the next day, was also named to the council.

Voroshilov, like Stalin, was a professional revolutionary who had not served in the Russian Army. He brought with him the fifth Ukrainian Army, which he had led since its activation in April. The army had been formed to provide organized resistance to the Austro-German occupiers of the Ukraine by the Council of the People's Commissars of the Donetsk-Krivoi Rog Republic.** It was made up of locally recruited detachments serving under elected leaders (Voroshilov at the time was commanding a detachment of irregulars, the 1st Lugansk Socialist Partisan Detachment). These detachments were variously organized and equipped, dependent on captured weapons, ammunition, and equipment; one can surmise that they were poorly disciplined. In addition to resisting the Austro-German occupiers, they were also contesting the forces of Ataman Pavel Petrovich Skoropadskii and the Ukrainian Rada, who were counting on the Austro-German occupiers to support the establishment of a Ukraine independent of Russia—soviet or imper-

---

*Military councils (voennye sovety), collegial command groups, were created officially for all *front* and army headquarters in September 1918. They were to consist of the *front* (or army) commander and two political officers. Later they were expanded to include the chief of staff. The military council was to participate in all phases of the military decision-making process. No order was considered to be valid unless it was signed by one of the members of the military council. The military council at Tsaritsyn was created with Lenin's approval, apparently anticipating the order that was to be isssued in September.

**The Donetsko-Krivorozhskaia Sovetskaia Respublika (The Donetsk Krivoi Rog Soviet Republic) had been created in the vain hope that the Austro-German occupiers would accept its establishment as evidence that the territory was not part of the Ukraine. At Lenin's urging the detachments were Ukrainianized; hence, the armies were named Ukrainian to further the fiction that the occupiers were meeting local and not Soviet opposition (Khromov 1983, 196).

ial. As Voroshilov and his troops were pushed out of the Ukraine, they were also to collide with Krasnov's White Don Cossacks, who were opposed to the installation of the Soviet regime in the Don region.

Voroshilov thus became Stalin's first military lieutenant and political-military subordinate, a relationship that was to last some thirty-five years, until the dictator's death in 1953. Voroshilov had become acquainted with Stalin in Stockholm in 1906 at the Fourth Party Congress, where they shared a room. Stalin's name then was Iosef Vissarionovich Diugashvili, (his party nickname at that time was Koba). He began to use the pseudonym Stalin in 1912. They became friends (Voroshilov 1971, 247, 248). In 1907, Voroshilov served with Stalin on the Baku Party Committee, organizing oil field workers.

## KLIM VOROSHILOV

Although Voroshilov had no professional military training, he fit the Bolshevik conception of the ideal Red Army commander. He was a true proletarian, born in conditions of extreme poverty and given a very limited education. He became a self-taught leader in the late-nineteenth-century labor movement in the industrially burgeoning Donets Basin (the Donbass).

Klim was born in a small cottage along a railroad right-of-way, the third child of a trackwalker. His father was of peasant stock and never rose above the level of farmhand–unskilled laborer *(batrak-chernorabochii),* to use Voroshilov's characterization (Voroshilov 1971, 13). Because of his father's feisty nature and the fluctuating economic conditions in the region, his father was frequently unemployed or was absent and searching for work in other areas. During these periods, Klim's mother attempted to provide for the family by taking in laundry or by hiring out as a cook and a domestic. Klim and his siblings were often hungry, barefoot, and half clothed. At the age of ten he was earning maybe ten kopecks a day working from six in the morning until dark picking iron pyrites from coal at a local mine.

Young Voroshilov was fortunate to receive two years of schooling at a village parochial school before the family's economic situation demanded that he return to work. His first job, obtained because he could read and write, was that of a messenger at a new metallurgical factory being constructed in the area. He was fourteen years of age. In addition to delivering messages within the factory, his duties included delivery and pickup on horseback of the factory mail at the post office, located eight kilometers away. At an early age the future commissar of the First Cavalry Army began developing equestrian skills.

### FIRST BRUSHES WITH AUTHORITY

Klim eventually gained employment as a machinist's helper, and he continued to improve his knowledge of the outside world by reading under the tutelage of his former grade school teacher. He also experienced his first arrest, and spent the night in jail for failing to evidence the proper respect to a local gendarme. From this episode, "a turning point in my life" (Voroshilov 1971, 81), he became convinced that the local gendarmerie personified the enormity, criminality, evilness, and mercilessness of the tsarist police regime (Voroshilov 1971, 84). After this encounter, Klim became a target for police attention, including frequent warnings about his conduct and surveillance, summons to the police station, and searches of his living quarters.

The various industrial enterprises of the Donbass were natural targets for Marxist agitators and organizers of Lenin's Russian Socialist Democratic Party, the forerunner of the All Russian Communist Party (Bolsheviks). Voroshilov joined in 1903, met Lenin in 1905, and by 1906 was participating in Party congresses abroad, representing the Lugansk Party Committee.

Voroshilov spent five months in jail in 1905 after he was arrested while preparing to lead a strike at the locomotive works where he was employed. He continued to be held after the tsar issued the manifest of 17 October 1905 on the grounds that he was subject to criminal charges because a policeman had been wounded during his arrest. Voroshilov was freed in December when thousands of Lugansk workers marched on the prison and demanded his release. Frightened by the demonstration, the authorities contrived "a small guarantee" in exchange for freeing Voroshilov—habeas corpus, revolutionary style (Voroshilov 1971, 197, 198). The agreement was that he would be tried subsequently. When his principal accuser was murdered in the interim, Voroshilov was acquitted.

## EXILE

The Bolsheviks were among the last to realize that the revolutionary fervor of 1905–06 had cooled. Voroshilov continued to prepare for the next clash with the authorities from his underground post as head of the Lugansk Party Committee and his open position as head of his factory trade union. He attended the Fifth Party Congress in London in May 1907, engaged in gun running and bomb making, and was rearrested in July for engaging in revolutionary activities and inciting workers to strike. He was sentenced to be exiled for three years in the Russian north—Archangelsk Guberniia. He soon escaped and fled to Baku, where he joined Stalin in attempting to organize and radicalize workers in the oil industry. When Voroshilov lost his job as a boilermaker, he was forced to leave Baku and return to Petersburg, where the police eventually found him and returned him to Archangelsk. This time he was sent to a village closer to the Arctic Circle. And this time he served his full term; he was released in July 1912.

Voroshilov was not permitted to live or work in Petersburg or Moscow, so he returned to the Donbass, where he soon took up the activities that he had left four years earlier: underground work with the Party; aboveground work with the trade unions, workers' cooperatives, and company credit unions. He conducted all this from his modest position as a baker in the factory cooperative—the only job he could get. His record as an agitator and organizer of labor unrest made him the object of close police surveillance. In March 1913, he was given a two-year term in exile, this time to the Cherdinskii region of Perm Guberniia, 470 kilometers north of Perm in the foothills of the Urals (Kardashov 1976, 81, 82). His wife, Ekaterina Davidovna, a fellow exile whom he met in the Archangelsk region in 1907, accompanied him to his place of banishment (Akshinskii 1976, 35, 36; Kardashov 1976, 82).

Voroshilov's term of exile was reduced by one year in 1913, ironically by the Romanovs, whom he was working to overthrow, as they celebrated 300 years of ruling the Russian Empire. Voroshilov showed his gratitude by continuing his Bolshevik activities in a weapons factory in Tsaritsyn, where he moved after failing to find employment in Lugansk. He was there when World War I began in August 1914. Voroshilov claims that, like other true Bolsheviks, he was opposed to the war from the moment it broke out despite the patriotic fervor with which it was greeted by the vast majority of workers. In Tsaritsyn, Voroshilov, assisted by another Bolshevik, Sergei Konstantinovich Minin, organized a consumers' cooperative to cover the dissemination of Bolshevik antiwar propaganda. In 1915, Voroshilov moved to Petrograd and continued his antiwar activities, avoiding military service as he worked as a master boiler-maker in a small factory. He was in Petrograd, which the Bolsheviks continued to call Petersburg, when the February Revolution broke out.

Lev Trotsky, writing from exile on the island of Prinkipo in 1929, analyzed Voroshilov's political attitudes and activities in terms of Trotsky's "internationalist Marxist" views.

> The life of Voroshilov illustrates the career of a worker revolutionist, with its leadership in strikes, underground work, imprisonment, and exile. Like many of the other [Soviet] rulers of today, Voroshilov was merely a national revolutionary democrat from among the workers, nothing more; this was most apparent in the imperialist Great War, and later on in the February revolution. In the official biographies of Voroshilov, the years 1914–17 are a great blank, as is true of most of the present leaders. The secret of this blank is that during the war most of these men were patriots, and discontinued their revolutionary work (Trotsky 1960, 440).

### FEBRUARY AND OCTOBER REVOLUTIONS

While in Petersburg, Voroshilov did not play a major role in the events surrounding the February Revolution. He did manage to insinuate himself into the confidence of the regimental committee of the Life Guards Izmailovskii Regiment, the reserve depot of which was stationed in the city. Although one of his Soviet era biographers claims that he participated in the drafting of the notorious Order No. 1, which did so much to undermine the reliability of the old army (Kardashov 1976, 89, 90), his name is not mentioned in what has been called "one of the best documented episodes of the Revolution" (Wildman 1980, 182, 187, 188). That order required all the units in the Petrograd garrison to elect soldiers' committees, subordinated all units to the Petrograd Soviet, and placed all unit weapons under control of the soldiers' committees. The order, which applied to the huge Petrograd garrison, effectively removed some 200,000 troops in the garrison from the control of the provisional government and transferred them to the Petrograd Soviet. The troops could not be sent to the front without authority from the Soviet because they were needed to "defend the revolution." The order was also dispatched to the troop units at the front and, although it did not apply to them, it further diminished their military effectiveness.

In late March, Voroshilov and his wife were sent by the Party Central Committee to Lugansk, where he was enthusiastically received by his old comrades. When he arrived, the Bolsheviks were in the minority in the Lugansk Soviet. By late September they were in the majority, and Voroshilov was chosen chairman. His biographer attributes this rapid growth in Bolshevik power in Lugansk to its strong Party organization and to Voroshilov's leadership, energy, firmness, and decisiveness (Kardashov 1976, 195).

After the Bolshevik seizure of power in Petrograd, Voroshilov, as chairman of the local soviet, found himself responsible for the institution and preservation of the new order in the city and its environs. The Don Cossacks, traditional privileged supporters of the tsarist regime, whose territories lay adjacent to the Donbass, were perceived as one of the principal threats to the new order. After the Bolshevik coup, the ataman of the Don Cossacks, Aleksei Maksimovich Kaledin, declared that the members of Lenin's government were criminals and that the Don Cossacks were independent (Seaton 1985, 220). Voroshilov increased the number of Red Guards in the city to 1,500; weapons were confiscated from the armed contingents of other parties; and a large Ukrainian nationalist unit was dispersed.

During the confused period between Trotsky's vain attempt to take Russia out of the war (10 February 1918), the resumption of hostilities by the Austro-German Army (18 February), and the actual signing of the Brest Litovsk peace treaty (3 March), the Bolsheviks frantically attempted to assemble forces to resist the advancing enemy. Under the terms of the treaty, the Bolsheviks agreed to make peace with the Ukrainian nationalists, in effect recognizing the Ukraine as an independent state (Mawdsley 1987, 33). The Central Rada, Ukrainian nationalists, signed a peace treaty with the Austro-Germans on the same day that Trotsky had attempted to declare a unilateral peace. As the Central Powers advanced into the Ukraine, the forces of the Rada were in their train. On 1 March they occupied Kiev and continued to move east.

At the end of February, Voroshilov was in Kharkov, where the Bolshevik leadership was attempting to organize resistance to the occupiers. Voroshilov returned to Lugansk, where he collected a detachment of some 640 volunteers. On 10 March, the 1st Lugansk Socialist Partisan Detachment, led by Klim Voroshilov, marched through the town and boarded a train for Kharkov. They were escorted by two armored trains that had been hastily constructed at the local locomotive works. The next night, after arriving in Kharkov, they joined the Fifth Ukrainian Army and were given the mission of covering the approaches to the north and east along the rail line from Bakhmach to Konotop (Kardashov 1976, 114).

On 18 March, Voroshilov and the Lugansk detachment received their baptism of fire at the rail bypass at the village of Duboviazovka, approximately fifteen kilometers east of Konotop. The engagement was typical of what the Germans called *der Eisenbahnfeldzug* (the railway campaign). The German general, Max Hoffman, found it to be the "most comical campaign" he had ever known (Mawdsley 1987, 34, 35). Voroshilov did not find the encounter amusing. Leading his troops from the makeshift armored train, he encountered head-on a party of Germans also mounted in an armored train. In the ensuing artillery exchange, the German train was damaged and could not move; however, it continued to fire on the Lugansk detachment and eventually destroyed its main gun, although the Red train was capable of retreating out of the range of the German artillery. The German train was soon repaired, and when it came in range of the Lugansk train—which had retreated to the bypass where several other Red train-borne detachments were halted—one of its rounds landed on a car carrying ammunition. The ensuing explosion, the continuing enemy fire, and a collision of trains attempting to withdraw all contributed to the panicky, disorderly retreat of the other detachments. The Lugansk detachment held its positions under Voro-shilov's threat to shoot anyone who attempted to leave. Under the cover of darkness they retreated, abandoning their makeshift armored train because its engine was damaged. The Lugantsy did remove their dead and wounded along with the operable weapons as they withdrew in the direction of Kharkov during the night.

The Lugansk detachment participated in a vain effort to defend Kharkov from Austro-German occupation. As the city was falling, Voroshilov led his detachment on a retreat to the south toward its home territory—the Donbass. There, in mid-April, Voroshilov volunteered to take command of a new Fifth Ukrainian Army, which would replace the army that had been shattered in the defense of Kharkov. The Fifth Ukrainian Army and parts of the Third Ukrainian Army established fortified positions around Lugansk and Iuzovka,* and they managed, under constant hostile pressure, to evacuate to Tsaritsyn dozens of trains loaded with supplies, military equipment, and refugees. As the occupiers attempted to halt the evacuations, Voroshilov led a 500-kilometer retreat along the rail line to join the defenders of Tsaritsyn.

## THE DEFENDERS OF TSARITSYN

The arrival of Voroshilov and his troops improved the Red situation around Tsaritsyn. The ranks of the city's defenders were also swelled by the arrival of thousands of Lugansk metalworkers and Donetsk miners. These reinforcements were not trained soldiers; although they were soon organized into units with designators resembling

---

*Iuzovka was named after the Welsh ironmaster John Hughes, who in 1870 built a large steel plant and coal mine there. In 1924, the name was changed to Stalino; in 1961, to Donetsk.

those of a regular army, they were regular in name only. Regimental commanders were selected by soldiers' committees, often from former noncommissioned officers with combat experience in the old army. From among these, some managed to enjoy lengthy careers in the RKKA and, eventually, in the Soviet Army. These careers, in some cases, seemed to progress not as a result of successes but rather in spite of some significant failures.

Semen Mikhailovich Budenny, who was to become one of the most renowned popular military heroes of the civil war, led his detachment of horsemen to Tsaritsyn in August 1918. The detachment was soon re-formed into a regiment. On the basis of his combat experience alone, Budenny, who started inthe tsarist military service in 1903 and served in the Russo-Japanese War and World War I as a senior noncommissioned officer, probably stood head and shoulders above his fellow regimental commanders. In a war that often became a series of mobile engagements along the rail lines—the main avenues of communication in central and southern Russia—the ability to maneuver large bodies of cavalry became decisive. The role of mounted troops was magnified not only by the nature of the theaters of operations and their lack of infrastructure but also because of the common cavalry heritage of the Reds and the Whites—the Russian Imperial Army. During World War I, that army maintained a constant million horses, partly to overcome the local transportation problems but also because the army continued to believe that cavalry units could still play a role on the battlefields of Eastern Europe despite firepower developments such as the machine gun and rapid-firing light field artillery, which eventually drove the horse soldier from the battlefield (Stone 1975, 134). Thus, the White armies, too, depended on large cavalry formations to provide mobile strike forces.

Another veteran of World War I who commanded a regiment at Tsaritsyn was Semen Konstantinovich Timoshenko. A private in the tsar's army, he joined the Reds in the initial battles against the White generals Kornilov and Kaledin in 1917, and in April 1918 he took command of the 1st Crimean Revolutionary Regiment.

Efim Afanas'evich Shchadenko, a Bolshevik Party member since 1905, commanded a detachment of Red Guards that joined the

Fifth Ukrainian Army in its retreat from Lugansk. Soon after arriving in Tsaritsyn, he was named the commissar of the staff of the North Caucasus Military District. Shchadenko arrived in the city with Voroshilov, and he soon made his presence felt. On 24 June the council declared a local mobilization of all twenty-one- and twenty-two-year-old workers, and it improved the work of the political enlightenment section to make it more lively and pertinent.

Red artillery at Tsaritsyn was commanded by Grigorii Ivanovich Kulik, who came to the besieged city with Voroshilov as elected artillery commander of the Fifth Ukrainian Army. In October 1918, when the Fifth Ukrainian Army was reorganized as the Tenth Army, Kulik became the commander of artillery of that army (SVE 4:517).

## FIRST CLASHES WITH TROTSKY

When Trotsky was appointed commissar for war in the spring of 1918, he knew that he did not have the experience or background to manage the complex task of directing the RKKA in the civil war while at the same time developing it into an "army of a new type." Although he admitted that he did not think himself a strategist in any sense, he also had little patience with what he called the "strategist-dilettantism" that flooded the Party as a result of the revolution. He, like Lenin, was a strong subscriber to Clausewitz's theory that war is a continuation of politics by other means. Trotsky claimed that in those cases where he did take a strategic position against that of the high command and the majority of the Politburo, his stance was based on political and economic considerations rather than those relating to pure military strategy. After all, he argued, questions of high strategy cannot be solved in any other way (Trotsky 1930, 350).

Trotsky also recognized that the thousands of military specialists from the old army had to be used if a modern army was to be created while a civil war was being fought. Although the majority of the former officer corps of the tsarist army opposed the revolution and joined the various White armies, many officers from the lower social orders did not sympathize with the tsarist aristocracy, were opposed to the continuation of the tsarist regime, or for patriotic reasons were willing to continue to fight to prevent the growth of German and other foreign influence in the old Russian Empire. In wishing to create a new regular army with the assistance of the military specialists, Trotsky had the support of Lenin, who, in the existing circumstances, saw that a modern army was absolutely necessary if the state was to survive.

Many of the old Bolsheviks clung to the Socialist belief that the state could be protected by a workers' militia and that the creation of a standing army should be avoided at all costs. For them, the standing army was a potential instrument of coercion that could be used to suppress the working class, as it had in 1905 and on other occasions in Russian history. For the younger revolutionaries who had experienced the harsh discipline of the tsarist army and the heady days of regimental committees and elected commanders, the idea of a new type of army sounded too much like the old one. The curses of the old discipline were still ringing in their ears when a new revolutionay discipline began to be introduced (Trotsky 1960, 437).

It was not accidental, as the Soviets would say, that Tsaritsyn would be the locus of what became the "military opposition." Stalin interpreted his mandates and his position as a member of the Politburo as authorizing him to report directly to Lenin, often on petty matters, bypassing Trotsky and the military chain of command. Stalin also demonstrated an early manifestation of his chronic suspiciousness, particularly of the military specialists whom Trotsky sent to assist in the development of a well-trained and disciplined army (Volkogonov 1989, book 1, part 1:90). The death by drowning of several former officers who had been imprisoned on a barge that sank in the Volga was considered by Trotsky to be particularly outrageous. Although one of the officers escaped before "the accident" and subsequently was found to be a traitor to the Red cause, the episode plus other evidence that *partizanshchina* was rampant among the city's defenders convinced Trotsky that Stalin had to be relieved (Trotsky 1960, 437, 438). *Partizanshchina,* a condition that may have been more irritating to officers of the old army than to a soldier-politician such as Voroshilov, implied an absence of military order and discipline; spontaneous reactions to military situations rather than carefully planned operations; appropriation of captured weapons and supplies on a first-come first-served basis rather than a distribution according to military need; and election of officers tending to turn unit command into a popularity contest. The military specialists clearly would consider these faults more serious than politicians such as Stalin and Voroshilov.

While Trotsky was endeavoring to convince Lenin to recall Stalin, the effort to incorporate Tsaritsyn's defenders into the new army continued. On 11 September 1918, the Southern *Front* was formed to provide operational and strategic control over four armies—the Eighth, Ninth, Tenth, and Eleventh—and other units engaged in the struggle against the troops of Krasnov and Gen. Anton Ivanovich Denikin, commanding the Armed Forces of Southern Russia. The Southern *Front* zone of responsibility stretched in a broad arc from south of Voronezh to the northern Caucasus. Pavel Pavlovich Sytin, a *general maior* (one star) in the old army, was placed in command of the *front;* Stalin, Voroshilov, and Sergei Konstantinovich Minin, a Bolshevik and former chairman of the Tsaritsyn Party committee, were appointed members of the military council. In early October, the defenders of Tsaritsyn became the Tenth Army, and Voroshilov remained in command. The Third and Fifth Ukrainian Armies ceased to exist.

Stalin and Voroshilov were soon at cross purposes with Sytin. Their differences reached a climax in late September when Sytin proposed to move the headquarters of the *front* from Tsaritsyn to the north and west to Kozlov (now Michurinsk), a location that militarily at least seems more logical than Tsaritsyn because it was not in immediate danger of being surrounded. Sytin also insisted on noninterference in operational matters by the members of the *front* military council (Stalin, Minin, and Voroshilov). On 1 October, the members of the military council petitioned the Military Council of the Republic to remove Sytin from command and to replace him with Voroshilov. Another message the next day, signed by Stalin, complained about the supply of weapons and ammunition to Tsaritsyn and asked, insolently it seemed, if the central military authorities considered it necessary to hold the south, repeating the assertion that the situation around Tsaritsyn was serious and demanding precise and unqualified instructions on these questions.

Trotsky's response on 3 October ordered that the *front* military council operate on the basis of noninterference by commissars in operational matters and that the *front* headquarters be moved to Kozlov. Trotsky added that if this was not done within twenty-four hours he would be forced to take "severe measures." The same day, Stalin and Voroshilov responded by raising the dispute to the highest level, demanding, in a telegram to Lenin, that the Party Central Committee review Trotsky's conduct in snubbing the most prominent members of the Party to please "traitors from the military specialists." Stalin also demanded a review of the question of the use of military specialists who came "from the camp of the non-party counterrevolutionaries" (Kardashov 1976, 146–48).

The tone of this exchange, with its challenge to the policy of using the military specialists, demanded Lenin's intervention. Stalin was recalled to Moscow on 6 October. He lost the argument as Trotsky continued to insist on his recall, which was finally accomplished in late October after Stalin was permitted to return to Tsaritsyn, presumably to save face. Trotsky also made a special visit to see Voroshilov, who admitted to him that Tsaritsyn executed only those orders they considered to be right. Trotsky threatened that, if in the future Voroshilov failed to execute military orders exactly as they were received, he (Trotsky) would have him arrested and brought to Moscow to be tried by court-martial. Voroshilov promised to obey, and Trotsky left him in command of the Tenth Army. Voroshilov's conduct and his attitude toward orders from higher commanders continued as before, and Trotsky removed him from command on 19 December 1918 (Kardashov 1976, 154; Trotsky 1930, 442).

## MILITARY OPERATIONS AROUND TSARITSYN

While Stalin was still in Tsaritsyn, Krasnov made two major attempts to seize the city. In the beginning of August he directed a three-pronged attack on the city from the west. By 11 August, the White Cossacks under Konstantin Konstantinovich Mamontov had reached a position west of the village of Voroponovo, about fifteen kilometers west of Tsaritsyn, where they were halted and thrown back with heavy losses. The White northern column met a similar fate, and by 29 August the Reds had driven them back to Karpovka and Kotluban. Unlike the Germans in 1942, White troops never did enter the city (Naida et al. 1957, 3:252–55).

There is no specific evidence that Stalin ever visited the front lines during these often desperate hand-to-hand engagements, although one of Voroshilov's biographers reports that on 16 July, prior to Krasnov's attack, Stalin, accompanied by Voroshilov, completed a reconnaissance in an armored train 270 kilometers along the rail line to Tikhoretsk. They concluded that if they had some large, well-organized units, they could secure it. Unfortunately, at that time there were no such units available (Kardashov 1976, 139).

Beyond this one foray into unfamiliar territory, the record does not indicate that Stalin wearied himself with visits to the forward positions, aid stations, assembly areas, and observation posts, which were usually undertaken by commanders to check on the execution of their orders and enable themselves to be seen for morale purposes (Volkogonov 1989, book 1, part 1:90, 91). Nor did he demonstrate any special military talent. He became known for his style of leadership: exerting pressure on his subordinates, usually from his headquarters, where he wrote reports; giving orders to his commanders and commissars in the most elementary of terms; challenging their revolutionary ardor; and threatening them with relief, trial, and death if they did not succeed.

In contrast, Voroshilov, writing in 1936 after Stalin had become the country's acknowledged leader, described the tense days of the White offensive in August 1918.

> You should have seen comrade Stalin at that time. As always, calm, deep in his thoughts, he literally did not sleep for days on end, dividing his most intense work between the combat positions and the headquarters of the army.
>
> The situation at the front became almost catastrophic. . . . But Stalin did not concern himself with it. He was consumed with one consciousness, with one thought—to conquer, to defeat the enemy no matter what it cost (Voroshilov 1937, 18, 19).

The absence of specific instances in Voroshilov's recollection, his record of subservience to Stalin, and his reputation for distortion of the historical record suggest that this account was an example of the panegyrical style that he used whenever he wrote about Stalin. Later, when it was possible to measure the results achieved against Voroshilov's promises and claims, his performance was to be judged in terms of two splendid Russian words—*shapkozakidatel'stvo* (literally, tossing one's hat in the air) and *ochkovtiratel'stvo* (literally, rubbing someone's eyes)—as he boastingly promised easy victories and pulled the wool over people's eyes.

In late September, while Stalin and Voroshilov were engaged in their vain challenge to Trotsky and the policy of using military specialists, Krasnov made a second attempt to take the city. This time he attacked the southern flank of the Tenth Army, striving to cut off Tsaritsyn from Astrakhan and the northern Caucasus. A diversionary attack to the north of the city reached and crossed to the left bank of the Volga, threatening the Tenth Army rear (SVE 8:402). During this offensive, Voroshilov, assisted at times by Kulik and Shchadenko, rallied the troops by his personal example and exhortations. On one occasion the forward elements of the Tenth Army headquarters were taken by surprise with the arrival of a raiding party of Cossacks at a rail station where Voroshilov was conferring with his staff and subordinate commanders. In the ensuing panic, Voroshilov ran outside, found an abandoned machine gun, and opened fire. Soon, joined by others, he drove off the invaders. There was never any question about Voroshilov's personal courage in the field.

The White effort to take Tsaritsyn reached its culminating point on 17 October. Having taken Voroponovo the previous day, the Whites approached Sadovaia at dawn. There, Voroshilov and Kulik decided to concentrate the bulk of the available Red artillery—some 100 guns. The combined firepower of these weapons plus a decisive counterattack of Red infantry forced the retreat of the Cossack attackers. Subsequently, tactical mistakes of the White commanders allowed Voroshilov to defeat the White Don Cossacks in detail and drive them thirty to forty kilometers from the city.

In the respite that followed Krasnov's second repulse, Voroshilov continued the effort to convert the Tenth Army into a regular army, forming divisions consisting of two or three brigades from the various detachments. One notable organizational development was the formation of a cavalry division, initially commanded by Boris Mokeevich Dumenko and then by Budenny (Kardashov 1976, 153).

## THE RELIEF OF VOROSHILOV

Voroshilov's record as an army commander as it was presented in days before glasnost did not seem to merit his summary relief from command in December. However, that public record did not include numerous official complaints about his performance as Tenth Army commander, which were hidden from researchers as well as the general public. As early as July, a military member of the Military Council of the North Caucasus Military District concluded that Voroshilov did not practice the elementary principles of troop leadership and that he was not infused with the spirit of duty and service. In October, Ioakim Ioakimovich Vatsetis, who had been appointed commander in chief of the RKKA in September, reported to Lenin that Voroshilov was ignoring his *front* commander and was leading the Tsaritsyn sector to a catastrophe (Khorev 1989, 3).

Following his relief, Voroshilov was sent to the Ukraine, where he joined the provisional revolutionary government of the Ukraine as commissar of internal affairs. That government had been formed immediately after Germany and its allies on the western front, faced with military defeat, sued for the armistice that went into effect on 11 November 1918. Among the conditions of that armistice were the annulment of the treaty of Brest Litovsk and the immediate evacuation of all German troops from all occupied territories (DeWeerd 1968, 407, 408). In the chaotic situation in which the Austro-German occupiers withdrew, the Bolsheviks avoided clashes with the former occupiers while attempting to oust the Ukrainian nationalists whom the Central Powers had installed as the government of the country. As commissar of internal affairs, Voroshilov was responsible at the local level to install organs of Soviet power in those areas where they had not existed previously and to organize the functioning of those local soviets that were already in existence. At the same time, he had to maintain order and protect the population against various armed bands that contested the imposition of Bolshevik authority. His duties as commissar for internal affairs were basically those of a police and counterintelligence nature and were similar to those of Feliks Edmundovich Dzerzhinskii, the head of the Cheka (the All Russian Commission for Combatting Counterrevolution and Sabotage). We are told that in his later years Voroshilov was fond of referring to himself as a "Chekist" (Khorev 1989, 4).

## THE MILITARY OPPOSITION

In early March, the Bolsheviks of the Ukraine elected Voroshilov to the Central Committee of the Ukrainian Communist Party. On 18 March Voroshilov was in Moscow attending the Eighth Congress of the Russian Communist Party as a member of the Ukrainian delegation (Kardashov 1976, 154–56).

One of the important policy resolutions Lenin sought to have adopted by the congress concerned the structure of the armed forces. He had accepted the necessity of creating a standing army. Although it would be called an army of a new type, it was to retain many of the characteristics of European armies. The election of officers was to cease; officers were to be appointed. Where they were available, the former officers of the old army were to be used. The military specialists were to be under the observation and control of political commissars. A resolution embodying these principles, if passed by the congress, would put an end to the active and passive obstructionism that the military specialists were encountering in the Red Army.

Opposition to this policy came from some forty delegates, among whom Voroshilov was perhaps the most prominent. Trotsky, the commissar for war and a strong advocate of the formation of a regular army and the employment of the military specialists, was an unnamed target of the opposition.

In an exchange during a closed session of the congress, which was not revealed to the public for years, Lenin addressed the brash Voroshilov directly.

> . . . collective command? That is staggering, a complete return to partizanshchina . . . that is not only bad but conceals danger . . . the old partizanshchina still lives in you and it is

heard in all of the speeches of Voroshilov . . . you can kill 60,000 but from the point of view of our general line can we give up 60,000? [From the floor Voroshilov interjected, "But how many did we kill?"] I know very well that you killed many . . . but in the sense of the party line, in the sense of awareness of the missions which were given by us it is clear that perhaps we would not have had to lose those 60,000 if there were specialists there, if there was a regular army there (Danilov 1989, 3).

The military opposition suffered a complete defeat at the congress, and we are told that as "befits a real communist" Voroshilov accepted the criticism of his errors without being insulted and, in the future, complied with the decisions of the congress (Kardashov 1976, 158).

Voroshilov's "friend" Stalin was not among the open opponents of Lenin's military policy, although he clearly sympathized with the opposition. According to Roy Medvedev, "He was trying to create the impression that Lenin and the Central Committee did not understand military affairs" (Medvedev 1972, 14). In a three-page discussion of this episode in a history of the civil war published in 1986, Voroshilov's name does not appear, and Stalin is quoted as emphasizing that "without a regular army the defense of the Soviet land is impossible, the army must be imbued with a spirit of discipline and in it there must be well installed political work" (Azovtsev 1986, 23). This was a risk-free statement that might have been compared with some of his insolent messages from Tsaritsyn to determine his real attitude toward the military specialists.

Following his removal from Tsaritsyn in October, Stalin continued to be sent by Lenin and the Central Committee to trouble spots, areas where his particular strengths would be most effective. His experience at Tsaritsyn gave him more confidence in his dealings with fellow members of the Central Committee and the government. He, after all, had been in the field and seen the realities of the civil war.

Stalin also continued to function as the people's commissar for nationalities, performing as representative of the center on occasions that crossed national lines. As a member of the military council, he participated in the formation of a mixed Russo-Ukrainian *front* south of Kursk, which was preparing to enter the Ukraine as the German and Austrian occupiers left after the armistice of 11 November 1918. He was recalled to Moscow on 20 November and led a "congress" of the Belorussian section of the Bolshevik Party as it resolved in late December, in the name of the workers and peasants of Belorussia, to form the Belorussian Soviet Socialist Republic (Naida 1957, 293).

## TO PERM AND PETROGRAD

In early January Stalin was sent with Dzerzhinskii to investigate the causes and find those responsible for the defeat of the Third Army and the fall of the city of Perm to the Whites on 24 December. Perm was the site of one of the Imperial Army's largest arsenals, which held 10 million rifle cartridges and enough machine guns and rifles to equip several divisions (Lincoln 1994, 313). The special commission convened in Viatka, where it proceeded quickly and decisively to order a group of those responsible to be tried by a military court. Those commissars and commanders whom the commission judged responsible for the defeat were removed from their positions. The commission also took steps to improve political work among the troops, strengthen discipline, and shore up the supply situation. As always, Stalin was suspicious of those commanders who came from the old army; when he determined that they had committed acts of treason, he proceeded harshly and mercilessly. He also found cause to criticize the role of the Revolutionary Military Council of the Republic (without naming Trotsky) for its "impermissibly criminal method of directing the *front* . . . paralyzing the *front* with its contradictory directives and taking from the *front* any possibility of coming to the assistance of the 3rd Army . . ." (Voroshilov 1937, 23). As a result of these actions, Stalin could report that the combat effectiveness of the Third Army had been restored and that it was in condition to counterattack to restore the situation (Volkogonov 1989, book 1, part 1:95, 96).

On 17 May, Stalin was sent with plenopotentiary powers to Petrograd to stiffen the defenses of the city in the face of a looming

White threat. The threat was magnified by the possibilities that the Whites might persuade either the Finns or the Estonians, or both, to join in attempting to capture the "cradle of the Revolution." Given the support that the Whites were hoping to receive from the British, and the fact of the support of a squadron of the British fleet operating out of Revel (Tallin), it is understandable that the dimensions of the threat were magnified in the minds of the Bolshevik leadership. The degree of magnification was multiplied by Stalin's chronic visions of spies and traitors in the city and among military specialists in the Soviet Seventh Army.

A small White-Russian force, then called the "Northern Army," was formed under German auspices at Pskov in October 1918. Estimates of the size of the force vary to a maximum of 25,000. After Germany collapsed in November, the Whites withdrew into the newly independent state of Estonia and attempted to regroup with British support. In May 1919, they moved back into Soviet-controlled territory accompanied by an Estonian division. The objective of the White move was to establish a base of operations outside of Estonia. The Estonians were chiefly concerned with capturing territory that could be used to bargain over boundaries with whomever the future rulers of Russia were. The Soviet Seventh Army, weakened by the dispatch of levies to other *fronts,* fell back in disorder to the city, to the alarm of its Bolshevik leadership, headed by Politburo member Gregorii Zinoviev (Mawdsley 1987, 196, 197).

Stalin proceeded to reorganize the defenses of the city and gave particular attention to the spies and traitors in the Soviet forces and in the city. But, as the Whites continued to advance, on 9 June he wired Lenin asking for reinforcements, saying that "the fall of Piter [Petrograd] was hanging by a hair . . ."(Naida 1959, 160). As a result of this message, Lenin the next day proposed and the Central Committee approved the designation of the Petrograd *front* as first in importance, and reinforcements were dispatched from the Eastern *Front.* By mobilizing the workers of Petrograd and shaking up and reinforcing the Seventh Army, the White advance was brought to a halt at Gatchina and Krasnaia Sela on 12 June.

However, the overall situation remained critical. On 13 June, the garrison of the fort, Krasnaia Gorka, on the shore of the Gulf of Finland revolted and invited the garrisons of other forts, including the naval base at Kronstadt, to join them. Two others did and seemed to provide a prime opportunity to secure a breach in the system of naval fortifications protecting Petrograd. The British naval squadron was not ready to take advantage of the revolt, and the White ground troops were not flexible enough or strong enough to move to help the rebels (Naida 1959, 162, 163). The forts were retaken by the Reds with an air, land, and sea assault on 16 June.

Stalin, who participated in the planning of the assault, boasted that he had ignored the opinion of naval specialists who said that the attempt to take Krasnaia Gorka from the sea was contrary to naval science (the battleships *Petropavlovsk* and *Andrei Pervozvannyi* [Andrew the First, called St. Andrew] bombarded the fort all day on 15 June) (Naida 1959, 163). Stalin, attempting to be coy, promised to act similarly in the future despite his reverence for science (Voroshilov 1937, 30).

Six days later, Stalin announced that a turning point had been reached in the situation. Deserters were crossing over to the Reds, the Soviet offensive was proceeding successfully, and the Whites were running. In early July, Stalin was recalled from Petrograd but not before he had sixty-seven officers of the Kronstadt garrison executed on 18 June (Voroshilov 1937, 30; Luckett 1971, 303).

The Whites had been pushed back from Petrograd, but they did succeed in creating a base outside of the borders of Estonia. In July, General Iudenich was named commander of the Northwest Army. In August, with the aid of the British and Estonians, he directed another attempt to capture Petrograd; it was timed to coincide with Denikin's drive on Moscow. Again, the Seventh Army began to fall back. Zinoviev in the city, citing the superior arms and equipment that the British had furnished the Northwest Army, asked for reinforcements, but they could be furnished only from other heavily engaged *fronts*. Lenin seriously considered abandoning the city. Trotsky, supported in this instance by Stalin, opposed this course of action; after changing Lenin's mind, Trotsky left for Petrograd on 16 October with a mandate to defend the city.

When Trotsky arrived in Petrograd, he found the city's leadership in a state of utmost demoralization, with Zinoviev the "very center of utter confusion." Iudenich was only ten to fifteen kilometers from the city. Trotsky, aided by the personnel from his train, took the lead in stiffening the resolve of the city's residents to defend themselves. In one instance, Trotsky mounted an available horse to turn back the members of a regiment who had panicked before a White attack and led them in a counterattack (Trotsky 1930, 429). By 21 October, the White advance had been checked. On 22 October the Red Army began an offensive that drove the Northwest Army back into Estonia, where its soldiers were disarmed and interned (some 14,000 were stricken with typhus) (Trotsky 1960, 431).

Soviet history makes almost no mention of these two short campaigns, especially Trotsky's role in the last and decisive one. As popularized by Voroshilov, Stalin was the victor over Iudenich when in fact Iudenich led the offensive that almost took Petrograd. And there is no record of Stalin at any time exposing himself on the battlefield.

## STALIN'S MILITARY STYLE

There apparently was no stigma attached to Stalin's recall from Tsaritsyn; he was credited by some with restoring the situation there and with having accomplished his original mission of ensuring the shipment of foodstuffs to the center. He also was convinced, perhaps by Lenin himself, that the military specialists were to remain a factor in the construction of the army. But nothing would change his chronic suspicion and inherent dislike of the former tsarist officers and the one who supported them—Trotsky. Stalin's conflicts with Trotsky would make him an attractive leader to the workers and peasants who made up the great mass of the Red Army and who found Trotsky's style and methods difficult to accept. Among these were Budenny, Shchadenko, Kulik, Timoshenko, and others who had been elected to command positions in the immediate aftermath of the Bolshevik seizure of power. They would be the dictator's willing collaborators for the rest of their careers. The experiences at Tsaritsyn, Perm, and Petrograd did not improve Stalin's grasp of military affairs. He would continue to practice his own style of leadership derived from his experience as an underground revolutionary. In that regard, it was hardly likely that his friend Voroshilov could or would try to teach him anything; Voroshilov was cut out of the same cloth, and it probably was already evident that he was destined to be Stalin's eternal subordinate.

# 3
# EGOROV
# THE ODD MAN IN

## THE MILITARY SPECIALISTS TAKE OVER

It must have been particularly galling to Voroshilov that the man who relieved him as commander of the Tenth Army, Aleksandr Il'ich Egorov, was in many respects the epitome of the military specialist. He had been a lieutenant colonel in the old army, where he had served with distinction from the time of his commissioning at the Kazan Infantry School in April 1905. He arrived at Tsaritsyn accompanied, according to Budenny, by eighty former officers. Budenny's subordinates predicted future betrayals from this entourage of military specialists (Budenny 1958, 112).

Egorov took command of the Tenth Army on 26 December 1918. Tsaritsyn was still enclosed in a semicircle with a radius of some twenty kilometers and the Volga at its rear. Conditions within the Tenth Army were "extraordinarily difficult." In addition, the army command element required reorganization, and the overall condition of the troops and the logistical support services was poor. Egorov had to search out the ways and means to hold on to what he called "the Red Verdun" (Kopylov 1962, 203).

Egorov did not have time to complete his reorganization before the Whites struck on 1 January 1919. By the middle of January they had tightened their semicircle around the city, and on 12 January they siezed Dubovka, on the Volga. When Egorov shifted Dumenko's provisional cavalry division to the north, the Whites seized Sarenta on 16 January. But this was to be their last success. The provisional cavalry division (led by Budenny after Dumenko became ill) drove

41

the Whites out of Dubovka and then executed a deep raid in the rear of the White positions. This raid, combined with the offensives of the Eighth and Ninth Armies to the north, raised the siege of Tsaritsyn, and by late March the Don Cossacks had been driven to positions south of the Manych River (Khromov 1983, 407). The Southern *Front* appeared ready to drive the Whites into the Black Sea.

Egorov, in a monograph published in 1931, explained why this did not happen. The Southern *Front* (approximately 100,000 troops) was not strong enough to attack without reserves along a 700-kilometer front. The units on the flanks of the *front*—Nestor Ivanovich Makhno's detachment of irregulars on the right (west) flank and the Tenth Army, commanded by Egorov, on the left (east) flank—were far from positions from which they could support the central armies. Finally, and perhaps most importantly, the troops were exhausted from inadequate equipment, massive epidemics, and the absence of an established and regular source of supplies. Desertions increased, and there were outrageous incidents and refusals to obey orders. In March, outbreaks against Soviet authority occurred in the Ukraine, and a Cossack uprising in the rear area of the Southern *Front* had to be suppressed by combat troops. And, as Egorov observed, the Whites were fighting for their very existence with their backs to the sea (Egorov 1931, 85, 86).

The Whites launched a counterattack that drove the Tenth Army back to the Sal River. In May, in a battle along the Sal, which, according to Egorov, "decided the fate of the Tenth Army" (Kopylov 1962, 203), Egorov led the attack of units of Budenny's cavalry division and successfully beat off the White effort to cross the Sal. Egorov was wounded in the action but remained at the scene until his deputy relieved him. Budenny recounts helping to bind Egorov's wound in the left shoulder soon after it happened. According to Budenny, Egorov placed him in command of that sector until his deputy could take command of the army. Budenny wrote that he had great admiration for Egorov and considered him an important military specialist, dedicated to the revolutionary cause. Budenny also recalled that Egorov carried himself modestly and did not flaunt his education. Budenny was especially taken with Egorov's bravery in battle (Budenny 1958, 180).

## EGOROV'S ROOTS

Aleksandr Il'ich Egorov, born in 1893 in the town of Buzuluk in the south Volga region, was the fourth and youngest child of Ilia Fedorovich and Maria Ivanovna Egorov. Ilia Fedorovich was of the *meschaninskoe soslovie* (petit bourgeois estate) in a town that, at the end of the century, would have a population of 13,289, of whom 12,680 were members of the Orthodox Church. The main occupation of the area was grain farming, although there were some cattle and sheep raised there. It was an area afflicted by frequent poor harvests and, in 1873, 1880, and 1891, crop failures. Poor harvests had persisted from 1887 to 1891. The result was that the local peasantry was burdened with huge debts to moneylenders for food and seed loans (Brokgaus and Efron Iva 1891, 860).

The exact circumstances in which Egorov grew up, his early education, and his military service are not known, due to discrepancies between an autobiography he wrote in 1926, presumably for official purposes (Kopylov 1962, 200–205), and the data provided by his Soviet biographer, A. Nenarokov. For example, in his autobiography Egorov claimed that he was born in 1895; Nenarokov, who had access to the autobiography, cites the year of his birth given on his birth certificate as 1893. Egorov describes his childhood as one of extreme poverty exacerbated by his father's addiction to alcohol. Nenarokov does not mention this potentially significant influence on the man. Egorov gives the impression that he obtained his education almost on his own and passed the secondary school examination without attending school *(eksterno)*. Nenarokov cites an enclosure to Egorov's application to volunteer for military service as a means of gaining admission to officer candidate school. The document certifies that he completed the sixth class of the classical gymnasium in Samara. It was signed by "one of the most experienced and well known pedagogues in the Don region" (Nenarokov 1973, 28).

More importantly and potentially more damaging to a senior officer serving in the Red Army of 1926 is Egorov's claim that he was forced to leave the Imperial Army sometime after 1905 because he was considered unreliable politically. Nenarokov, in direct contradiction to what Egorov wrote about himself in 1926, names the units, their locations, and the dates during which Egorov served in them, establishing that Egorov remained on active duty from the time he was commissioned in 1905 until that army disintegrated during the revolution. That service included such activities as dispersing demonstrations, suppressing uprisings, and controlling striking peasants—activities that his political masters in 1926 would have considered to be counterrevolutionary (Nenarokov 1973, 14, 15).

There is no indication in the accompanying article of the purpose of the autobiography. The original was held in Egorov's personnel file in the directorate of cadres in the Soviet Ministry of Defense. As a senior officer who participated in the validation of candidates for officer positions in the Red Army after the October Revolution, Egorov must have known that he was taking a risk in concealing or distorting the facts of his military and social background. Possibly, he was advised that despite his civil war record, he should cover up the counterrevolutionary aspects of his tsarist army service if he wished to continue to serve in the Red Army. If so, whoever provided this advice planted a potentially devastating discrepancy in the files of the future marshal.

In the autobiography, Egorov wrote that his father was a *gruzchik* (freight loader and stevedore) and that he and his brother frequently took the older man's place when he was too drunk to work. Whatever *petit bourgeois* activity his father engaged in to support his family, Aleksandr, growing up in the midst of rural poverty, could hardly have avoided becoming aware of its consequences. His eventual political leanings were undoubtedly influenced by the experiences and observations of his youth.

Given the poor economic prospects for the region, it is hardly surprising that Aleksandr chose the army as an escape route. In 1901, he volunteered to enlist as a soldier in the Imperial Army with the expectation that if his service was satisfactory, he could apply to enter the Kazan Junkers Infantry School. His application was accepted, and he served in the 4th Grenadier Nesvizskii Regiment until entering the Kazan Infantry School in the fall of 1902. He encountered no academic difficulties there, but during the wave of unrest that swept through Russia during the Russo-Japanese War, he became associated with those who were opposed to the monarchy. In 1926, he was to claim that he began to share the views of the Socialist Revolutionary (SR) Party as early as 1904. The SR Party advocated confiscation of land from the large landowners, the church, and the nobility and its distribution to the peasantry. Consequently, the SR Party enjoyed the support of the overwhelming majority of the peasantry, who continued to dream of completing the emancipation of 1861, which they believed had provided them with only half of the land to which they were entitled.

Although Egorov was demoted one grade in Junker (cadet) rank in April 1905 for participating in a gathering in sympathy for "political criminals," he was allowed to complete the course. On 22 April 1905, he was commissioned a *podporuchik* (equivalent to a second lieutenant) with seniority from 9 August 1904, awarded because of his high relative standing in his class. He was assigned to the 13th Life-Grenadier Erivan Regiment, stationed near Tbilisi (Nenarokov 1973, 13).

### A LIFE FOR THE TSAR

Egorov served in the Caucasus for six years during the period of revolutionary unrest that swept the country during and after the Russo-Japanese War (1904–5). He was sent to Baku for patrol and guard duty, assisted the civil authorities in Tbilisi, did temporary duty in Gori (Stalin's birthplace) to suppress the uprisings of 1906, and guarded the lines of the Caucasian Railroad from 1907 until 1910. This was a period when Stalin and the Georgian Bolsheviks were conducting raids on banks, treasury transports, and army units. Altogether 1,150 acts of terrorism were recorded in the Caucasus between 1905 and 1908. The most notorious robbery or expropriation took place in Tbilisi; it yielded 250,000 rubles, which were clandestinely transferred to the Bolshevik treasury abroad. Stalin's role in these activities was important, although it has never been clearly defined (Deutscher 1949, 87). There is no evidence that the young *poruchik* (Egorov was promoted and also decorated in 1908) ever came into direct contact with the future dictator during his tour of duty in the Caucasus.

In April 1911, Egorov was transferred to the 132d Bendery Infantry Regiment, which was returning to the Kiev Military District following service in Baku. He took with him Varvara Vasil'evna, whom he had married in the spring after a three-year courtship. In March 1912 their first child was born, a daughter, Tatiana. A photograph exists on the back of which the happy father wrote: "Dear Grandfather: Maybe you will now come to visit us, to look at me. Your Tatusia." There is no evidence that the old man, who would not bless the marriage, ever accepted the invitation.

During this period, Egorov, through a fellow officer, was given free access to the newly opened Kiev Conservatory, where he studied voice. Egorov had dreamed of going to a conservatory to train his "beautiful, resonant, baritone" voice. According to Nenarokov, this opportunity excited him more than his promotion to staff captain and assumption of command of a company—two days before Austria-Hungary declared war on Serbia (Nenarokov 1973, 14–20).

## THE EASTERN FRONT, 1914–17

"The pits of our stomachs contracted and our hair stood on end when we attacked for the first time on 13 August 1914," Egorov recalled later. The attack was successful: sixty Austrian soldiers and two officers were captured. Staff captain Egorov was awarded an honorary weapon. It was the first entry into what was to become an outstanding war record. During the next two years, Egorov was decorated six times and, demonstrating that these were earned decorations, was wounded five times. On four of these occasions, Egorov either returned to the front earlier than was prescribed or he refused hospitalization, although he was urged to accept it by medical personnel. Only on 20 July 1915, when he was evacuated unconscious, did he remain in the hospital more than a month.

After being promoted to captain, Egorov was given command of a battalion in a reserve regiment stationed in Tver (Kalinin during the Soviet period) for four months; he then spent two months training *praporshchiki* (warrant officers) in Riga. When he returned to his regiment, the 132d Infantry, it was in defensive positions along the Western Dvina. These positions were relatively close to the capital, Petrograd, when the February Revolution exploded. The ministers of the provisional government in Petrograd attempted to cope with the Petrograd Soviet and, after Lenin's return to Russia in April, with the peace program of the Bolsheviks. At the front, Egorov's regiment was subjected to a flood of agitators from Petrograd and Riga pleading various causes. Although the revolution was considered a calamity by the army high command and a predominate portion of the generals and higher ranking officers, for Egorov it was an opportunity to resolve the internal contradictions that had plagued him since 1904. He declared himself a Socialist Revolutionary and was elected to the 32d Division Soldiers' Committee, where he headed the SR fraction and wholeheartedly took up the challenges posed by the revolution's influence on the army (Nenarokov 1973, 25, 26; Frenkin 1978, 71).

As Allan K. Wildman has observed: "The soldiers were not indiscriminate in removing their superiors and happily submitted to popular and respected officers" (Wildman 1980, 235). Egorov's war record and his political beliefs would have earned him respect, and his background would have given him the understanding and sympathy for the needs and yearnings of his predominately peasant troops. The soldiers' committees, analogous in form and intent to the soviets, appeared at every level of command following the February Revolution and the broad dissemination of Order No. 1 of the Petrograd Soviet. By the end of March the soldiers' committees in the frontline units were fully legitimized when the high command realized that they could be useful in calming the mutinous disorders that were occurring, including the lynching of officers, desertions, arrest and removal of officers, chaos on the railways, and refusals to obey orders (Wildman 1980, 187, 246).

As the committees evolved, they were given certain functions, such as supervising commissary accounts and mediating soldier-officer conflicts. Most committees over time developed a pronounced pro-Soviet and Socialist coloration. The work of the committees attracted many intellectuals in uniform, and the committees were eventually composed of very few peasants. The committees also, according to Wildman, developed a strong bias in favor of reconstituting military discipline on the new "democratic" foundations (Wildman 1980, 248). The peasant soldiers, who formed the overwhelming majority of the Russian Army in 1917, although they were in the minority on the committees, had no interest in continuing to fight. They saw in the revolution an opportunity to acquire land; strongly influenced by rumors from the rear that the transfer of land was imminent, they deserted by the thousands. For the peasant soldier, the hunger for land and the longing for peace combined into an irresistible urge to quit the front and return to his native village (Frenkin 1978, 194–96).

The provisional government's response to the burning questions of peace and land was to temporize: the land question would be settled after a constituent assembly decided on the form of the new government and the peace question by continuing to honor Russia's obligation to her allies. These policies did not satisfy the peasant's hunger for land or his desire for peace. And they drove Egorov into the ranks of the Left SRs and ultimately to the Bolsheviks.

The collapse of the Russian Army's June offensive has been called the turning point of the revolution (Kvartadze 1967, 111–17). The offensive, planned at an interallied conference at Chantilly, France, in November 1916, was undertaken in an effort to restore the morale of the army, to strengthen the authority of the provisional government, and to fulfill alliance obligations. None of these goals was accomplished. Russian losses in dead, wounded, and missing soldiers were more than 150,000 men. Both army morale and the prestige of the provisional government declined even further. The Germans and Austrians, utilizing divisions transferred from France and Italy, drove the Russians farther to the east. The Northern *Front*'s Fifth Army launched a secondary attack on 10 July in support of the Southwestern *Front*'s main effort, which achieved some insignificant success. However, the troops not only refused to continue the advance but also blocked the introduction of other units into the battle (Kvartadze 1967, 111–17).

Of the tumultuous events of the summer of 1917, the unsuccessful attempt by Gen. Lavr Georgievich Kornilov to seize Petrograd in August helped Egorov understand that the counterrevolutionaries were intent on establishing a military dictatorship and restoring the monarchy. This affair also exacerbated the issue of whether the SRs should continue in coalition with the bourgeois parties. In September, the Left SRs voted with the Bolsheviks against renewing the coalition. In October, some Left SRs joined the Bolshevik-led Military Revolutionary Committee when it was formed and assisted the Bolsheviks in the siezure of power. After the siezure, the Left SRs favored the creation of a broad Socialist coalition. The

SR Central Committee, however, expelled from the Party all who had participated in what became known as the October Revolution and all who had remained at the Second Congress of Soviets, during which the composition of the Lenin-led Bolshevik government was announced. The Left SRs formed a separate party in November 1917 and became junior partners in a coalition with the Bolsheviks until the summer of 1918.

During these events, Egorov continued to play an active role in the politics of the army at the front. In August he was elected to the Twelfth Army Soviet of Military Deputies; in early September he became a member of his division's demobilization committee, which was charged with considering the sensitive question of demobilizing older classes of soldiers. After the Bolshevik seizure of power on 7 November 1917, Egorov was elected a division delegate to a First Army Congress, which convened five days after the Bolshevik coup. Late that evening, a telegram was read to the congress from Aleksandr Fedorovich Kerensky, the head of the provisional government, ordering the dispatch of the most capable combat troops to Pskov to assist in returning the provisional government to power. The congress unanimously rejected the order.

The next day, the First Army delegates to the Second All Russian Congress of Soviets returned from Petrograd and announced the composition of the new government to the First Army Congress. When Egorov was given the floor, he called for the formation of a single Socialist government, demonstrating that, in those days, he still shared the "erroneous" (according to his Soviet biographer) views of the Left SR leadership. However, even before cooperation with the Bolsheviks was agreed to by the Left SRs in Petrograd, Egorov and others in the lower organizations cooperated with the Bolsheviks. Egorov, along with fourteen of his Left SR comrades, was elected to the First Army Executive Committee. At the conclusion of a stormy session, Egorov led the delegates in the singing of "Dubinushki" (the Song of the Volga Boatmen, the contemporary equivalent of "We Shall Overcome") (Nenarokov 1973, 31).

On 9 November, Egorov was promoted to colonel; later that same month he was sent to Petrograd as a delegate from the First Army to the Central Executive Committee of the Second Congress of

Soviets. His name was also included on a list of officers, civil servants, doctors, and soldiers "completely devoted to the new order" as candidates to replace disaffected individuals in the central institutions of the Defense Ministry. As was the case with other governmental ministries, only the lower ranking employees of the ministry appeared for work on the first days after the Bolshevik seizure of power. The business of supplying the troops at the front was handled by no more than a dozen Party workers. The disruption in the ministry and Kerensky's order to organize an advance on Petrograd had an immediate effect on the supply system; soldiers at the front began to starve and horses collapsed. The Bolsheviks forced the military and civil servants of the provisional government to return to work but were soon charging senior officers with sabotaging the operations of the Defense Ministry and attempting to organize opposition to the new regime in the field forces (Korablev 1970, 168).

Egorov left for Petrograd on 22 November. There he was selected for membership on a commission that chose the age groups to be demobilized and that designated military activities to be discontinued. In December, co-opted to the military section of the Central Executive Committee, he participated in and voted with the Bolshevik faction developing the draft principles on which to base the formation of a new Socialist army (Nenarokov 1973, 32, 35). Here Egorov came to the attention of Avel Enukidze, a Georgian Bolshevik who claimed Party *stazh* (seniority) from 1898. On Enukidze's recommendation, Egorov remained with the military section as a "needed worker." Enukidze "guided and defined" all of Egorov's activity at this stage of his career (Nenarokov 1973, 34, 35).

## CREATING AN ARMY OF A NEW TYPE

When the negotiations at Brest Litovsk broke down at the end of January and the Germans resumed their advance, Egorov returned to the front and desperately tried to organize resistance. In a popularized sketch of Egorov, I. Mukhoperets claimed that during this period of German advances, crumbling Soviet resistance, and disarray in Petrograd, he encountered Egorov leading a demolition detachment attempting to slow the German advance by blowing bridges on their route (Mukhoperets 1969, 73–75). Nenarokov does not confirm this episode but does say that Egorov was forming detachments of Red Guards as an "instructor-organizer" at this time (Nenarokov 1973, 36). These detachments of troops attempted to halt the German advance, but there is no record, other than that of Mukhoperets, of exactly where and how Egorov contributed to the events that during the Soviet period were annually celebrated on 23 February—the Day of the Soviet Army and Fleet.

On the morning of 24 February, after an exhausting series of debates in the Central Committee of the Bolshevik Party, before the Petrograd Soviet and the Central Executive Committee of the Council of People's Commissars (Sovnarkom), Lenin signed the telegram to the German government that accepted the German peace terms. The Soviet delegation, however, did not reach Brest Litovsk until 28 February because a railway bridge had been destroyed by Red Guards (directed by Egorov?) trying to check the German advance. According to John Wheeler-Bennett, there was no more vilified man in Russia or Europe than Lenin after the terms of the treaty were made public (Wheeler-Bennett 1938, 264, 265). The leading Left SRs resigned from the government, but Egorov disagreed strongly with this action. Four months later he wrote:

> Having carried on my shoulders the entire yoke and weight of the conditions of the last war and having combat experience, I did not share the view of the CC [Central Committee] of the party of the Left Socialist Revolutionaries on the question of the conduct of the war and the building of an army.

This statement was part of Egorov's letter published in *Pravda* on 16 July 1918 renouncing his membership in the Left SR Party and announcing his intention to seek to join the Bolsheviks (Nenarokov 1973, 36). However forthright Egorov's public declaration of his attitude toward the war and the Bolshevik Party was, it would not be sufficient to save him twenty years later when he was accused of calling Lenin an "adventurer" and an "agent" of the Germans during a speech to the delegates of the First Army Congress in November 1917 (Khor'kov 1992, 6).

The departure of the Left SRs from the government did not detract from Egorov's standing in the military section of the Central Executive Committee. On Enukidze's recommendation, Egorov was entrusted with the forming and training of units of the new army. In April, he was detailed along with I. I. Vatsetis, a future commander in chief of the Red Army, to inspect military units and evaluate courses for instructors in Moscow and the Moscow Military District. After an inspection in Tver at the end of April, Egorov reported that "morale in the urban units of the Red Army is bad, there is a complete absence of discipline and internal order . . ." The main reasons for this were the "inadequate attention on the part of local Soviets and social organizations to recruiting the army and the appointment of former officers and instructors the Red Army men distrusted" (Nenarokov 1973, 39).

To remedy this situation, Egorov proposed to the commissar of war, Trotsky, that all candidates for commissions be given the closest scrutiny and that opportunities be given to all to present reasons why a candidate should be accepted or rejected. This and others of his suggestions were reflected in a directive of the Supreme Validating Commission. On 7 May, Egorov was named chairman of the commission, which considered candidates for the positions of regimental commander and higher, as well as corresponding positions throughout the military establishment. The commission's recommendations were forwarded to the commissar of war for final approval. Among the first to be validated was Mikhail Nikolaevich Tukhachevsky, who had been a lieutenant in the old army and had spent most of the war as a prisoner of war in Germany. Tukhachevsky was designated a military commissar in the Moscow region of the western screening force (Nenarokov 1973, 38).

Administrative support of whatever Soviet forces could be put in the field was initially handled by a hodgepodge of ad hoc and former tsarist agencies until 8 May 1918. At that time their functions were all assumed by the All Russian Main Staff, headed by a chief and two commissars. This staff was to be an executive organ managing matters such as mobilization, formation, quartering, and training of troops, and developing tables of organization and equipment, field manuals, instructions, and directives. All local military-administrative elements were subordinate to this staff. Egorov had a large role in its formation, and he and N. I. Bessonov were its first two commissars. Its first chief was N. N. Stogov, who switched his allegiance to the Whites at the end of the summer (Popov 1967, 96).

Egorov also functioned concurrently as head of the evacuation section of the People's Commissariat for Demobilization, conducting negotiations with representatives of Germany and her allies for the exchange of prisoners of war (Nenarokov 1973, 39).

In August 1918, Egorov, observing with apprehension the Red Army's failures in the field, provided an analysis of the reasons for them and recommended on how to avoid them in the future. In a note to N. I. Podvoiskii, at that time an influential member of the Supreme Military Council, he cited the main reasons for the Red Army's defeats: the absence of a unified plan of operations, the absence of appropriate technical organization and preparation, shortages of modern equipment, and shortages of experienced commanders. Egorov recommended "urgent measures" to alleviate the situation, including the formation of a military-revolutionary defense staff headed by Lenin, and declaring the entire territory controlled by the new regime to be in a "military-revolutionary situation," that is, under martial law. He also recommended some purely military measures, including the development of a general plan of operations and keeping in mind that the enemy now had the initiative and that the technical shortcomings of the army would not permit an immediate offensive. On 20 August, he submitted a report to Lenin, including a recommendation that a commander in chief of the Soviet forces be named because "only a single will can direct operations; under the influence of various and even useful advice it [the high command] always loses its clarity and decisiveness and the organs directed by it will act with uncertainty . . ." (Popov 1967, 99). In his report he also criticized sharply the activities of the Supreme Military Council.

> In the Supreme Military Council "for" and "against" are based on such strong and irrefutable facts that one opinion destroys the other and as a result the matter does not move. In such a system, any independence, any rapid decision, any bold risk without which one cannot conduct any war, will be turned down (Popov 1967, 99).

On 26 August, Podvoiskii sent a telegram to the Supreme Military Council with copies to Lenin, the chairman of the Central Executive Committee, and others urging the formation of what he called a *stavka* without delay. On 2 September, the Central Executive Committee declared the country a "military camp." It also formed the Revolutionary Military Council of the Republic (RVSR), chaired by Trotsky, as the body directing the combat operations of the Red Army. The Supreme Military Council was disbanded. On 6 September, the RVSR named Vatsetis, who had been in command of the Eastern *Front,* as commander in chief (Popov 1967, 100).

## ARMY COMMANDER

Egorov had participated in the dissolution of the old army, the drafting of founding principles, and the selection of officers for the new army. Now he had helped shape the high command of the Soviet Republic. From his vantage point in Moscow, he felt the crisis atmosphere surrounding Lenin and his regime. There appeared to be no doubts about his reliability, even though he was a former officer and an SR. He was now anxious to take the field against the regime's numerous enemies. He may also have had his fill of administration and paperwork. The attempted assassination of Lenin on 30 August intensified his desire to return to combat duty. The next day he submitted a request for duty at the front, which was approved. He was designated commander of the Ninth Army.

The Ninth Army was defending the approaches to Tsaritsyn. Like the Tenth Army, the Ninth consisted mainly of partisan detachments named for their commanders. On Egorov's arrival at army headquarters, he proceeded to strengthen the army staff, wiring the commander in chief to send some General Staff officers. He also asked for candidates for the posts of chief of staff, chief of operations, and chief of intelligence. For the latter post, Egorov wanted a Communist qualified in intelligence. As former chairman of the Validating Commission, he knew the various available former officers well and did not hesitate to call for them. He also organized the army supply section, halting all attempts by subordinate unit commanders to decide their supply problems on their own (Nenarokov 1973, 46, 47). As Egorov was to recall later, "I had to begin the organization of an army consisting of partisan detachments . . . it took extraordinary efforts to bring those partisan detachments not only to obedience and subordination to a single will but also to give them the polish of regular units" (Kopylov 1962, 203).

Egorov was not able to complete the task of converting the Ninth Army into a "polished" regular unit. At the end of October 1918, he became seriously ill; although he tried to return to his post, he was hospitalized until late December. Then, not fully recovered, he was ordered to Tsaritsyn to take command of the Tenth Army from Klim Voroshilov. Although there is no evidence that the two met at this time, under these circumstances they certainly must have become aware of each other. This initial contact, direct or indirect, was not likely to foster a warm subsequent relationship.

We have already recounted Egorov's success in raising the siege of Tsaritsyn. His efforts there must have been appreciated, for on 9 July 1919, when he returned to duty after recovering from the wound he received on the Sal River in May, he was given command of the Fourteenth Army, the redesignated Second Ukrainian Army (Nenarokov 1973, 53), again relieving Voroshilov (SVE 8:469). When Egorov took command, the army was part of the Southern *Front,* defending before Briansk the onslaught of Denikin's Volunteer Army. Denikin's situation had improved markedly in Egorov's absence. He had received a considerable replenishment of arms, ammunition, and supplies from the British and had conducted a mobilization among the Cossack population in the north Caucasus (Azovtsev 1986, 133). The Whites had captured Tsaritsyn, Ekaterinoslav, and Kharkov and were driving toward Voronezh. Encouraged by these successes, Denikin ordered his forces to move on Moscow (Egorov 1931, 100–105).

## THE DEFEAT OF DENIKIN

Denikin's advance raised fears in Moscow that the Whites coming from the south would join forces with those of Adm. Aleksandr Vasilevich Kolchak in Siberia. This concern was one of the reasons the new commander in chief, Sergei Sergeevich Kamenev,* chose

---

*Kamenev relieved Vatsetis on 8 July 1919. Vatsetis was arrested but eventually was released. Bonch-Bruevich, who had a poor opinion of Vatsetis, considered Kamenev "hesitant and phlegmatic," with a habit of always leaving something unsaid, of never finishing what he started to say, and never fully implementing operational decisions. Bonch-Bruevich refused to serve under him (Bonch-Bruevich 1966, 330–37).

to make his main effort down the Volga to prevent the linkup of Denikin and Kolchak.

Egorov's Fourteenth Army, in an offensive scheduled to begin on 15 August, was to assist in the main effort with attacks along its front. However, before the offensive began, the Whites attacked at the junction of the Thirteenth and Fourteenth Armies and forced both to retreat. The offensive of the remainder of the *front*, although thrown off balance, appeared to the *front* commander, V. N. Egorev, to have had some initial success. However, a White cavalry raid led by K. K. Mamontov and a series of White counterattacks brought the offensive to a halt and in some sectors caused the Red Army to retreat. On 7 September, the Whites captured Kursk, drove out elements of the Thirteenth Army. The Fourteenth Army, still under the influence of *partizanshchina* and the unsystematic way that its predecessor, the Second Ukrainian Army, had been formed, could only provide limited support to the Thirteenth Army. Nevertheless, Egorov was optimistic about the army's future. Desertions had been reduced to a minimum, cases of failure to carry out orders disappeared, and the arrival of fresh troops promised that the army would soon be combat ready (Egorov 1931, 111–25).

## FRONT COMMANDER

On 26 September, the situation on the Southern *Front*, according to Egorov, "was assuming the dimensions of a catastrophe . . ." (Egorov 1931, 133). To avoid it, the *front* was divided in two by assigning the armies on the left, eastern flank to the newly created Southeastern *Front*. The Southern *Front* retained the Eighth, Thirteenth, and Fourteenth Armies, and the Twelfth Army was subordinated to it on 16 October. On that date the *front* numbered some 130,000 men, equipped with 2,689 machine guns and 599 artillery pieces. Of the 130,000 men, there were 17,500 cavalrymen; as the Russians of that era would describe the force, it consisted of 112,500 bayonets and 17,500 sabers (Egorov 1931, 141). Egorov was given command of the *front* and Stalin was assigned as the member of the *front* Revolutionary Military Council (RVS). As the member of the RVS, Stalin was obliged to observe all of Egorov's activities and validate all of his orders.

At this juncture in his 1931 account, Egorov inserted an excerpt from Voroshilov's *Stalin i Krasnaia Armiia* (Stalin and the Red Army) in the following glowing terms: "The Party and the working class in that period of truly enormous significance places one of its best and most devoted to the proletarian revolution fighters in the most important combat sector, I. V. Stalin, and on his shoulders places the entire weight of leading the struggle against Denikin. An exhaustive evaluation of the giant and outstanding work of Stalin we find in the following pages of that marvelous historical outline of Voroshilov . . ." (Egorov 1931, 141). The excerpt from Voroshilov's book describes how Stalin recommended to Lenin that the previous operations plan be scrapped and that a new one devised by Stalin be substituted for it. Stalin's objection to the old plan was that it entailed making the main effort through the territory of the Don Cossacks, which would serve to rally them against the Red Army and drive them into the arms of Denikin, making him the "savior of the Don." Stalin proposed to split Denikin's forces with a drive through Kharkov and through the Don Basin to Rostov on the Don (Egorov 1931, 141). Egorov apparently agreed with Stalin's proposal, but there is no indication that he participated in its formulation. In his 1926 autobiography, Egorov stated flatly that "the operational plan for the offensive was developed by me . . ." (Kopylov 1962, 204).

As the Red Army prepared for a counteroffensive, the Whites continued to advance. Under orders from the commander in chief, Egorov directed the Thirteeth and Fourteenth Armies to counterattack even though they had not completed their concentration. The attack of the Thirteenth Army was a complete failure, resulting in heavy losses and further retreat. Egorov placed the responsibility for this on the army commander, A. I. Gekker, who did not understand his mission, failed to evaluate the situation on his front correctly, and was incapable of using the relatively strong strike force available to him. Subsequently, Gekker asked to be relieved of his duties because he could not cope with them. He was not relieved immediately, however; he remained in command until February 1920.

The Fourteenth Army had some success. The fact that it had delayed the enemy, remained steady even when retreating in some places, and in all cases had its units supporting one another in accordance with directives gave Egorov the feeling that a turning point had been reached. Subsequently, the Red Army recaptured Orel on 20 September in a series of remarkable small unit actions by the Latvian brigades (Egorov 1931, 144).

The Thirteenth Army, after a number of false starts and reinforced by the Estonian Division, began its offensive on 26 October. In a series of battles that cost 3,000 casualties, the army moved slowly to the southeast with what Egorov observed to be new confidence in its ability to win. Progress of the Fourteenth Army accelerated early in November when it exploited the success of a cavalry raid led by V. M. Primakov. By the middle of November, both armies were advancing on a broad front (Egorov 1931, 171–72).

Cavalry actions also played a critical role in the combat actions of both sides on the eastern flank of the Southern *Front*. Mamontov led another successful raid in late September against a weakened Eighth Army whose commander independently ordered a withdrawal to reorganize and replenish his forces, thus exposing Egorov's left flank. Here another independent action, this time by Budenny, saved the Southern *Front* from disaster. Budenny's cavalry corps, of some 7,500 sabers and 500 bayonets, was subordinate to the Southeastern *Front* and was under orders to cross the Don and move northwest. Instead, hearing of Mamontov's raid, Budenny decided not to cross the Don but to move north aiming to intercept the White cavalry. When the CINC, S. S. Kamenev, was informed what Budenny was doing, he could only comment, "It is very sad that this is the way that your people execute orders. Now there is nothing left but to agree with your decision [to approve Budenny's move]" (Egorov 1931, 152). On 7 October, Budenny had moved into the zone of the Southern *Front*, and his corps had been transferred to that command. This was *partizanshchina* on a grand scale, but as Egorov was to observe in another context, "victors are not brought to trial" (Egorov 1931, 169). The appearance of Budenny's corps on the southern flank of the White cavalry, plus assistance from the Southeastern *Front*, helped restore the combat worthiness of the Eighth Army. By 12 October, the army's condition had improved to the point where Egorov could order it and Budenny's cavalry to counterattack the Whites. On 13 October, Budenny's corps came into direct contact with Mamontov's troopers and began to push them in the direction of Voronezh. By 24 October, Voronezh was recaptured through the combined efforts of Budenny's cavalry and the infantry.

By mid-November, the Whites were in full retreat, but they were giving ground grudgingly and occasionally counterattacking. After Budenny's capture on 16 November of Kastorniia, a rail junction approximately 100 kilometers west of Voronezh, it became clear to the *front* command that the presence of the cavalry corps at the juncture of the Thirteenth and Eighth Armies provided an opportunity to drive to the south and divide Denikin's forces in two. On the west would be the remains of the Volunteer Army and on the east would be the Don Cossacks.

As Budenny moved south, the decision was made to expand his corps into an army. Egorov gives credit for "this idea of genius" to Stalin (Egorov 1931, 181, 192, 206, 207). The First Cavalry Army was established on 11 November 1919, according to Voroshilov "despite and even against the wishes of the center . . ." (Voroshilov 1937, 39).

The Twelfth Army, on the right flank, now began to play a more active role. In September and October, the army's main operational function was to reconnoiter the activities of the Polish forces in the Ukraine and to provide reinforcements for the other armies of the Southern *Front*. The army's task was made easier because the Poles and Denikin, despite having a common enemy—the Bolsheviks—could not agree on a plan to proceed against them. As the *front* entered the pursuit phase of the operation, the Twelfth Army was ordered to clear the right bank of the Dnieper of Denikin's troops. Due to the poor condition of the army, its ability to advance hinged largely on the progress of the Fourteenth Army, on its left.

As the collapse of Denikin's forces became imminent, the Southern *Front* pursuit was measured by the successes of Budenny's Cavalry Army. In an attempt to halt him, White units were moved from the Tsaritsyn *Front*. But the transfers were too late; Denikin's forces were in complete disarray. Taganrog and Rostov on the Don were occupied by 10 January, and the remnants of the Volunteer Army and the Don Cossacks were scattered into the Caucasus and the Crimea and on both sides of the Dnieper (Egorov 1931, 213).

After the defeat of Denikin, the Southern and Southeastern *Fronts* were reorganized and renamed to reflect their new missions. The Twelfth, Thirteenth, and Fourteenth Armies remained under Egorov's command in what was now called the Southwestern *Front;* Stalin remained the member of the *front* military council. The Southeastern *Front* became the Caucasus *Front* and the First Cavalry Army and the Eighth Army were assigned to it. Egorov and the Southwestern *Front* were given the mission of liquidating the remaining White forces west of the Dnieper, particularly in the city of Odessa, preventing the Whites from entering the Crimea from the north, covering the Kiev region in the event of an offensive by the Poles, and securing the north shore of the Sea of Azov. Egorov established his headquarters in Kharkov (Nenarokov 1973, 58).

*Front* operations in the next two months consisted mainly of skirmishes on both sides of the Dnieper involving the Thirteenth and Fourteenth Armies. Odessa was captured in February, and by midmonth the entire west bank of the Dnieper had been cleared of Whites. In early March, the Thirteenth Army moved to Perekop on the isthmus connecting the Crimean peninsula to the mainland and to Chongar and the bridges crossing into the Crimea, attempting to force its way onto the peninsula. The army was beaten back by the White defenders. After the event, the army's failure to capture the Crimea was attributed to a shortage of men and equipment, a failure of command and control in the echelons from regiment to army, a loss of surprise, and the inclement weather (Azovtsev 1986, 210, 211). The *front* commander, Egorov, shared in the army's successes and must have taken part of the blame for its failures. But it was the army commander, A. I. Gekker, who was relieved during this operation.

### EGOROV'S FIRST COLLABORATION WITH STALIN
Despite the Thirteenth Army's failure to capture the Crimea, Egorov's first collaboration with Stalin had to be considered a success, one that by 1931 he was only too eager to attribute to Stalin. Egorov had also demonstrated the ability to work with Voroshilov and Budenny, who on their own had joined the Southern *Front* to defeat the White cavalry leader, Mamontov. Their reward was the cre-

ation of the First Cavalry Army. This leadership team and its apparent military skill seemed to have found the recipe for success in the Russian Civil War. And, in a development that was to influence subsequent events, Stalin assumed a proprietary attitude toward the First Cavalry Army.

# 4
# TUKHACHEVSKY
# THE NOBLE REVOLUTIONARY

Egorov's campaign, with the First Cavalry Army in the vanguard, appeared to have ended organized resistance to Bolshevik rule in European Russia. As the campaign came to an end, Trotsky began the conversion of some of the armies in the field that were not actively engaged to "labor armies." The first of what ultimately became eight labor armies was the Third Army of the Eastern *Front*, which in January 1920 was converted into the First Revolutionary Army of Labor. The plan was that the personnel of these armies would be used in rebuilding the civilian economy while retaining the organization and equipment of the other Red armies and that they would be sufficiently trained to rapidly return to military service in the event of an emergency (SVE 7:126, 127).

Such an emergency developed almost at the same time that the first field armies were undergoing conversion. After being driven out of Rostov on the Don, Denikin's battered forces retreated to defensive positions behind the Don and the Manych. They were joined there by elements of the Don Army, which was retreating before the Southeastern *Front*. In mid-January, the Southeastern *Front* (now renamed the Caucasus *Front*), reinforced by the transfer of the Eighth Army and the First Cavalry Army from the Southern *Front*, launched a series of frontal attacks, which the Whites threw back with heavy Red casualties. The First Cavalry Army was especially hard hit; it suffered 3,000 casualties. Budenny and Voroshilov complained to the RVS of the Republic that the Caucasus *Front* commander, Vasilii Ivanovich Shorin, who had been a colonel in the old army, did not know how to employ cavalry. The RVS of the Republic responded by appointing Mikhail Nikolaevich Tukhachevsky to command the Caucasus *Front*. Tukhachevsky had been a highly successful army commander on the Eastern *Front* and had been cooling his heels temporarily on the staff of the Southern *Front* (Ivanov 1990, 137, 138).

## TUKHACHEVSKY—THE NOBLE REVOLUTIONARY

Mikhail Nikolaevich Tukhachevsky was born in February 1893 to the peasant wife of a hereditary nobleman on a small estate approximately 100 kilometers northeast of Smolensk. The family, for financial reasons, moved to Penza and later to Moscow, and Tukhachevsky attended schools in those cities. At eighteen he entered the First Moscow Cadet Corps, from which he graduated in 1912 at the head of his class and then entered the Aleksandrovskoe Military School in Moscow. In July 1914, he finished that school, again at the top of his class. Because of his high class standing, Tukhachevsky was given the rank of *gvardii podporuchik* (guards second lieutenant) and the reward of choosing the regiment in which he would serve. His choice was foreordained—the Life Guards Semenov Regiment, a regiment founded by Peter the Great in which his great-grandfather had served in the War of 1812 (Ivanov 1990, 20–25).

The start of World War I curtailed Tukhachevsky's graduation leave, and he was forced to join his regiment as it moved to the front. His active service during the war was also shortened when he was captured by the Germans at Lomza, Poland, in early 1915. In some six months of active service he succeeded in earning six decorations. In early 1917, after several unsuccessful attempts, he managed to escape from the prisoner-of-war compound in the fortress at Ingolstadt, cross into neutral Switzerland, and eventually reach St. Petersburg on 27 October 1917, ten days before the 7 November seizure of power by the Bolsheviks. In November he rejoined his regiment, then part of the Southwestern *Front*, where he was given command of a company. Early the next year, probably before Tukhachevsky had time to become accustomed to or evaluate the new order within the army brought about by the revolution, the Life Guards Semenov Regiment was disbanded and its officers were demobilized. Guards *podporuchik* Tukhachevsky was unemployed (Ivanov 1990, 12–14).

Possibly because of the mixed nature of his parents' social background and the experience of growing up in relative poverty, Tukhachevsky, although entitled to the privileges of his noble birth, was not sympathetic to the tsarist regime and voluntarily sought ways to serve the revolution. The early aptitude he had shown for the military profession shaped his postrevolutionary efforts to continue in that field. For obvious reasons it was not easy for a former guards officer and a nobleman to overcome the prejudice and suspicion with which former officers were regarded in the aftermath of the revolution. Fortunately, Tukhachevsky found a sponsor in a boyhood friend who was a member of the All Union Central Executive Committee (VTsIK). He recommended Tukhachevsky to Avel Safronovich Enukidze, chief of the military section of the VTsIK. The military section was the link between the Central Committee (the Politburo) and the ministries dealing with military matters. Tukhachevsky was recruited as one of Enukidze's assistants. He made a name for himself by his reporting and recommendations on the initial steps the regime was taking to rebuild Soviet defenses (V. M. Ivanov 1990, 18).

Tukhachevsky became a member of the Bolshevik Party in April on the recommendation of his highly placed boyhood friend. The revolt of the Czech Corps in late May changed dramatically the military situation on the Volga, and Tukhachevsky was one of those Communists who were sent to the Eastern *Front* to assist its commander. After his arrival he was given command of the First Army.

His "army" consisted of all the volunteer detachments and units in the area of Simbirsk, Syzran, and Samara. There were 80 such units in all, numbering 20 to 250 troops. They were spread over a broad front, providing valiant but scattered opposition to the Czechs and their White allies. The latter had seized the opportunity afforded by the Czech "revolt" to oppose the spread of Bolshevik power. Tukhachevsky's troops, who lacked transportation, operated along the rail lines. To find officers for his units, Tukhachevsky ordered all demobilized officers residing in Simbirsk *guberniia* (province) to report to him in the city of Simbirsk for possible service in his army. Those failing to report were to be turned over to a military field court. One week later a nationwide mobilization of military specialists was ordered in Moscow. In the course of July 1918, Tukhachevsky mobilized 2,000 former officers in Simbirsk and Penza (Ivanov 1990, 50–52). In this fashion the Red Army was staffed with the military specialists it needed.

## THE NOBLE REVOLUTIONARY TAKES THE FIELD

The almost tragic affair with Murav'ev had an unsettling effect on the First Army as various versions of it began circulating among the troops. In particular, it added fuel to the inherent suspicion that surrounded the military specialists. Tukhachevsky, in spite of having been arrested and almost shot on Murav'ev's orders and having demonstrated his loyalty in helping to smother Murav'ev's attempted treachery, was arrested a second time. He was soon released, but the problem of the intense suspicion in the ranks of former officers was ameliorated only over time, in no small measure through the efforts of V. V. Kuibeshev and O. Yu. Kalnin, seasoned Bolsheviks who were appointed members of the First Army's military council. Political help was also needed to facilitate the mobilization of additional servicemen in the First Army area. The deployment of the military commissariats that would eventually perform this function was not completed until the end of 1918. By the end of July the army, which was to have 4 infantry divisions numbering 27,000 each, was able to muster 3 divisions with severely reduced tables of organization and equipment. The total strength of the army was around 13,500 men, with 50 artillery pieces, 230 machine guns, 2 armored trains, 7 armored cars, and an airplane. Initially, these divisions were named according to the localities from which they were mobilized: Penza, Inza, and Simbirsk. When the infantry divisions were given numbers, they were numbered, respectively the 20th, the 15th, and the 24th. These were the first regular divisions in the Red Army.

Tukhachevsky was forced to devote considerable attention to the problem of the army's transport. In these early days, railroad cars provided most of it as well as living quarters for the troops. But in early August, Tukhachevsky was directed, in Lenin's name, to take measures to move the troops into the field and to procure horses and wagons to haul the army's supplies. His efforts to fulfill this order were complicated by a worsening of the military situation on the army's front. The enemy, taking advantage of the uncertainty among the troops caused by the Murav'ev incident, attacked and captured Simbirsk, Lenin's birthplace. First Army troops also withdrew from Bugul'ma. Striving to save Simbirsk, Tukhachevsky, who was in Penza mobilizing former officers, returned to his army's headquarters in Inza. En route he encountered the 4th Latvian Regiment which was on a train, and directed it to Simbirsk. He also attempted to divert to Simbirsk an engineer detachment retreating from Ufa. The engineer troops, who were demoralized from previous defeats, were on the edge of panic, which infected their commander. He protested Tukhachevsky's order on the grounds that placing engineer troops in the line was an incorrect use of specialized troops, and he demanded that his unit be allowed to continue to Kazan to be reorganized. Tukhachevsky convinced the engineers to fight by appealing to the Party conscience of the troops and calling on them to follow his personal example and go to Simbirsk.

A more dangerous situation developed in the 4th Latvian Regiment. They were being moved to the reserve after heavy fighting around Syzran. When they were ordered back into the line at Simbirsk without a rest, they refused, and their commanders could not budge them. Again, only the personal intervention of Tukhachevsky caused the Latvians to change their minds and return to the fray. However, all of Tukhachevsky's efforts were in vain, and the Whites took the city on 22 July. The army's left flank was exposed, and the road to Inza, the army headquarters, was open. Under orders from Vatsetis, the Southern *Front* commander, Tukhachevsky shored up the defensive positions around Inza by having constructed a series of strongpoints that could support each other by fire. Tukhachevsky was convinced that this system of defense was superior to a network of trenches in continuous lines. In this case his theory was not tested.

While the defenses were being constructed, the First Army set about the task of winning back the city of Simbirsk. Tukhachevsky, at the same time, was required to defend himself for the army's failure to hold the city. Vatsetis provided some defense for the army commander, reporting that the army was numerically weak. But Vatsetis severely criticized the young commander for "roaming around the rear areas and not remaining in his headquarters . . . ." This message provoked an immediate response from Tukhachevsky, who informed Vatsetis that he had spent most of his time in the forward positions, that he had been at Penza to re-form units that had run, and that he should collect artillery and engineers. When Vatsetis did not answer Tukhachevsky's telegram, Tukhachevsky and his political commissar, V. V. Kuibeshev, sent him another, asking that restrictions on his movement from his headquarters be removed. Vatsetis replied with a short message that in effect lifted any restrictions on Tukhachevsky's movement from his headquarters. (Because of Tukhachevsky's youth and the low rank he held in the old army, he often found himself in disagreement with the former generals and colonels who were now his superiors in the new army. Regardless of the vast difference in former ranks, Tukhachevsky did not often yield, and he had numerous critics if not ill-wishers among the military specialists in the high command [Ivanov 1990, 49–65].)

The First Army required three attempts to retake Simbirsk. The failures of the attacks on the city launched on 3 and 9 August were attributed to the fact that the army had not completed its organization and the troops were not prepared for offensive operations. After the failure of the second attack, Trotsky threatened to have Tukhachevsky tried. The intervention of Kuibeshev, who appealed directly to Lenin, saved the young army commander. Lenin ordered that the First Army complete its organization and only then be committed to offensive operations.

On 25 August, the army was considered in condition to attempt partial offensive operations in order to improve its position for the attack on Simbirsk. The successful execution of these partial attacks not only improved the operational situation of the army, it also restored the combat spirit of the troops.

The third attempt to retake Simbirsk began on 9 September, while the Fifth Army's operation to regain Kazan was still in progress. Simbirsk was first surrounded on two sides before being stormed on the twelfth. By dawn of that day, one regiment, with the assistance of local railroad workers, had occupied positions in the rear area of the White troops so that in effect the town's occupiers were almost completely surrounded. The result was the complete rout of the enemy and the capture of almost a thousand prisoners, three aircraft, ten artillery pieces, supply wagons, and other trophies. In their haste to withdraw, the Whites left the railroad bridge over the Volga intact.

Tukhachevsky considered the capture of Simbirsk to be an intermediate objective, and before its capture he ordered the commander of the army's strike force, Gai Dmitrievich Gai, to be prepared to pursue the Whites across to the left bank of the Volga. The absence of river craft and the fortuitous capture of the railroad bridge made almost obligatory its use as the fastest, albeit the most risky, means of crossing the river. The bridge was almost one kilometer long and under observation by White artillery observers over its entire length. The Whites attempted to discourage a night attack by igniting an oil barge to illuminate the bridge during the hours of darkness. Tukhachevsky's solution was to send an unmanned locomotive over the bridge followed closely by an armored train and the infantry of the 2d Brigade of Gai's Simbirsk Division covered by the available artillery batteries. The attack was successful, and on the night of 15 September the White defenders abandoned their artillery and retreated to positions thirty to thirty-five kilometers from the Volga.

The next day, Gai's troops came under attack by White troops retreating south from the fall of Kazan and White reserves drawn from the east. These attacks continued for the next week while on the right bank of the river Tukhachevsky converted Simbirsk into a fortified area. He also sent additional forces over the Volga, threatening a deep envelopment of the counterattacking Whites. By 28 September the White forces had been almost completely destroyed, and the remnants had retreated to Bugul'ma, almost 160 kilometers to the east.

The victory at Simbirsk and the operations over the Volga that followed it suddenly propelled Tukhachevsky into the forefront of the Red commanders in the civil war. More importantly it strengthened his confidence in himself. He also developed confidence in his staff, realizing that it was impossible to do everything himself and that he had selected reliable assistants. The failures of his first two months in command were behind him; having demonstrated restraint and perseverance, he had proven that he was fully prepared for army command (V. M. Ivanov 1990, 66–79).

## VICTORIES AT SYZRAN AND SAMARA

Even before the Whites had been cleared from the Simbirsk area, Vatsetis ordered an offensive designed to recapture Syzran and Samara. The main effort in the operation was to be made by the First Army assisted by one division of the Fourth Army and ships of the Volga flotilla. The entire operation involved around 16,000 troops, 61 artillery pieces, 263 machine guns, 7 armored riverboats, "a floating battery," and 7 armored sloops. This was a combined operation of considerably more complexity than that which Tukhachevsky had just completed. The area of operations was also much larger than that involved around Simbirsk. Tukhachevsky did enjoy a numerical superiority one and a half times that of his opponents.

The attack was launched by the Inza, Penza, and Vol'sk (from the Fourth Army) Divisions toward Syzran on 14 September. The Simbirsk Division, which had been reinforced with units from the Inza and Penza Divisions, continued operations east of Simbirsk. The First Army divisions moved slowly south toward Syzran until the Simbirsk Division, having driven the Whites from Simbirsk to the east, made two forced marches of more than fifty kilometers per day and, on 3 October, successfully attacked the Whites who were defending the Aleksandrovsk railway bridge over the Volga east of Syzran. This victory cut the escape route to Samara of the White troops on the right bank of the Volga, causing a panic-stricken retreat and bringing the campaign to a close. Syzran fell on the same day, and Samara fell four days later. With the fall of Samara, the Volga was cleared for navigation, and the shipment of oil and foodstuffs to the starving upper regions of the Volga Basin was resumed. Lenin urged that shipments be maximized in the days remaining until the winter freeze (Naida 1957, 245, 246).

After the capture of Samara, Tukhachevsky moved the First Army headquarters to Syzran where, for the first time since the onset of combat operations, he and his staff were quartered in other than bivouac conditions; they took over a large private dwelling. He took advantage of the break in the fighting to review with his staff and commanders the previous army operations, searching for lessons for the future while the First Army prepared for the next offensive.

Awards and decorations were passed out, including an inscribed gold watch to Tukhachevsky. The lull in his combat service lasted until mid-November 1918, when he was called to Moscow and informed that he was to be transferred to the Southern *Front* as deputy commander (Ivanov 1990, 83, 84).

## ON THE SOUTHERN FRONT

Tukhachevsky's transfer to the Southern *Front* was related to the recognition in Moscow of the growing White threat in the south of the country. By late 1918, the White forces were preparing to complete their conquest of the whole North Caucasus. By early February 1919, this had been accomplished by forces under the overall command of Anton Ivanovich Denikin, known as the Volunteer Army. On 8 January 1919, Denikin became commander in chief of the Armed Forces of Southern Russia, which included the Volunteer Army. In contrast, General Krasnov's Don Cossacks had moved out of Don Cossack territory as far north as Liski Junction, about fifty kilometers south of Voronezh, where the combat-weary, outnumbered Cossacks were brought to a halt. This—plus the failure of the third Cossack attempt to take Tsaritsyn in January and the withdrawal of the Austro-German occupation troops from the Ukraine, exposing the western portion of the Don region to Red Army incursion—had a crushing effect on Cossack morale, causing mass desertions and surrenders (Mawdsley 1987, 161–65).

Tukhachevsky did not join the Southern *Front* until early January 1919. This was due, according to one of his biographers, V. M. Ivanov, to the lack of enthusiasm among the senior military specialists (many of whom had been generals in the old army) for the assignment of a former *poruchik* to the high post of deputy *front* commander. Ivanov notes that of the sixty-two military specialists who commanded armies during the civil war, Tukhachevsky was the only one who had not risen above the rank of *poruchik* in the tsarist army; of seventeen military specialists who commanded *fronts* during the civil war, again, Tukhachevsky, who was to command the Caucasus *Front* later in 1919 and the Western *Front* in 1920, was the only former *poruchik.*

Tukhachevsky did not remain at *front* headquarters for long. On 24 January he took command of the Eighth Army, the political section of which, incidentally, was headed by a woman, a veteran Bolshevik, Rozaliia Samoilovna Zemlachka. The Eighth Army, when Tukhachevsky took command, was commencing a pursuit of beaten White Cossack units. By the end of January, the army had crossed the upper Don River and was continuing the pursuit energetically when, in early February, it began to encounter units of Denikin's Volunteer Army. On 1 February, the CINC, Vatsetis, gave the Southern *Front* what was in essence a new mission: after completing the destruction of the Don Cossack Army and seizing the area of the upper and middle Don regions, the *front* was to develop an offensive aimed at Novocherkassk and Rostov, on the Don. These objectives required the right wing of the *front*, particularly the Eighth Army, which had been moving directly toward the Donbass, to wheel to the south. In the process, a gap of more than seventy kilometers developed between Innokentii Serofimovich Kozhevnikov's group and the right flank of the Eighth Army.* At this point a difference of opinion developed between Tukhachevsky and the Southern *Front* commander, Vladimir Mikhailovich Gittis, who had been a colonel in the old army. Gittis believed that Kozhevnikov's group could cope with the White forces in the Donbass and that the Eighth Army should be directed toward the southeast to complete the destruction of the Don Army. On 16 February, the CINC ordered the Eighth Army to join with Kozhevnikov's group and move toward Rostov. The Eighth Army received no reinforcements despite the appearance before it of increasing numbers of the well-armed troops of Denikin's Volunteer Army.

This difference of opinion did not remain within the Southern *Front* family for long. Tukhachevsky wrote a letter to the RVS of the Republic "not as a commander...but as a communist, concerned over any failure of the revolution . . ." (Ivanov 1990, 90). It was his opinion that the *front* commander had erred in his selection of the direction of the main effort from the very beginning. The main effort should have been to drive to Rostov via the shortest distance, through

---

*The Donbass (the basin of the Donets), an industrial area, should not be confused with the Don region, the homeland of the Don Cossacks, which lies to the east of the Donbass.

the Donbass. This would have secured the *front*'s rear area, since the population of the industrialized Donbass was sympathetic to the Red Army. Moving through the Don region required the diversion of troops to put down Cossack uprisings (Ivanov 1990, 90).

Despite Tukhachevsky's disagreement with Gittis, and some inclement weather at the end of February, he led the Eighth Army to the Donets in early March. Their advance was halted at Likhaia by the spring thaw and by the general exhaustion of the troops (Ivanov 1990, 92).

## RETURN TO THE EASTERN FRONT

This pause, and the appearance of a new threat in the east in the form of the armies of Adm. Aleksandr Vasilevich Kolchak, provided an opportunity for Tukhachevsky to extricate himself from an unsatisfactory command situation. The Eastern *Front* became the most important *front*, and Tukhachevsky requested to be returned there. It is not clear which channels he used to forward his request—military or Party. As we have seen, he was quite capable of playing the Party card when it suited his purpose. According to V. M. Ivanov, the request was sent to the RVS of the Republic, but "in the Central Committee of the party they treated his request with understanding . . . " (Ivanov 1990, 93), and the Central Committee "recommended" that Tukhachevsky be given command of the Fifth Army of the Eastern *Front*. This convoluted treatment of Tukhachevsky's transfer request suggests that the author was trying to avoid the use of Trotsky's name. As chairman of the RVS of the Republic, Trotsky had to approve the transfer of an army commander. Whatever the case, the transfer was approved, and Tukhachevsky took command of the Fifth Army on 24 March.

Kolchak, a former commander of the tsarist Black Sea Fleet, had been declared "supreme ruler of the Russian state" after a military coup against the Provisional All Russian Government in Omsk on 18 November 1918. The Provisional All Russian Government represented a compromise of the various political entities that were disenfranchised by the Bolshevik seizure of power in 1917 and the subsequent dismissal of the Constituent Assembly.

The Eastern *Front*, after Tukhachevsky's departure for the Southern *Front* in January 1919, had continued its advance in the center and the south until February. By that time the *front* had taken Ural'sk and Orenburg, both seats of Cossack hosts *(voiska)*. In the center, the Fifth Army had taken Ufa, and farther north the Second Army had taken Izhevsk and Votkinsk. At the north end of the *front* zone of action, the Soviet Third Army had lost the important city of Perm in November (causing Stalin and Dzerzhinskii to be sent to find the causes). The Reds did not go deeper into Siberia at that time because of the usual factors: the enormous distances between populated areas that had to be traversed by exhausted troops in the Siberian winter, supply and evacuation became more and more difficult as the troops moved farther from the center, and as the *front* moved east it lost its priority on replacements and equipment (Mawdsley 1987, 104, 111, 132, 133).

When Tukhachevsky rejoined the Eastern *Front*, it had been commanded by S. S. Kamenev since September 1918. The *front* stretched some 1,800 kilometers from the Caspian Sea to the north Ural tundra. In the beginning of March, the *front* numbered some 100,000 troops, 1,880 machine guns, and 375 artillery pieces. Kolchak's force was between 130,000 and 145,000 troops, 1,300 machine guns, and 200 artillery pieces. The length of the *front* and the relatively light density of the forces on both sides made the theater of operations ideal for mobile warfare, and the Whites had a 2:1 superiority in cavalry (Naida 1959, 51).

Kolchak's Western Army attacked the center of the Eastern *Front* on 4 March, advancing along the railway from Cheliabinsk toward Simbirsk and Samara using sledges to traverse the snow-covered steppes. Ufa was taken on 14 March, and by the end of April the Whites had advanced to within ninety kilometers of the Volga. During the same period Kolchak's Siberian Army in the north had advanced 150 kilometers from Perm toward Viatka (Mawdsley 1987, 134). Here, again, operations were slowed by the spring thaw, which occurred later in the northern and central Urals. These advances raised concerns in Moscow, heightened because they were unexpected, that Kolchak would link up with Denikin in his drive on Moscow from the south.

When Tukhachevsky took command, the Fifth Army was in critical condition. In the previous defensive battles it had lost almost half of its personnel; its 26th and 27th Divisions were defending on a broad front against two corps of Kolchak's Western Army. The troops were tired and demoralized after their long retreat. There was a shortage of officers and political commissars. Units of the army were retreating in disorder to the Volga, and contact with G. D. Gai's First Army had been lost. There was a 150-kilometer gap between the army's left flank and the Soviet Second Army, to the north. A White advance to the Volga would threaten the center of the Eastern *Front* and facilitate the linkup of Kolchak and Denikin, putting the country's central regions in peril (Naida 1959, 50–57).

As the White offensive approached the Volga, the *front* commander (S. S. Kamenev) and the CINC since September 1918 (I. I. Vatsetis) considered various counterattack options to halt the White advance while Moscow was engaged in mobilizing reinforcements and supplies. For the counterattack, it was decided to adopt a proposal put forth by the commander of the Fourth Army, Mikhail Vasilevich Frunze, to concentrate the forces on the right flank of the 1,800-kilometer-long front into a single command and to strike at the left flank of the extended White Western Army. On 10 April, Frunze was given command of the force that was to be called the southern group of the Eastern *Front.* The group was to include the First, Fourth, and Fifth Armies and the Turkestan Army.*

### THE DEFEAT OF KOLCHAK

By 20 April the combat readiness of the Fifth Army had been restored, and by the end of the month the army was ready for offensive operations. A gap had been identified between the two White corps facing the Fifth Army, and Frunze decided to take advantage of it without waiting for the total concentration of his reinforcements. The operation began on 28 April and by 30 April the Fifth

*The Turkestan Army was formed on 5 March 1919 by a directive of the commander of the Eastern *Front.* It consisted of the Orenburg Rifle Division and the 3d Cavalry Division. The 24th and 25th Rifle Divisions were assigned to that army from May to June 1919. The army was disbanded on 15 June 1919. The creation of this army appears to have been a control device to allow these units to operate under a single command on the southern flank of the long eastern front. There is no indication that its creation was authorized by the Revolutionary Military Council of the Republic or the commander in chief.

Army had taken the Buguruslan railroad station. Units of the army under heavy artillery fire from the Whites crossed the Bol'shaia Kinel and entered the town of Buguruslan. During the advance the White 7th Infantry Division was severely mauled.

The Whites in the meantime had pushed toward the Volga, capturing Sergievsk and causing alarm at *front* headquarters that the Whites were going to roll up the army's left flank and cut the line of communications with Samara. To counter this threat, Kamenev shifted the axis of the southern group's advance from northeast to north. The Fifth Army was given the mission of taking Bugul'ma, thereby severing White communications to the east.

By 4 May, to avoid being cut off, the Whites had assembled some 30,000 troops to defend Bugul'ma. Tukhachevsky's plan was to attack the city from the south and the west. His strength was around 22,000, and in his operations order he instructed his unit commanders not to weaken themselves by keeping too much of their force in reserve. His studies of the operations of the old army in World War I had convinced him that there was a tendency to hold too much of an attacking force in reserve, thereby reducing the impact of the forward echelons. His operations orders often included injunctions against reducing the firepower and offensive weight of attacking units.

On 6 May the attack was launched, and by 13 May the town had been taken. Remnants of the White defenders managed to escape over the Ik River, barely avoiding the deep envelopment forces that Tukhachevsky had dispatched to block them. In the course of seven days the Fifth Army had advanced up to 150 kilometers and defeated the main forces of Kolchak's Western Army (Ivanov 1990, 101, 103). The army, which during March and April had been retreating and was exhausted by difficult defensive battles, experienced a rebirth. The morale of the troops improved and their confidence in victory was restored (Naida 1959, 109).

## A CHANGE IN FRONT COMMAND

The forward momentum of the southern group of the Southern *Front* was halted temporarily by the appointment of Aleksandr Aleksandrovich Samoilo, a former general, to replace S. S. Kamenev as commander of the Eastern *Front.* Kamenev had disagreed with the

CINC, I. I. Vatsetis, over the conduct of Eastern *Front* operations, and at his insistence Kamenev had been relieved. The new *front* commander decided that the *front* operations plan should be changed, and upon assuming command he ordered that the Fifth Army, which had grown to six divisions, should be detached from the southern group and move to the north toward Menzelinsk and force the Kama River. Samoilo's orders apparently reflected the operational dispute between Vatsetis and Kamenev. That is, Vatsetis considered the White Siberian Army, which was moving toward Moscow from the north, to be a greater immediate threat to link up with Denikin than was the White Western Army from the east. By moving the Fifth Army to the north, he would threaten the left flank of the Siberian Army and lead to its defeat or withdrawal.

Frunze and Tukhachevsky protested this change in plan, both believing that the Western Army before them should be completely defeated. They urged that Frunze's ongoing operation, including the Fifth Army, against Belebei and Ufa should be completed, the Western Army destroyed, and the Siberian Army defeated later by a deep envelopment from the south. In the course of this dispute, Samoilo changed his directives to the Fifth Army several times, causing Tukhachevsky to inform Samoilo on 15 May that he disagreed with his directives and that his decision was "unenergetic." On 21 May Tukhachevsky sent Samoilo another message complaining that he had received five missions in ten days, each altering the previous one, and asking the *front* commander to please observe the field manual, which required that all directives be well thought out before they were issued. Samoilo wanted to have Tukhachevsky brought to account for lack of respect for a senior officer, but his military council would not support him. The dispute finally reached Lenin; it was resolved by sending Samoilo back to army command and restoring Kamenev to command of the Eastern *Front* (V. M. Ivanov 1990, 103–105).*

---

*In July 1919, Kamenev replaced Vatsetis as commander in chief. Frunze replaced Kamenev as Eastern *Front* commander. In August the situation in Turkestan was deemed more grave than that on the Eastern *Front*, and Frunze was sent there to command the Turkestan *Front*.

During the contretemps over future operations, the southern group had taken Belebei on 17 May and in the process had sent Kolchak's strategic reserve, the well-equipped 1st Volga Corps, commanded by Gen. Vladimir Oskarovich Kappel, reeling back toward Ufa. There it was divided into three groups with the mission of defending the Belaia River line (Khromov 1983, 622).

In effect the return of Kamenev meant that Frunze's and Tukhachevsky's recommendations on the further course of the campaign against Kolchak in the east would be carried out.

The Fifth Army was again subordinated to Frunze's southern group of the Eastern *Front,* and the offensive on the Urals was continued. On 29 May, Lenin put the mission of the *front* in the starkest of terms: "If we don't conquer the Urals by the winter then I consider the collapse of the revolution inevitable" (Ivanov 1990, 106).

The southern group had renewed operations against Kolchak's Western Army on 25 May, ordering the Fifth Army's 26th Division to cross the Belaia River south of Birsk in order to prevent a White flotilla from interfering with operations against Ufa to the south. In these actions the Fifth Army administered another severe defeat on a remnant of the White 1st Volga Corps, effectively removing it from further participation in the White defense of the Urals. These actions secured the left flank of Frunze's southern group and caused him to change the direction of the main effort against Ufa. The capture of a bridgehead at Krasnyi Iar, north of the city, enabled Frunze to move the group reserve over the river, and Red Army units reached the city on 9 June.

After capturing Birsk, units of the Fifth Army moved rapidly to the east to the Ufa River, sealing off the escape routes from the city, which fell on 19 June. The road to the southern Urals was open. In the north, as Frunze and Tukhachevsky had anticipated, the retreat of the Western Army had forced the Siberian Army to cease active operations on the Kazan and Viatka axes, facilitating the offensives of the Second and Third Armies toward the northern foothills of the Urals.

## THE CAPTURE OF ZLATOUST AND CHELIABINSK

The campaign against Kolchak moved much faster than Lenin could have hoped. The Fifth Army's next objective was Zlatoust, the key to the southern Urals. For this mission the 24th Division was added to the army's order of battle, which included the 26th, 27th, and 35th Rifle Divisions and a separate cavalry brigade. The total strength of the army was about 22,000 troops, 90 artillery pieces, and 500 machine guns. At the beginning of this phase of the campaign, the north wing of the army was stretched along the Ufa River; the south wing was east of the city, having crossed the Belaia River. The northern divisions—the 35th, 27th, and the bulk of the 26th—faced the problem of forcing the Ufa in the face of White opposition and then proceeding to push into the Urals. Tukhachevsky's decision was to utilize all of the passes through the mountains, including the roadless and pathless valley of the Iuriuzan River, even though communication between his advancing columns would be difficult if not impossible.

The 26th Division began its attack on the night of 25 June and in three days, led by a regiment commanded by Vitoft Kazimirovich Putna, had penetrated into the mountains 120 kilometers. There, the division encountered superior White forces and held them off for three days before the 27th Division, which had lagged behind on a parallel route, joined the battle. It ended on 8 July with the withdrawal of the Whites to areas around Zlatoust. The city was captured on 13 July by the 26th and 27th Divisions in a simultaneous three-sided attack. Trophies included 3,000 prisoners, 8 artillery pieces, 32 machine guns, 3 armored cars, 30 locomotives, and 600 wagons. The Whites also abandoned large stores of grain, food, and other raw materials as they withdrew to Cheliabinsk.

The fall of Cheliabinsk followed two and a half weeks later, on 4 August, as the Fifth Army resumed its pursuit of the demoralized forces of Admiral Kolchak. White combat losses and defections gave the Fifth Army numerical superiority for the first time in the campaign, and Tukhachevsky pressed his advantage. Combining frontal attacks, envelopments, and turning movements, the Fifth Army took the city, 13,000 prisoners, 100 machine guns, 32 locomotives, and 3,500 wagons (Khromov 1983, 220, 649).

The river Tobol was the next important defensive line on the route to the depths of Siberia, and it was here that the remnants of the White defenders of Cheliabinsk withdrew in haste. Tukhachevsky, sensing that the Whites were in serious disarray, urged his weary troops to engage and conclusively defeat the retreating Whites before they could be reconstituted and replenished by the Western Allies. As it was, by the end of August, Kolchak had reinforced his armies and formed a new Cossack Corps. The new Eastern *Front* commander, Vladimir Aleksandrovich Ol'derogge, a former general, was not aware that this had occurred, and on 16 August he ordered the Third and Fifth Armies to force crossings of the Tobol and to pursue the Whites toward Petropavlovsk. He also ordered that one division of the Fifth Army be placed in *front* reserve for possible dispatch to the south.

Tukhachevsky protested the weakening of his army, and he protested more vigorously when Ol'derogge disapproved his concept that the main effort should be made by the Third Army while the Fifth Army protected the *front* right flank and the open steppe to the south, known to be occupied by hostile Cossacks. Ol'derogge insisted that the Fifth Army make the main effort along the Kurgan-Petropavlovsk railroad, and Tukhachevsky was required to follow Ol'derogge's orders. Both armies successfully crossed the Tobol on 20 August and managed to move 180 kilometers to the distant approaches to Petropavlovsk in ten days. There they were met by fierce counterattacks on the right flank of the Fifth Army, which drove them back to their bridgeheads over the Tobol by the end of September.

The Eastern *Front* temporarily took up defensive positions along the Tobol and used the period through 14 October to reinforce and regroup. By then the Fifth Army strength had increased to around 37,000 troops, and Tukhachevsky used almost half of the army strength to envelop the left flank of the Whites.

By 21 October, Kolchak's troops had suffered heavy casualties and were withdrawing along the entire front. For the Whites the constant threat of having their line of retreat cut by the envelopment of their left flank led to a panicky retreat and a collapse of morale. By 29 October one of Tukhachevsky's divisions was entering Petropavlovsk, and the next day the Fifth Army had captured the town. The crushing defeat of the Whites before Petropavlovsk removed any hope that Kolchak may have had of regaining the strategic initiative.

Tukhachevsky rejected the pleas of his division commanders to allow the troops some rest before continuing on to Omsk—Kolchak's headquarters. The result was that Kolchak's troops were incapable of offering organized resistance; on 12 November, Kolchak and his government fled Omsk. On the evening of 14 November, units of the Fifth Army entered the city. The 30,000-man garrison surrendered without a battle, and White ammunition dumps were captured intact. In a month-long campaign, the Fifth Army had moved from the Tobol to the Irtysh—more than 600 kilometers—while forcing three rivers. The average rate of advance of 20 kilometers a day in the face of White opposition was a phenomenal pace, considering the infrastructure of the region and the absence of motorization and mechanization.

For the capture of Omsk, which marked the collapse of the Kolchak threat from the east, the Fifth Army was awarded an extra month's pay and allowances. Tukhachevsky was given a saber with a golden hilt and the order of the Red Banner affixed. At the time, the order was the highest award for outstanding combat service given to members of the high command of the active army. The 27th Division was given the right to add the name of Omsk to its title. In November, Tukhachevsky was ordered to Moscow for reassignment.

## FIRST ENCOUNTER WITH STALIN

Tukhachevsky arrived in Moscow at the end of November, expecting to receive a new assignment and then depart immediately for his new duty station. Both the Southern and the Southeastern *Fronts* were engaged with Denikin's forces, and Tukhachevsky was anxious to participate in the action. Instead there was an unaccountable delay in assigning him to a new post, which Tukhachevsky attributed to continued doubts about his command capabilities among senior military specialists who had so far outranked him in the old army. While he waited for his orders, Tukhachevsky, at Lenin's request, put in writing his views of the military specialists. He found that the old officers could not and did not wish to understand class warfare. Therefore they could not appreciate that the class composition of the local population had to be considered in calculating the possibilities for reinforcing during an offensive and for securing rear areas and supply routes during operations (Tukhachevsky 1964, I:7). Earlier he had reported to the RVS of the Republic that it was difficult to find good commanders among the older military specialists and that it was time to move Communists into the senior command positions (Tukhachevsky 1964, I:7, 8). According to Tukhachevsky, the younger officers in the old army were the best prepared at the start of World War I, but many of them had been killed or were now serving in the White forces. Many of the officers who had joined the Red Army had received accelerated wartime training and were now serving in relatively senior positions. Tukhachevsky's conclusion was that, with the exception of those who had served on the General Staff and other staffs, workers and peasants who had command experience should now be placed in command positions.

On 22 December, Tukhachevsky was assigned command of the Thirteenth Army, at that time commanded by Anatolii Il'ich Gekker and part of the Southern *Front*. The *front* commander, as we have seen, had had problems with Gekker, and it is not unreasonable to assume that Egorov had requested a replacement for him. However, Stalin, as the member of the RVS of the Southern *Front*, had the deciding voice on whether or not Tukhachevsky could be placed in command of the army, and he apparently withheld his approval. Tukhachevsky's friends and comrades would later recall that Stalin was never friendly with Tukhachevsky; they would later speculate that Stalin's attitude may have been due to Tukhachevsky's noble background and Stalin's known distaste for former tsarist officers and his envy of the renown that Tukhachevsky had gained in the east, or some combination of these factors. Whatever the reason, Tukhachevsky was not given any assignment by the Southern *Front,* and on 19 January he wrote the RVS of the Republic asking for any available assignment even if it were not at the front.

Tukhachevsky's letter may have arrived in Moscow around the time that Budenny and Voroshilov were complaining that the Caucasus *Front* commander was not employing his cavalry properly and causing the First Cavalry Army to suffer an inordinate number of casualties. On 24 January, Tukhachevsky was appointed temporary commander of the Caucasus *Front,* and on 3 February he arrived in Saratov to take command. In addition to the First Cavalry Army, the *front* consisted of the Eighth, Ninth, Tenth, and Eleventh Armies.

On that same day, Stalin, who had also received Voroshilov and

Budenny's complaint about the incompetent employment of the First Cavalry Army, called Budenny and gave the impression that he had somehow been influential in changing the command of the Caucasus *Front*. To Budenny he described Tukhachevsky as the "conqueror of Siberia and the victor over Kolchak..." (Ivanov 1990, 138). Stalin clearly exaggerated his role in effecting the change in command. He never explained his reluctance to employ Tukhachevsky; subsequently, when the Caucasus *Front* needed reinforcements, he was apparently reluctant to make them available.

## THE DEFEAT OF DENIKIN

Soon after Tukhachevsky assumed command of the Caucasus *Front*, he was joined by Grigorii Konstantinovich Ordzhonikidze (Sergo), a veteran Bolshevik who had been an organizer of the partisan movement in the Caucasus. Sergo's temperament complemented that of Tukhachevsky, and the two became fast friends. Quickly grasping the operational situation on his *front*, Tukhachevsky ordered a halt to ongoing operations and prepared new offensive plans to deliver an unexpected blow. Because Denikin's right flank along the Manych River appeared weaker than his left along the Don, Tukhachevsky decided to regroup his forces and begin his offensive over the Manych. The First Cavalry Army was moved from the left flank to the right by means of a forced march, which the Whites did not detect until the actual attack began. Because Tukhachevsky realized that time was of the essence, he decided to begin his attack with the available forces and not to await the reinforcements that had been promised the *front* from the Ukraine.

The operation commenced on 14 February. On the left flank, the Eighth and Ninth Armies attempted to cross the Don and the Manych, without success. On the right flank, the Tenth Army crossed the Manych that day, and the First Cavalry Army forced a crossing the next day. The First Cavalry Army and the Tenth Army were to advance on to Tikhoretzkaia, the hub of Denikin's rear area and communications. Denikin, recognizing the threat to his rear and his communications, withdrew his reserve from his left flank to meet the First Cavalry Army threat. The reserve, numbering some 10,000 to 12,000 horsemen, met Budenny with some 10,000 sabers reinforced with three rifle divisions of the Tenth Army in a series of battles. They developed into the largest cavalry engagement of the civil war—25,000 troopers—on the Manych steppes between Egorlykskaia and Belaia Glina. By 25 February the Red cavalry had routed their foes. The Red victory in this battle was the culminating point of the operation. The defeated White cavalry ceased to exist as an organized force.

While the battle was developing near Egorlykskaia, Denikin's left flank forces attacked, crossed the Don, and captured Rostov, on the Don. This setback alarmed Moscow. Lenin, knowing that the Caucasus *Front* was outmanned by Denikin's troops, queried Ordzhonikidze directly on the condition of the *front*, and to Stalin he sent a series of messages directing him to facilitate the movement of reinforcements to the Caucasus *Front*. Despite the urgency of the situation, Stalin demurred, asking to be called to Moscow to explain his reluctance to comply with Lenin's and the CINC's requests. Finally, exasperated, Lenin ordered him categorically to dispatch a division to the Caucasus *Front* and to stop "squabbling" (Ivanov 1990, 144, 145).

On 21 February, Tukhachevsky was rebuked by Kamenev because he had not awaited the arrival of reinforcements before he began his attack. Kamenev, concerned over the "catastrophic" situation at Rostov, doubted that the Tenth Army's operations would be felt on the Rostov axis. Tukhachevsky responded that he had attacked to preempt the Whites and assured the CINC that all was not lost. He also dismissed the loss of Rostov, saying that if Rostov had been a village, no one would have been concerned about it. On 23 February, Tukhachevsky was proven right as the Eighth and Ninth Armies retook the city (Azovtsev 1986, 206). Denikin had been forced to withdraw the reserve that would have been used to exploit the capture of the city and beat off the Red counterattack.

Five days after being rebuked by the CINC, Tukhachevsky could report to him that the situation had improved markedly. White cavalry had been decisively defeated, and Rostov was back in Red Army hands. By 4 March, Ordzhonikidze could report to Lenin that the enemy's resistance had been broken and that the headquarters of the *front* was moving to Rostov. Tikhoretzkaia fell on 9 March, and

Ekatarinodar on the Kuban on 17 March. Major elements of Denikin's forces were evacuated to the Crimea by the Allied fleets as the Red Army entered Novorossiisk on 27 March. Tukhachevsky could repeat Caesar's famous words—*veni, vidi, vici.*

As early as February 1920 it became apparent to Lenin that there was a strong possibility of a conflict with Poland, and he urged the RVS of the Republic to devote attention to preparing and strengthening the Western *Front.* The next month, when the issue with Denikin had been decided, Kamenev proposed that command of the Western *Front* be given to Tukhachevsky, who "was capably and decisively conducting the last operations for the destruction of the armies of Denikin . . ." (Ivanov 1990, 150).

# 5
# THE SOVIET-POLISH WAR, 1920

As an episode in the seventy-four-year history of the Soviet Union, the short war between newly independent Poland and the revolutionary Soviet state does not appear to merit much attention. The almost inevitable conflict to settle claims over what has been a contested border through the centuries did settle the border issue for almost twenty years. But the war was about more than a border. It was about the existence of an independent Poland, it was about the class structure of that state, and it was about the religion that would prevail there. The war took on a degree of ferocity matching that of the fraternal struggle that was finally winding down in the central confines of the Russian heartland.

For those Red Army commanders who were to be leading actors in the Soviet-Polish drama—Tukhachevsky, Egorov, Budenny, Voroshilov, Iakir, and Uborevich—the future evaluation of their performance was destined to be fateful, although they did not realize it at the time. And, if Soviet attitudes toward the independent Polish state that emerged from the war can be deduced from the consistency with which their propagandists referred to Poland as *panskaia Pol'sha* (landowner- or gentry-ruled state), then Soviet participation in the brutal third partition of Poland in 1940 and the execution in the Katyn Forest of thousands of Polish officers should not have been a surprise.

Soviet historians called the war "the struggle with the last creatures of international imperialism." During Stalin's lifetime it was called the "third campaign of the Entente." In either case the title was consistent with Soviet propaganda claiming that the Polish offensive that started the war was planned and directed by France, Great Britain, and the United States. More recent accounts continued to make this claim, primarily on the basis that the Allies equipped the Poles and furnished military advisers. What Soviet historians chose to ignore was that by the end of 1918, Allied policy toward Poland was intended to make that newly reconstituted state a barrier against Russia and a check on Germany. Allied military assistance was furnished supposedly only for defense, and the Allies were opposed to the Polish initiation of hostilities in 1920 (Davies 1972, 89–92).

Hostilities between the Poles and the Soviets really began in early February 1919 with a clash of Soviet and Polish troops moving into the vacuum created by the retirement of German occupation troops from the borderlands of Russia and Poland. In the next year the two sides conducted negotiations while skirmishes continued in the area. In April 1920, the head of the Polish state and marshal of Poland, Jozef Pilsudski, dreaming of a Polish, Lithuanian, and Ukrainian federation, signed a treaty with the Hetman of the Ukraine, C. V. Petliura. The next day Pilsudski launched an offensive aimed at the capture of Kiev. Pilsudski's political bargain with Petliura recognized the right to exist of an independent Ukrainian state. In return, Petliura and his adherents marched with the Poles, prepared to assume the governance of the Ukraine (Wandycz 1969, 192).

Soviet sources credit the Poles with achieving surprise and with having a threefold advantage over the defenders (Azovtsev 1986, 260). The defenders' task was further complicated by Ukrainian and anarchist partisans operating in the rear areas of the Red Army units. By 6 May, the Soviet Twelfth Army had been driven from Kiev while the Fourteenth Army, commanded by I. P. Uborevich, retreated slowly to the south, covering the approaches to Kremenchug and Odessa. The Southwestern *Front* was also covering the arrival and concentration of Budenny's First Cavalry Army, which had begun marching from the North Caucasus in early April under orders to concentrate on the right bank of the Dnieper in the vicinity of Uman by 18 May (Azovtsev 1986, 261).

The relative strengths of the opposing forces during these operations cannot be established with certainty. It is probable that the Poles had numerical superiority initially due to an erroneous estimate by the Polish General Staff that the bulk of the Soviet forces were in the Southwestern *Front*. Based on this estimate, Pilsudski hoped to destroy the major portion of the Red Army and then leave the defense of the Ukraine to Petliura and his troops (Wandycz 1969, 190–91). Soviet sources provide no explanation of why the Red Army troops were taken by surprise. Negotiations between the two fledgling governments had been under way since the previous year, but Polish attitudes, particularly on the border question, were not encouraging to the Soviets. Late in January, the Soviet high command issued an alert order that read in part, "the general task remains the same—stubborn defense of the front line accompanied by local counterattacks" (Wandycz 1969, 174, 192).

In mid-February, Boris Mikhailovich Shaposhnikov, chief of the operations directorate of the Field Staff of the RKKA, provided the high command with an estimate of the situation on the Polish front, outlining the probable forces that would be involved and the measures that should be taken to meet the potential Polish threat. The estimate concluded that Poland might receive help from Lithuania and Latvia but that Romania had no territorial interest in a war with Soviet Russia and was unlikely to enter the conflict. The northern theater was expected to be the main theater of operations, with the Ukrainian theater of secondary significance. Because the Red Army in mid-February was still engaged in the Caucasus and in southern Russia, Shaposhnikov recommended an active defense by the Western *Front* until forces could be freed to join in a general offensive against the Poles. The estimate did not foresee that Pilsudski would accept Petliura and the Ukrainians as allies, nor did it anticipate that the initial Polish effort would be in the direction of Kiev (Kakurin and Melikov 1925, 66–70). When the Poles in early January 1920 began reinforcing their troops facing the Soviet Southwestern *Front* and on 5 March captured Mozyr and Kalinkovichi, cutting the rail line between the Southwestern and Western *Fronts*,* the Red Army had every reason to assume an alert posture.

At Smolensk in early March, the Soviet high command decided, on the basis of Shaposhnikov's estimate and Polish actions in the in-

---

*This move was recommended by French marshal Foch when consulted by the Polish General Staff on possible terms of an armistice with the Soviets (Wandycz 1969, 160).

tervening period, that the main effort would be made by the Western *Front*. Egorov's Southwestern *Front*, reinforced by the First Cavalry Army from the Caucasus, was to tie down the Poles by moving toward Brest. The CINC's (Kamenev's) rationale for the shift of the Cavalry Army to the Southwestern *Front* was his belief that success in the forthcoming operations would depend on the rapidity with which the Southwestern *Front* could operate along the Berdichev-Rovno-Kovel-Brest axis. In a telephone conversation with Egorov on 18 March, Kamenev repeated that the Western *Front* would be the main area of operations. He also observed that the Polesie (Pripyat Marshes) was so large that it would be impossible to obtain complete coordination between the two *fronts*.* Therefore, the overall direction of the campaign must be in the hands of the high command. When Egorov asked for some idea of the operational plans of the Western *Front* to aid him in formulating his own plans, he was told, "First stage Minsk. Then coordinated actions with you. Understand?" (Kakurin and Melikov 1925, 73).

Based on this limited information, Egorov drew up his plan for the employment of his *front* against the Poles. According to his estimates, the Poles outnumbered his forces. If the *front* was to move toward Brest, reinforcements, in addition to the Cavalry Army, would be required. Kamenev agreed and promised that, if reinforcements were not available from the Caucasus, the Southwestern *Front*'s mission would be changed to one of active defense (Kakurin and Melikov 1925, 74).

While these plans were being developed, White forces in the Crimea were being strengthened. Baron Petr Nikolaevich Vrangel had taken command of Denikin's Kuban forces in the Crimea and, calling his army "White Guards," proclaimed a more liberal political program than that of his predecessor. He faced the Reds with an army that seemed better equipped in aircraft and motor vehicles (Naida et al. 1960, 51). The Red military high command did not con-

---

*The Polesie is a 60,000-square-mile region of extensive riverlands, ponds, and canals in a countryside of meadows, birch groves, and willow glades. As Norman Davies observes, "It is fine duck shooting country but not the place for an army on the move" (Davies 1972, 33).

sider the White forces in the Crimea to be a serious threat until, prod-
ded by Lenin, Kamenev told Egorov that the liquidation of the White
forces in the Crimea was to take precedence over the Polish sector
of the front. The Thirteenth Army was to be reinforced with six
brigades drawn from the "internal *fronts*" specifically for operations
against Vrangel. The Southwestern *Front* was also to be reinforced
with an infantry division and a rifle brigade; however, these units
were not to be used in the Crimea but held in reserve and used only
in the event of a Polish attack. The distances separating the reinforcing units from the Crimea were such that Egorov calculated that
it would take a month before an attack against Vrangel could be
launched.

The Southwestern *Front* plan of attack, approved by the CINC,
called for the attack to begin on 18 April and the operation to be concluded by the end of the month with the complete occupation of the
Crimea. The condition of the rail net made it impossible to meet this
schedule. As it became increasingly clear that the Poles would attack,
the CINC removed all restrictions on the employment of the reinforcing units and directed Egorov to liquidate the White Guards in
the Crimea even if it meant temporarily weakening the forces facing
the Poles. When the Polish offensive did begin on 28 April, the preparations to oust Vrangel from the Crimea were halted. As it was, the
Thirteenth Army was still not ready to begin offensive operations; it
had only some 12,700 effectives available, whereas the White Guards
were estimated to have twice that number.

## STALIN REJOINS THE SOUTHWESTERN *FRONT*

In late May, Stalin rejoined the military council of the *front*. He had
been performing various special missions for the Politburo and the
*Sovet Truda i Oborony* (the Council of Labor and Defense, or STO).
The STO was established in November 1918 initially to deal with military economic questions. Chaired by Lenin, the STO soon became
involved in the strategic direction of the war effort. In the spring of
1920, the STO assigned Stalin the task of finding supplies, weapons,
and ammunition for the Western *Front*. When he returned to the
Southwestern *Front*, he was charged with taking all necessary measures to improve the combat capabilities of Budenny's First Cavalry

Army (Voroshilov was still the member of the Cavalry Army's military council) (Naida et al. 1960, 84, 101).

The successful command combination that had defeated Denikin was now in place. Stalin's success against Denikin had increased his confidence in his own military abilities. It had also reinforced his estimate of the capabilities of the Cavalry Army. That he was given special instructions to improve the combat capabilities of Budenny's army suggest that others in Moscow were also impressed with the Red troopers. But success seemingly confirmed his judgment that the military high command and its civilian overseer, Trotsky, were weak if not traitorous. Stalin's alarm at the prospect of fighting on two fronts soon became evident. In early June he suggested to Lenin that either an armistice be concluded with Vrangel so that portions of the Thirteenth Army could be used on the Polish front or, if the situation did not permit that, an offensive to liquidate the White Guards should be authorized. Lenin's answer to Stalin's proposal was a diplomatically worded rejection saying that the proposal was so serious that it would have to be studied carefully.

Baron Vrangel's forces conducted a successful amphibious landing on the north shore of the Sea of Azov on 6 June. The inadequacies of the defenders, including the absence of an overall plan of defense, enabled the Whites to expand their bridgehead and to move toward Melitopol, fifty kilometers to the north. By 8 June, the Thirteenth Army situation was considered so critical that a division that had been ordered to the Polish front on 7 June was ordered to retrace its steps and reinforce the Thirteenth Army. After its retreat, which ended on 24 June, the army was now split in two by the Dnieper River. But the fact that the army was still in existence meant that the path was not open to the Whites to the rear areas of the Red armies engaged with the Poles (Naida 1960, 105, 116). In late June and early July, the Thirteenth Army, now commanded by R. P. Eideman, conducted unsuccessful attacks against the White Guards, demonstrating that the Thirteenth Army was still too weak to defeat them.

## THE KIEV OPERATION

The Southwestern *Front*'s military situation improved markedly when, on 14 May, the Western *Front*, commanded since 29 April by

M. N. Tukhachevsky, attacked due west into what is now Belorussia. Tukhachevsky's initial successes forced the Poles to shift units from the Ukraine. With the aid of those units, the Poles counterattacked and by early June had driven the Western *Front* back to their initial positions. In the meantime, S. S. Kamenev had met with Egorov in mid-May in Kharkov to plan the Southwestern *Front* counterattack. The plan envisioned a double envelopment of Kiev with the Twelfth Army crossing the Dnieper north of the city and the Cavalry Army crossing to the southeast, trapping the Polish Third Army and portions of the Polish Second Army. As the plan was refined, the First Cavalry Army was to make the main effort. The Fourteenth Army was to support the operations of the Cavalry Army while the Thirteenth Army was to continue to block the exit of Vrangel and the White Guards from the Crimea (Azovtsev 1986, 267–71).

The execution of this plan is an excellent illustration of what Clausewitz has called "friction in war" and a measure of the operational capabilities of the Southwestern *Front.* The offensive was planned to begin on 26 May, but only the Fourteenth Army attacked on that day. The Twelfth Army had not completed regrouping and preparing a combat crossing of the Dnieper. A small group from that army attempted a crossing north of Kiev, without success. Subsequently, the army attempted a frontal attack (not the planned envelopment), which also failed. The First Cavalry Army moved 100 kilometers to the line of contact with the Poles and attacked on 27 May on a 60-kilometer front; it succeeded in inflicting some casualties on Polish covering forces. Budenny and his troopers had moved out without preparation and little rest after a 1,200-kilometer march from the Caucasus to the Uman area. Soviet historians have observed that these battles revealed serious shortcomings in the conduct of an offensive.

Egorov and the *front* command, after analyzing the results of these battles, instructed the army commanders in what should have been obvious: successful offensives require detailed preparation; frontal attacks on prepared positions are costly; and strike groups should be used on the main axis of advance. The Twelfth Army was ordered to cease its frontal attacks on Kiev, to leave a covering force in front of the city, and to cross the Dnieper north of Kiev as originally planned (Naida et al. 1960, 195, 196).

To correct shortcomings in the operational and administrative procedures of the Cavalry Army, Egorov urged Budenny to appoint L. L. Kliuev as chief of the army staff. Kliuev, a graduate of the General Staff Academy, had been a colonel of the General Staff of the old army and had joined the Red Army in 1918. Budenny had encountered him at Tsaritsyn, where he had been chief of staff of the Tenth Army after the departure of Voroshilov. Although Budenny accepted Egorov's recommendation, it is clear from Budenny's description of subsequent Cavalry Army operations that Kliuev was usually far from the combat action and from participation in day-to-day operational decisions (Budenny 1958, 112). How well Kliuev managed the supply and administration of the army is not clear. What is clear is that the army managed to keep moving while complaining continually about the support it was receiving from the rear.

These initial failures gave Stalin and Egorov the impression that the First Cavalry Army could not accomplish its mission without additional infantry support. Accordingly, Stalin requested that the army be reinforced with two more infantry divisions from the Caucasus. The request could not be accommodated because the two divisions in question were already en route to the Western *Front.* The Southwestern *Front* then changed the objective of the Cavalry Army from seizure of the Kazatin-Berdichev area to the capture of Fastov—that is, from a deep objective to a much shallower one.

Arguing that the seizure of Fastov would involve the army with the right flank forces of the Polish Third Army and that the army would not be able to operate in the enemy's deep rear areas as envisioned in the original plan, Budenny and Voroshilov obtained Egorov's permission to return to the original objective—the Kazatin-Berdichev area. The change in objectives was approved even though Stalin had already informed Lenin of the change in the original plan (Budenny 1958, 99).

The army resumed the attack on 5 June and, even without additional infantry, penetrated the Polish front to a depth of between fifty and sixty kilometers. But after cutting the rail line between Fastov and Kazatin, the army had no further orders, no communication with *front* headquarters, and no information about the progress of the Twelfth and Fourteenth Armies. Budenny considered two possible objectives for continuing the offensive: attempt to seize the rail hub at Kazatin, or move in the direction of Berdichev and Zhitomir. Seizure of the rail hub was the objective given in the *front* directive of 23 May, but a prisoner reported that the city's Polish garrison had been strengthened. Budenny reasoned that the seizure of Kazatin could involve the army in a prolonged battle, whereas the seizure of Berdichev and Zhitomir would split the Polish forces in two. Budenny chose the latter objective, which was taken on 7 June (Golubev 1966, 86, 87). These moves caused the collapse of the Polish forces in the Ukraine.

Later, Pilsudski recalled that government operations, even in places hundreds of kilometers from the front, were disrupted by a general feeling of panic caused by rumors of the impending arrival of Budenny's horsemen. In the opinion of V. K. Triandafillov, one of the creators in the 1920s of the theory of *glubokii boi* (literally, deep battle), the panic was a hallmark of this type of operation. The seizure of Berdichev and Zhitomir and its consequences were considered one of the progenitors of Soviet theories of deep battle (Triandafillov 1936, 163). That Budenny's troopers inspired panic in the local populace may have been due in no small measure to their undisciplined conduct after their arrival at their objectives. Trotsky, early in Budenny's Red Army career, while the Cavalry Army was still a corps, demanded that Stalin take severe measures to correct units under Budenny's command because they were looting the civilian population and there was drunkenness in the unit staffs to the extent that unit cohesion was threatened (Volkogonov 1992, book 1:238). During the Cavalry Army's retreat from Poland in 1920, a series of pogroms was conducted as the army passed through Jewish settlements within what had been the Pale (Volkogonov 1992, book 2:290).

Egorov at *front* headquarters did not recognize the possibilities that Budenny's initiative presented. The Cavalry Army was in position to continue the attack to the north and east to cut off the main escape route of the Polish Third Army—the rail line between Kiev and Korosten—or to the southwest to strike the Polish Sixth Army in its flank and rear. Budenny, still without orders, instead moved to the south to Fastov to aid I. E. Iakir and the 45th Division. This move was unnecessary, for Fastov had already been taken by Iakir by the time the Cavalry Army arrived. Twenty years later, Budenny claimed that Egorov was misinformed by Iakir and placed the blame on him for the failure to surround and destroy the Polish Third Army.*

From Fastov, on 10 June, Budenny proposed that his army be given Borodianka on the Kiev-Korosten rail line as its next objective, but Egorov ordered him to retake Zhitomir, a countermarch that was accomplished on 12 June, not without Cavalry Army losses. By this time Budenny was convinced that the Polish Third Army had escaped, and he turned his attention to the Polish Sixth Army, still located south and west of Kazatin. He proposed to Egorov, by radio, that the Cavalry Army be given Starokonstantinov as an objective, enabling him to strike the Poles in the flank and rear. This proposal was also turned down. Instead, he was directed to pursue the Third Army into the wooded, swampy Korosten region. There, by 17 June, the Poles succeeded in restoring the integrity of their front with the aid of two divisions from Belorussia and were occupying positions approximating those they had occupied at the start of their April offensive (Budenny 1958, 106, 107).

The Cavalry Army's success, even though it was not fully exploited, allowed the Twelfth Army to cross the Dnieper north of Kiev. The city was retaken on 12 June as the Fourteenth Army maintained pressure on the Polish troops to the south, preventing reinforcement of the forces around Kiev. The Soviet high command, anticipating that the Poles would continue to retreat, ordered Egorov to pursue the Third Army along parallel routes to the west toward Rovno. The Poles, however, chose to defend intermediate positions as they retreated, and it took the Cavalry Army until 27 June to capture Novograd Volynsk, 100 kilometers due east of Rovno.

On 27 June, the Southwestern *Front* revised the timetable for the offensive, ordering the Cavalry Army, assisted by the Twelfth Army, to take Rovno by 3 July. The Poles, however, counterattacked, and Rovno was not taken until 12 July. Budenny's success facilitated the advance of the Fourteenth Army, which captured Proskurov on 9 July (Naida 1960, 110, 112, 141).

---

*The accusation appeared in a serialized version of Budenny's memoirs published in the magazine *Don*. It was not repeated in the book-length version.

After taking Rovno, Budenny requested at least seven days' rest to replace lost equipment, bring up supplies, and restore combat capabilities. He also requested that Egorov visit the army while it was in Rovno. Egorov proposed instead that Budenny talk with him on the long-distance line, which was located in Berdichev, some 200 kilometers away. That conversation never took place. When a new directive was received, anticipating a renewed offensive on the fourteenth, five days later, Voroshilov went to Berdichev. After talking with *front* headquarters, he phoned Budenny from Berdichev to inform him that the army could rest but that the directive had to be fulfilled (Budenny 1958, 205, 210).

As the Southwestern *Front* pursued the retreating Poles, Tukhachevsky's Western *Front*, after a pause, resumed the offensive in mid-June, and by 11 July had retaken Minsk and Mozyr. The Western *Front*'s next objective was Belostok; the Southwestern *Front* had as its next objective Brest Litovsk. The two *fronts* were thus converging in the direction of Warsaw. By mid-July, the Western *Front* had completely cleared the borderland regions of Poles and were on the boundaries of ethnic Poland.

The military successes of the Red Army caused a change in the outlook of the Soviet political leadership on Soviet war aims. Initially conceived and publicized as a defense of the revolution against a Polish Army trained and equipped by the forces of counterrevolution, the Soviet counterattack was now seen as an opportunity to install a government of workers and peasants in Warsaw and to move the boundaries of revolution west to the borders of Germany. In Lenin's words, the Red Army would "probe with bayonets Poland's readiness for a socialist revolution . . ." (Volkogonov 1994, book 1:184). Kamenev was authorized to continue the offensive into Poland (Naida 1960, 141, 150).

### THE DECISION TO CAPTURE L'VOV

The decision to continue the offensive into Poland was informed by an optimistic appraisal of the Red Army position prepared by Kamemev on 15 July. The Western *Front* had reported that the left flank of the Polish forces was defeated and that events were moving with "head-spinning rapidity" (Budenny 1958, 226). At a meeting with Tukhachevsky in Minsk on 21 July, Kamenev had agreed with the Western *Front* appraisal and concluded that Tukhachevsky could take Warsaw by 12 August with three of his four armies (Naida 1960, 150). Overlooked in the enthusiasm for a push on Warsaw was Egorov's message of 22 July reporting "serious opposition," especially on the L'vov axis. Because of this and an assessment that the Western *Front* could take Brest Litovsk, Egorov requested that he be authorized to shift the center of gravity of his offensive from Brest Litovsk to L'vov. The request was approved the next day. As a result the two *fronts* began moving apart instead of moving to support each other as the Western *Front* moved closer to Warsaw. Latter-day Soviet historians were to comment that in these decisions the high command and the field commanders overevaluated the capabilities of their forces (Naida et al. 1960, 150).

Budenny claims that he was not convinced that the Poles were beaten and that he had expressed his doubts to Egorov. Budenny observed that, although the Poles were retreating, their losses were not severe. Egorov responded that the Polish forces facing the Western *Front* were defeated and it would not be necessary to help that *front* anymore. He also confirmed that the capture of L'vov had been authorized by the commander in chief. Budenny learned later that the commander in chief's optimism resulted from the meeting with Tukhachevsky at Western *Front* headquarters in mid-July. Tukhachevsky at that time did not object to the change of direction of the Southwestern *Front* and, on 19 July, he recommended to the CINC that he consider using the Cavalry Army in a strike along the southwest axis in a manner similar to the way that G. D. Gai's Cavalry Corps was being used around the northern flank of the Polish forces defending Warsaw. Kamenev informed Tukhachevsky that that was how he intended the Cavalry Army to be employed (Budenny 1958, 226).

A new Southwestern *Front* directive ordered the Cavalry Army to seize the L'vov–Rava Russkaia area by 29 July after defeating the Polish forces that it was then in contact with in the Krements-Dubno area. The Twelfth Army was ordered to continue to advance on the Cavalry Army's right flank, and the Fourteenth Army was to continue its advance on the Cavalry Army's left flank. On 28 July, the Cavalry Army was still 100 kilometers from L'vov. Budenny informed *front* headquarters that (1) the Poles were still offering stubborn resistance, (2) the army was worn out from the preceding battles, (3) the troops were starving—the basic rations were unripe apples and new potatoes, (4) there was no grain for the horses, and, (5) there was a shortage of ammunition. Under these conditions, it was impossible to cross two rivers, the Bug and the Styr, and then occupy a strongly fortified city such as L'vov in two days. Egorov apparently was not convinced; on 30 July he again expressed his dissatisfaction with the Cavalry Army's progress toward L'vov. This time Budenny reported a strong counterattack by the Poles and claimed that only by eliminating the Polish forces in his area could he resume his advance toward L'vov. This message was telegraphed to *front* headquarters at Kremenchug, because there was no voice contact between the two headquarters at that time (Budenny 1958, 237, 246).

The Cavalry Army occupied Brody on 26 July after what Budenny describes as a series of exceptionally difficult battles. In the version of Budenny's memoirs published in the magazine *Don*, V. M. Primakov, then commanding the 8th Chervonnyi Cossack Division, is faulted for his inactivity and unresponsiveness as a main cause of the difficulty. Budenny requested an investigation of Primakov's "criminal conduct" and his court-martial. Egorov and Stalin apparently did not act on Budenny's recommendation (Todorskii 1962, 88). Resuming the advance the next day, the Cavalry Army met head-on the Polish Second Army, which had been assigned the task of either stopping or slowing down Budenny's horse soldiers. Pilsudski in his account wrote that he had decided that he could deal with Tukhachevsky and the Western *Front* only if the "motive force in the south" were liquidated (Pilsudski 1929, 120, 121). By 2 August, the Cavalry Army had made little progress and was on the verge of losing Brody.

## THE WARSAW-L'VOV CONTROVERSY

In Moscow on that day (2 August), the Politburo considered the situation that had developed as a result of Vrangel's successes and the anti-Soviet uprisings in the Kuban. Stalin was instructed to form a new Revolutionary Military Council with either Frunze or Egorov as the military commander for a new *front* that was to be created to deal with the problem. Tukhachevsky's Western *Front* was to remain intact and absorb the Southwestern *Front.* This decision was the basis for a directive of the CINC, Kamenev, on 3 August that it was now time to combine the two *fronts* by transferring the Twelfth Army and the First Cavalry Army to the Western *Front.* Tukhachevsky was ordered to establish communication with those armies.

Stalin responded on 4 August with two messages to Moscow. In a private message to Lenin, in what might today be called the "back channel," Stalin expressed disagreement with the Politburo decision, whereas in a message in the "front channel," he provided his interpretation of the commander-in-chief's directive. What was intended, he wired, was the transfer of the Twelfth and Fourteenth Armies and First Cavalry Army to the Western *Front.* The Southwestern *Front* headquarters and staff, including its military council, would remain intact and be renamed the headquarters of the new Southern *Front.* Stalin's interpretation was accepted by the Revolutionary Military Council of the Republic in Moscow and approved at a plenary session to the Central Committee on 5 August (Naida et al. 1960, 153).

In his back channel message to Lenin, Stalin again exposed the dark side of his personality, the crudeness that Lenin would cite in his last testament. Stalin wired that the Politburo should not be wasting time with "trivialities" *(pustiaki)* such as the division of responsibilities of the Western and Southwestern *Fronts.* He went on to inform Lenin that he could work at the front only for a maximum of two more weeks, and that a substitute for him should be found. Stalin warned that the commander-in-chief's promises could not be trusted and that, in the matter of peace with Poland, Lenin should be aware that Soviet diplomacy sometimes very successfully undid the results of Soviet successes.

Lenin's immediate response requested the rationale for Stalin's opposition to the new frontal subordinations. Lenin stressed the necessity of dealing with Vrangel and asked Stalin to suggest a candidate for his position. He also asked for the specifics of the commander-in-chief's unfulfilled promises. He denied the charge that Soviet diplomacy, which was subordinate to the Central Committee, had ever frustrated Soviet military successes (Kuz'min 1962, 54).

Whatever Lenin's personal reaction to Stalin's pique, on 4 August he asked Stalin for his evaluation of the military situation, specifically referring to Budenny's problems and to those forces opposing Vrangel. Stalin replied that the delays being experienced by Budenny were temporary and did not signify that the balance was shifting toward the Poles, whom he described as weak and in need of rest. Stalin asserted that Vrangel would be defeated in the near future if the commander in chief would reinforce the Thirteenth Army with cavalry (Naida 1960, 152, 153). The Central Committee, presumably after considering these appraisals, decided to continue the offensive to complete the defeat of the Polish Army and to "aid the workers and peasants in their struggle for social liberation" (Naida et al. 1960, 153). In other words, to bring the revolution to Poland.

On 6 August, the commander in chief ordered Egorov to prepare the three armies for transfer to the Western *Front,* and he specifically directed that the Cavalry Army be allowed to rest to prepare for a decisive new strike (Naida 1960, 153). On the previous day, Budenny had informed Egorov that his army was in need of rest to restore the troops, their horses, and their equipment and that he had placed two cavalry divisions in reserve. Egorov responded that he could not acquiesce to Budenny's request and ordered that the offensive toward L'vov be continued (Budenny 1958, 282, 283).

The Cavalry Army attacked the next day, but the two cavalry divisions and one infantry division remained in reserve. Voroshilov was dispatched to Berdichev, now some 240 kilometers to the rear, to inform *front* headquarters on the direct line about the army's condition. While awaiting word from Voroshilov, Budenny was directed on 8 August to regroup, with the aim of bringing the cavalry units into the reserve and replacing them with infantry divisions. Budenny was unable to execute this order because two of the cavalry divisions and one of the infantry divisions were already in contact with a very active enemy. The other infantry division was in need of reinforcement and refurbishment (Budenny 1958, 284).

For the next two days, the front before the First Cavalry Army was unusually quiet. Voroshilov returned from Berdichev, where he had spoken by telephone with Egorov. According to Budenny, Egorov told Voroshilov that in the near future the Cavalry Army would be transferred to the Western *Front*. Voroshilov was also told that as long as the army was subordinate to the Southwestern *Front*, its mission would be the capture of L'vov (Budenny 1958, 288, 289).

That same day, 10 August, a Polish orderly was captured who had in his possession a document dated 8 August that ordered the Polish 1st Division to retreat to the Western Bug River. The unusual quiet for the past two days was thus explained. The Poles had broken contact and were re-forming, probably opposite the Western *Front*. The information was immediately passed on to *front* headquarters. Budenny, instead of immediately moving to regain contact with the retreating enemy, chose to continue to enjoy the midsummer sunshine as he visited his resting troops, who were reshoeing their horses, sharpening their sabers, and receiving new equipment. Budenny even describes dancing with the troops, recalling his "dashing youth." He admits no concern over losing contact with the Poles but did expect that he would be ordered to resume his advance toward L'vov.

On 12 August, the Southwestern *Front* order directed the Twelfth Army to seize the area Rava Russkaia and Tomashev, fifty to eighty kilometers northwest of L'vov. The Fourteenth Army was to support the Cavalry Army from the south as it

> . . . in the shortest possible time destroys the enemy on the right bank of the Bug, forces a crossing of the river and on the shoulders of the fleeing remnants of the Third and Sixth Polish Armies seizes the city of L'vov (Budenny 1958, 292–94).

This was a startling order, considering the previous directives of the commander in chief and the decisions of the Central Committee. In 1929, Egorov attempted to explain the reasoning behind his order by citing the great divergence at the very basis of the conceptions *(zamysly)* of the CINC and the *front* Revolutionary Military Council (read: Stalin) over how to achieve the defeat of Pilsudski's army. The CINC wanted to score the decisive victory over the Poles on the Warsaw axis; he considered operations around L'vov to have secondary importance to the fate of the Polish campaign. The Southwestern *Front*, according to Egorov, considered the capture of L'vov of exceptional importance and sought to find the solution to the Polish problem in a combined strike at Warsaw and through L'vov toward the rear of Warsaw (Kuz'min 1962, 55).

It was, of course, possible to make the argument that a thrust through L'vov would have been a better way to defeat the Poles; in effect, it would have been an envelopment of the Polish right wing. What Egorov did not answer was under what authority he and his political commissar, Stalin, were acting in proceeding against the orders of not only the commander in chief but the supreme political authority as well. This question was particularly acute for Egorov, who two years before had argued successfully for the appointment of a commander in chief empowered to make such decisions. This was also the same Egorov who was the foe of *partizanshchina*, now himself engaging in the practice not with an undisciplined detachment but with an entire *front*.

There is no evidence that Egorov or Stalin had had face-to-face contact with the Cavalry Army or its commander since early June, which undoubtedly contributed to the absence of reality surrounding the *front* order. The *front* headquarters at this time was at Aleksandrovsk (today's Zaporozh'e), some 800 kilometers from the region in which the First Cavalry Army was operating. At that distance it was probably easy for Egorov to ignore Budenny's pleas for rest and replenishment. And, as is evident from a message that Egorov and Stalin sent to Kamenev from Aleksandrovsk, there was also another reason to keep the First Cavalry engaged around L'vov. They wanted the army to be assigned to the new Southern *Front*, which Stalin had proposed to be commanded by Egorov and to which he, Stalin, had expected to be named member of the *front* military council. Whether Stalin expected Lenin to relieve him, as he had requested in his back channel message, we do not know (Kuz'min 1962, 58).

### STALIN BECOMES RECALCITRANT

On 11 August, the commander in chief sent two messages concerning the future employment of the First Cavalry Army and the Twelfth Army. The first asked Egorov's opinion on halting operations against L'vov and proposed that the Twelfth Army attack toward Liublin while the Cavalry Army assembled around Zamost'e. But this message was not a directive in that it requested Egorov's opinion on the matter. The second message was a directive: the Twelfth Army was ordered to proceed toward Liublin immediately; there was no mention of the Cavalry Army.

Neither message was received by Egorov until 13 August because of encoding-decoding problems. On that day, Egorov responded that the armies of the *front* were already engaged with the Poles in the direction of L'vov and could not comply with the commander-in-chief's order, except that the right flank of the Twelfth Army would be ordered to press somewhat to the north to provide assistance to the Western *Front*. Kamenev responded by ordering the First Cavalry Army and the Twelfth Army subordinated to the Western *Front* effective at noon on 14 August (Kuz'min 1962, 61).

Egorov drafted an order to the two armies directing them to comply with the CINC's order, but because Stalin refused to cosign the order, it was not valid. Stalin also sent a telegram giving his reason for refusing to approve the order.

> Your last directive 4774/op 1052/sh needlessly overturns the established grouping of forces in the region of these armies which have already taken the offensive; the directive should have been issued three days ago, when the Cavarmy was in reserve or later after the seizure of L'vov, at the present time it only confuses matters and inevitably causes needless delay for the purpose of a new regrouping ... (Kuz'min 1962, 62, fn. 52).

Stalin's refusal to sign the order provoked a prompt reaction in Moscow. He was ordered to return there to discuss his differences with Kamenev, and on 17 August he left for Moscow. In Moscow, Stalin requested to be relieved of "military work"; he was relieved of his duties as a member of the Revolutionary Military Council of the Southwestern *Front*. However, he remained a member of the RVS of the Republic (Kuz'min 1962, 62, 63).

Egorov, in the meantime, attempted to have R. I. Berzin, another member of the *front* military council, cosign the order. Berzin, who was working with the *front* rear area units, also refused to sign the order, on the grounds that he was not familiar with the issues. Only after receiving instructions from the deputy chairman of the Revolutionary Military Council of the Republic, E. M. Sklanskii, did he agree to sign the order. The First Cavalry Army and the Twelfth Army were transferred to the operational control of Tukhachevsky and the Western *Front* as of noon on 14 August, but the order said nothing about halting the offensive toward L'vov (Kuz'min 1962, 63, 64).

Tukhachevsky did not succeed in reaching Budenny with a valid order until 16 August. Communications were hindered because they had to be relayed through the Southwestern *Front*. Also, the order, as received, had no countersignature by a member of the RVS of the Western *Front* and was therefore not valid (Budenny 1958, 315). By that time Budenny was across the Bug, fifteen kilometers east of L'vov. Budenny had issued orders to his divisions to continue the attack the next day. Two infantry divisions of the Fourteenth Army that were to replace the Cavalry Army before L'vov, according to the Western *Front* order, were far from L'vov. The Twelfth Army had nothing available to replace the Cavalry Army units if they were withdrawn. Budenny concluded that the defeat of the Poles defending the city was necessary before his army could be withdrawn from the approaches to L'vov (Budenny 1958, 319–21).

Budenny continued the attack on L'vov until 19 August, moving to within five to seven kilometers of the city on three sides. On that date, he received another order from Tukhachevsky, dated 17 August, to move as rapidly as possible to the vicinity of Vladimir Volynskii. Budenny also learned that the Poles had begun their counterattack against the Western *Front*'s left flank on the sixteenth. The order and the Cavalry Army's situation before L'vov presented Budenny with a complex problem. He did not believe that his withdrawal would now influence the Polish attack on Tukhachevsky's left flank, and he continued to believe that the capture of L'vov would force the Poles to send reinforcements to block the Cavalry Army's further progress toward Warsaw. He attempted to communicate these considerations to Tukhachevsky, who was in Minsk, but the next morning the previous order was repeated. The Cavalry Army began withdrawing from before L'vov on 20 August and arrived at its designated concentration area on 28 August.

In the meantime the Poles continued their counterattack, and by 25 August their southern strike force had reached the Western Bug, in places fifteen kilometers east of Brest Litovsk. At this time a lull in the fighting occurred all along the front and the Soviet high command attempted to restore the combat fitness of the shattered armies of the Western *Front*. Some armies had lost a good portion of their artillery during the retreat, and some units had been forced to cross into East Prussia, where they were interned by the Germans (Naida 1960, 157–60).

Despite these crushing defeats, Egorov and Tukhachevsky remained in command of their respective *fronts* and, with the exception of Stalin, the military councils remained the same. An armistice in the war with Poland was signed on 12 December 1920, leading to the peace of Riga, concluded in March of the next year. Military operations on the right bank of the Dnieper did not cease, however, as opposition to Soviet rule continued. In one of his reports, Egorov claimed that the opposition he was dealing with was being directed by Ataman Petliura from the territory now controlled by Poland. The Soviets believed that the mission of these forces was to engage the Red Army troops that would otherwise be employed against Vrangel in the Crimea.

The mission of crushing Vrangel and his White Guards in the Crimea was given to the Southern *Front*, which was established on 21 December 1920, with Mikhail Frunze in command. The Thirteenth Army (now commanded by Uborevich), which had been struggling with the White Guards, passed to Frunze's command; the Southwestern *Front* retained the Twelfth and Fourteenth Armies. Egorov launched a general offensive on 10 November that forced the remnants of the Ukrainian opposition back to the lines held by the Poles—where they were disarmed. By 15 November, Kamenev was congratulating Egorov on his victory (Nenarokov 1973, 61, 62).

This short campaign and the concurrent defeat of Vrangel by Frunze and the Southern *Front* brought the civil war to an end. In December 1920, Egorov's service to the Soviet state was praised in a message from the Southwestern *Front* Revolutionary Council (R. I. Berzin, S. I. Aralov, and N. N. Petin) to Trotsky, the chairman of the Revolutionary Military Council of the Republic. The message praised the personal qualities that had contributed to Egorov's success as a commander: the ability to evaluate the military situation correctly; clarity and boldness in defining his mission; tirelessness and a strong will; ability to use all types of weapons and equipment; continuous study of the latest in military thought and theory; and broad, creative initiative. The members of the *front* military council recommended that Egorov be enrolled in the General Staff and awarded a gold pistol, which he received in February 1921. Although he was subsequently enrolled in the General Staff, the Soviet Army opted not to have a General Staff at this time.* In 1935, when it was decided to name the existing Red Army Staff the General Staff, he became its first chief.

## THE AFTERMATH OF THE POLISH WAR

For the next decade, the crushing defeat that Pilsudski's Polish Army inflicted on Tukhachevsky's Western *Front* and the role of Budenny's First Cavalry Army in the episode were the subjects of "lively" discussions among the Soviet military over who was to blame. Soviet military historians took part, but the main discussants were those who played leading roles in the fiasco: Egorov, Kamenev, Tukhachevsky, and Shaposhnikov. During the intense political battles over who was to be Lenin's successor, the defeat before Warsaw became an issue between Trotsky and Stalin. After Stalin became the victor, criticism of the command of the Southwestern *Front* ceased, and the actions of Egorov and Stalin were the only ones considered to have been correct. In 1929, Voroshilov, now commissar of defense, would write that the failure before Warsaw was the result of the traitorous orders of Trotsky and his adherents (Volkogonov 1992, 291). Eventually, Voroshilov would claim that the liberation of Kiev and the right bank of the Dnieper, the deep penetration into Galicia, and the organi-

---

*The Red Army did not have a General Staff at this time, although creation of such a staff was proposed. A list of officers considered qualified for high-level staff duty was maintained to provide a pool of officers as needed. In the fall of 1918 there were 526 former General Staff officers serving in the Red Army. Matvei V. Zakharov, a former chief of the Soviet General Staff, observed that these were the best prepared of the old officer corps (Zakharov 1989, 5, 6).

zation of the operations of the First Cavalry Army were all to a large degree due to the wise and skillful leadership of Stalin. "Only the failure of our troops before Warsaw thwarted the Cavalry Army . . . located ten kilometers from L'vov . . ." (Voroshilov 1937, 41).

The issue was reopened in 1956 after Khrushchev's famous speech to the Twentieth Party Congress. The Central Committee plenum's resolution of 5 August 1920 approving the transfer of the Twelfth and Fourteenth Armies and First Cavalry Army to the Western *Front* was published for the first time. In 1962, the message containing Stalin's rationale for not cosigning Egorov's orders transferring the First Cavalry Army and the Twelfth Army to Tukhachevsky's command was published.

Egorov's account of the operation, entitled *L'vov-Varshava*, appeared in 1929. It was intended, according to its author, to expose the "legend" of the fateful role of the Southwestern *Front* in the concluding stage of the Soviet-Polish war. Egorov "attempted" to prove that the transfer of all the armies from the Southwestern *Front* to the Western *Front* was not thought through by the commander in chief in time and became snarled in purely administrative difficulties. Budenny's army was ordered to be placed in reserve on 6 August, but the CINC did not inform Egorov what he had in mind for its future employment. The CINC did not know the situation at the front (and for that matter neither did Egorov), and his orders were received after long delays. In addition there were technical reasons (encoding-decoding problems) why Kamenev's instructions were delayed until 13 August. Egorov claimed that by that time it was already too late to move the Cavalry Army to positions that could threaten the rear and flank of the counterattacking Poles. Egorov, in short, placed all of the responsibility for the failure of the operation on the commander in chief and the Western *Front* command (Kuz'min 1962, 51). In 1992, with the publication of the second volume of Dmitrii Volkogonov's biography of Trotsky, it was revealed that Egorov, in the manuscript of *L'vov-Varshava*, had made some negative comments concerning Stalin's refusal to cosign his order of 13 August 1920. Egorov's treatment of the issue "alarmed" Voroshilov when he read it in 1928. He alerted Stalin to the problem and suggested that the dictator reread the passage and either call him or "make some noise" about it. Stalin apparently did so, and, despite Egorov's protest, the offending passage was deleted from the book (Volkogonov 1992, 2:291, 292).

Egorov, who seems to have accepted the optimistic evaluations of Tukhachevsky and Kamenev of the capability of the Poles to defend Warsaw, devoted most of his command attention to the threat posed by Baron Vrangel and the putative threat posed by a Romanian intervention. The displacement of the *front* command posts from Kharkov to Kremenchug to Aleksandrovsk, each closer to the Crimea and farther from Budenny, is a clear indication of the locus of Egorov's major concern. His failure to visit the Cavalry Army, even when requested to do so by Budenny—to appraise the army's condition, to encourage its efforts, and to evaluate its commanders—was a violation of his own principles of command. In his monograph on the campaign against Denikin in 1919, he wrote that success can be achieved only by live, continuous leadership of the high command and frequent personal exchanges with subordinates while assigning missions. Had he followed this policy in the Polish campaign, he might have realized that the missions the army was being given in late July and early August were beyond its capabilities. Allowing Budenny to operate virtually on his own may have been a result of the growing mystique of Cavalry Army invincibility, which was spreading in the upper echelons of the Red Army high command. The role of Stalin in Egorov's command conduct and the extent to which he was under the influence of the future dictator is not clear. In June, Stalin seemed to have been more concerned over Vrangel and the possibility that the Romanians might attempt to take advantage of the Polish attack. He may have been very influential in keeping Egorov close to his command post in the event that either Vrangel or the Romanians would attempt to move against the rear of the Southwestern *Front*. And visits to the *front* were not a part of Stalin's command style. He had not done it often during the defense of Tsaritsyn, and he would leave Moscow to visit a *front* headquarters only once during World War II.

The majority of the reviewers of Egorov's book rejected his analysis of the campaign. Among those who were considering a review rebutting Egorov's conclusions, but who apparently did not write one, was B. M. Shaposhnikov, who, as chief of the operations section of the All Russian Main Staff, was involved in the planning and coordination of the Red Army's operations and may have drafted some of the operations orders in question.

It was probably no accident that many of those who perished in the purges, including Tukhachevsky, Iakir, and Uborevich, played a role in this campaign. Until Khrushchev's revelations at the Twentieth Party Congress, Voroshilov's version of what happened before L'vov remained the only acceptable version, and those who knew better remained silent.

Dauria Station, 1928. Officers of the 5th Separate Kuban Cavalry Brigade of the Red Banner Separate Far Eastern Army. The headgear the officers are wearing was popularly called *budenovka,* recalling the First Cavalry Army commander, Budenny.

Halhin Gol, August 1939. Corps Commander Zhukov addresses his troops. Zhukov considered that his performance at Halhin Gol saved him from becoming a victim of Stalin's purges.

Stalingrad, January 1943. The Don Front commander Col. Gen. Rokossovsky (left) and member of the front military council Maj. Gen. Telegin. Rokossovsky's forces defeated the German Sixth Army and captured its commander, Marshal von Paulus.

Marshal A. M. Vasilevsky in full dress uniform. Together with Zhukov he coordinated the defense of Stalingrad and the subsequent counterattack. Zhukov and Vasilevsky also coordinated the German defeat at the Kursk salient in 1943.

First Belorussian Front 1944. Marshals G. K. Zhukov, K. K. Rokossovsky and General P. I. Batov. Stalin placed Zhukov in command of the *front* in 1945 and it played a key role in the capture of Berlin. Rokossovsky attributed the change in command to Zhukov and the episode led to an estrangement between the two officers.

Marshals Rokossovsky and Zhukov 1945. Rokossovsky's arrest in 1937 and his three-year imprisonment enabled Zhukov, who had been his subordinate, to overtake him in rank and become his superior.

Marshal Vasilevsky, probably when he was chief of the Soviet General Staff. Vasilevsky, despite frequent absences from Moscow as representative of the *stavka*, remained in that post until February 1945.

August 1945. Northern Group of Forces Commander in chief Marshal Rokossovsky (left) and his first deputy, Col. Gen. Batov. Batov commanded the 65th Army under Rokossovsky during the war.

Moscow, June 1945. On the Mausoleum: Marshals Govorov, Konev, Rokossovsky, Vasilevsky, and Politburo member Malenkov during the Victory Parade.

Marshal N. D. Iakovlev and son Nikolai Nikolaevich. Marshal Iakovlev was head of the Main Artillery Directorate from 1941 until 1948. His son was a prolific author and English language translator.

The commanders of the western *fronts* in 1945. (Seated) Konev, Vasilevsky, Zhukov, Rokossovsky, Meretskov. (Standing) Tolbukhin, Malinovsky, Govorov, Eremenko, Bagramian.

Moscow, June 1974. Funeral of Marshal G. K. Zhukov. Marshal Grechko (in uniform), Politburo members Suslov, Brezhnev, and Podgorny. They are carrying the urn containing Zhukov's ashes which was eventually placed in a niche in the wall of the Kremlin.

# 6
# STALIN ROUTS TROTSKY

Vrangel's defeat supposedly marked the end of the civil war. Now the Bolsheviks, having attained power by exploiting the longing of the masses for peace, land, and bread, were faced with redeeming their promises in a country ruined and exhausted from four years of world war followed almost immediately by four years of civil strife. And to say that the civil war was ended is to categorize the events at Tambov and Kronstadt in 1921 according to some new definition of fraternal conflict.

Trotsky was to claim that he realized in late 1919 that the economic policy known as "war communism" had to be modified. Under that policy, grain and other foodstuffs were requisitioned from the peasants by the government in return for arbitrarily fixed prices well below the open market level. Peasants refusing to sell to the government on these terms were branded as "kulaks" and "counterrevolutionaries" as well as being subject to the search and seizure of their farms. Trotsky urged some degree of restoration of the home market: the peasants had to be offered some incentives, other than artificially low, fixed state prices, to surrender their grain. Lenin opposed Trotsky's proposal (Trotsky 1930, 461–64). The "New Economic Policy" (NEP), which ameliorated the lot of the peasantry, was not announced until March 1921.

## THE ANTONOVSHCHINA

In early 1921, a widespread peasant revolt erupted in Tambov Guberniia (province) led by a Socialist Revolutionary, A. S. Antonov. The Politburo, after trying combinations of coercion and economic incentives to quell the revolt, decided in April to seek a military solution to the problem. Mikhail Tukhachevsky was placed in command of the Soviet forces in the province (around 50,000 regular troops) and given one month to end the insurrection. He tried mightily but did not succeed. Operating under a mandate that authorized the exercise of almost unlimited force, Tukhachevsky's troops smashed and scattered the insurgents. The troops were authorized to burn villages from which opposition emanated. Peasant huts were blasted at point-blank range. No prisoners were taken. To force the surrender of the male members of a family, women and children were taken hostage and held in miserable conditions. During this campaign the modern concept of the concentration camp became a harsh reality in Soviet Russia as early as May 1921.

When remnants of scattered bands of the malcontents and other "bandits" fled their villages for refuge in nearby forests, occasionally debouching to raid passing targets of opportunity for food and plunder, Tukhachevsky ordered the use of poison gas to destroy them. Antonov and his brother were tracked down and shot in June 1922. Peasant disorders on a lesser scale continued throughout 1922 in farming communities as widely spread as Orel and Tobolsk. Red Army losses during those two years were 171,185, giving some idea of the scale and ferocity of these conflicts. All of these steps were taken with the full knowledge and approval of Lenin and the Politburo (Volkogonov 1994, 91, 131, 156–58).

## THE REVOLT AT KRONSTADT

Perhaps an even greater shock to the Soviet regime was the outbreak of a revolt in early March 1921 at the strategic naval base at Kronstadt, located on Kotlin Island, at the head of the sea approaches to Petrograd. Marxist ideology had conditioned the Bolshevik leadership to anticipate opposition from the more prosperous peasants to the dictatorship of the proletariat, but the outbreak among the sailors of Kronstadt, who had played a critical role in the Bolshevik seizure of power in 1917, took the leadership by surprise. After the fact, a rationale was developed that the Kronstadt garrison had been replenished in the interim with troops and sailors from the villages who were influenced by the reports they were hearing from home of hunger, disorders, and violent reprisals.

The imminent breakup of the ice in the Gulf of Finland made it imperative that if military action were taken it be taken immediately. On 2 March, the Council of Labor and Defense (STO) declared a "siege situation" in Petrograd, reestablished the Seventh Army under the command of Mikhail Tukhachevsky, and sent the 27th Omsk Division to the city. After giving the rebels an opportunity to lay down their arms under an amnesty, but receiving no response, the Seventh Army launched its first attack on 8 March. It was unsuccessful. A second attack across the ice by a significantly reinforced Seventh Army on 17 March succeeded in reaching the fortress. Tukhachevsky ordered the use of poison gas against the battleships *Petropavlovsk* and *Sevastopol.* The revolt was considered over by noon the next day. The rebels suffered more than 3,000 casualties, and about 8,000 insurgents succeeded in escaping into Finland. Soviet casualties were about 4,000. The second offensive was notable in that some 300 military delegates sent from the Tenth Party Congress participated in the assault. The congress was suspended until the Kronstadt affair was settled. Among the delegates who participated in the storm of the fortress were Klim Voroshilov and Ivan Stepanovich Konev (SVE 4:479, 480; Murav'eva 1992, 2).

### STALIN AND TROTSKY—THE IRRECONCILABLES
Neither Trotsky nor Stalin claimed a leading role in these events. Trotsky, as commissar for war and navy and chairman of the Revolutionary Military Council of the Republic (RVSR), was involved in the selection of the commander and the assembly of the necessary forces. His role in suppressing the Kronstadt mutiny, though, was greater than he later cared to admit. He arrived in Petrograd on the night of 4–5 March 1921 and issued an ultimatum to the Kronstadt garrison and the crews of the rebellious ships. When it was rejected he ordered that the rebel fortress be reduced at all costs. When the rebels were finally overwhelmed, he ordered the use of utmost force in dealing with the survivors. In 1938, he was to attribute the brutality with which the uprising was suppressed to Dzerzhinskii and the Cheka (Payne 1977, 239–44).

Stalin, despite his action (or inaction) before L'vov, remained on the Politburo, a member of the RVSR, and commissar of nationalities. Aleksandr Il'ich Egorov, who in 1920 seemed to connive with Stalin to engage the First Cavalry Army in the attempt to take L'vov and thus thwart the CINC's orders to move Budenny's army to the Western *Front,* was also apparently forgiven and given command of the Kiev Military District. He did not participate in the suppression of the Kronstadt revolt, but after the Kronstadt events he was transferred from command of the Kiev Military District to Petrograd and took command of that military district on 17 April 1921 (Nenarokov 1973, 71, 73).

Relations between Stalin and Trotsky remained cool. In the popular estimation of the leadership, Trotsky was esteemed second to Lenin. So long as Lenin was alive and competent, that probably was in fact the relationship within the Politburo. Stalin, who initially felt himself uncertain in the face of Trotsky's eloquence, haughtiness, and self-confidence, eventually became convinced that much of what he saw lacked substance and that Trotsky was a poseur who could turn a phrase. His capabilities as a fiery speaker during the revolution and the civil war generated enormous popularity for him, and many saw him as the future leader of the Party. But, faced with the monotonous problems of daily peacetime governance, the orator's brilliance began to fade.

For Trotsky, the important thing was the gesture, the slogan, not the routine work of effective administration (Volkogonov 1989, book 1, part 1:117).

For his part, Trotsky considered Stalin to be his intellectual inferior. He could not bring himself to develop a working relationship with the Georgian despite Lenin's entreaties, and he rebuffed Stalin's tentative attempts to meet him halfway. Trotsky also began to become more concerned about his own health, almost obsessively so; he took a two-month leave in the spring of 1920 for medical treatment, and he spent much time hunting in the Moscow area. For Trotsky, the attraction of hunting was that it worked on his mind "like a poultice on a sore" (Trotsky 1930, 430). Accidents that occurred on hunting trips were eventually to cost him dearly for those "poultices."

In late 1921 the symptoms of Lenin's illness—headaches, insomnia, and fatigue—grew worse, and he left Moscow for a nearby sanitorium. By March 1922 his headaches continued to worsen and he was ordered by his doctors to take a prolonged rest. In May, Lenin had his first stroke. Trotsky, who had torn the ligaments in his foot while fishing, was disturbed that he was not informed of it until two days after the episode. Stalin, the new general secretary, was beginning to test the advantages of his office.

Retrospectively, Trotsky realized that his political health was linked to Lenin's physical health. With Lenin at the helm, Trotsky was confident that he was second in command and that Stalin and his supporters would be deterred from moving openly against him. But, as Lenin's health grew worse, Stalin entered into an alliance *(blok)* with L. B. Kamenev and G. Zinoviev, the principal object of which was to prevent Trotsky from succeeding to the leadership.

When Lenin returned to work in October, he became disturbed over the growth in the size and influence of the bureaucracy, which, according to Trotsky, he attributed to Stalin's activities as general secretary. And he offered Trotsky a *blok* against bureaucracy and Stalin (Trotsky 1930, 479). Volkogonov, citing Lenin's dominating position in the Party, doubts that he would have felt the need to recruit Trotsky to curb Stalin. In early March 1923, Lenin again (according to Trotsky) became disturbed over Stalin's machinations in Georgia, where the general secretary had organized (with the assistance of Feliks Dzerzhinskii and Sergo Ordzhonikidze) a coup d'etat against the best section of the Georgian Party (Trotsky 1930, 483). To counter Stalin, Lenin, who by this time had already determined that the general secretary had too much power and too little restraint in using it, enlisted Trotsky in an attempt to reverse Stalin's Georgian policy. Trotsky, who now was suffering from lumbago, tried to recruit Kamenev, who was preparing to represent the Politburo at a conference of the Georgian Party. After showing Kamenev materials prepared by Lenin critical of Stalin's activities in Georgia, Trotsky hoped to persuade Kamenev to speak against Stalin at the Georgian conference. While Kamenev was traveling to Tbilisi, he was informed by Stalin that Lenin had again lapsed into paralysis. Kamenev, knowing that he would not have to contend with the authority of Lenin, carried out Stalin's policy at the conference (Trotsky 1930, 486).

As Lenin grew more helpless, Stalin became more aggressive in moving his people into key positions and cementing his alliance against Trotsky in the Politburo. Eventually, Trotsky found himself isolated in that body. In September 1923, a plenum of the Central Committee directed that an executive organ be established in the Revolutionary Military Council, of which Trotsky was still the chairman. Stalin, Voroshilov, and others were added to the council over Trotsky's protest. In a letter to the Politburo he declared that the plenum's decision was in effect the creation of a new council. One of the conclusions of a subsequent plenum was that as military commissar he should devote more attention to military matters and less to opposing the Politburo majority. Despite knowing that he was in a hopeless minority, Trotsky continued to inveigh against the Stalinist bureaucracy. This activity provided Stalin with grounds to accuse Trotsky of fractionalism and opposing the Politburo and the Central Committee—activities prohibited by Party statute.

## THE MILITARY REFORMS OF 1924–25

In this atmosphere of political combat, the Red Army, which at the end of the civil war had reached a strength of some 5.3 million men and women, was reduced in three stages to 600,000 by February 1923. The demobilization was conducted in the midst of unparalleled economic hardship in the country, including famine, which one researcher, writing in 1958, characterized as "the most difficult period in the history of the Soviet armed forces . . ." (Berkhin 1958, 20). As anyone who has experienced the precipitous demobilization of a large national army would have anticipated, the combat effectiveness of the Red Army declined rapidly. This inevitable decline coincided with a waning in Trotsky's interest in military administration, his inexplicable political apathy, and his nagging health problems, providing an opportunity for his opponents to remove him from control of a potentially important power base—the leadership of the armed forces.

In June 1923, it was decided to conduct a comprehensive examination of the condition of the Red Army. A special military commission was formed; it was chaired initially by Valerian V. Kuibeshev, a member of the Politburo since 1922, and subsequently by Sergei Ivanovich Gusev, another old Bolshevik who had served as a member of the military council of several *fronts* during the civil war. The commission, known as the Military Commission of the Central Control Commission (TsKK) and the Workers and Peasants Inspection (RKI), was drawn from organizations that Stalin had been involved with from their inception following the seizure of power in 1917.

Not surprisingly, when the commission reported the results of its inspections toward the end of 1923, it found that neither the Red Army nor the fleet were combat ready, due to a combination of serious shortcomings that began at the very top of the defense establishment. Deficiencies in the central command organs included:

•The direction and training of the army were unsatisfactory.

•The structure of the RKKA Staff did not correspond to the mission of readying the defense of the country and direction of the armed forces.

•There was no central supply organ serving the ongoing supply of the army or assembling mobilization reserves and preparing economic organs for war.

•Existing tables of organization and equipment for troop staffs did not correspond to actual requirements, leading to the overworking of staffs.

•Existing organizations of rifle and cavalry formations did not answer the requirements of peacetime or their eventual combat employment.

•There was no unified plan for preparing the engineer defense of the country.

•A number of shortcomings were noted in the organization of technical troops, which had a negative effect on their training and development.

•The fleet had no combat capability.

•There were large shortages in the temporary as well as in the permanent command staff, reaching up to 50 percent in some units.

•Turnover was one of the major plagues of the Red Army, reaching up to 50 percent in some units.

•There were large shortages of weapons and equipment, and much of what was available was in disrepair.

•Training was unsatisfactory.

- Commanders, especially the younger ones, were not qualified. Their personal living situation was very difficult.
- The supply situation was catastrophic.
- Political work in the armed services was unsatisfactory (Berkhin 1958, 57, 58).

Consistent with Communist Party practice, the next step was to take up the matter of the condition of the Red Army at a plenary session of the Central Committee. The problems of the army became the main topic for discussion at a plenum that began in mid-January 1924. On 14 January, a "highly authoritative" commission was formed to determine the reasons for this situation. The commission was chaired by Sergei Gusev, who had chaired the military commission of the TsKK and the RKI. Among its highly authoritative members were Mikhail Frunze, Klim Voroshilov, N. S. Unshlikht, and the inevitable "others." This commission, after doing "tremendous work" and "deeply studying the situation in the army, especially questions of turnover of personnel and the condition of supply . . . ," was ready to report to the plenum on 3 February (Berkhin 1958, 60). Not unexpectedly, Gusev's report followed the thrust of the report of the military commission of the TsKK and the RKI. After a broad discussion of the question, the plenum authorized the commission to continue its work. On 4 February the Revolutionary Military Council established a commission headed by Frunze and including Voroshilov, Unshlikht, S. S. Kamenev (still commander in chief of the Red Army), and P. P. Lebedev (chief of Staff RKKA) to work out a plan to conduct the military reforms (Zakharov 1989, 24, 25).

One of the earliest recommendations of the commission was the appointment of a new Revolutionary Military Council with new leadership. On 11 March, Frunze was appointed deputy chairman of the Revolutionary Military Council; the next year, on 26 January 1925, he was appointed chairman of the RVS, replacing Trotsky. Klim Voroshilov, described in 1958 as "an outstanding figure of the Bolshevik party and the Soviet State and one of the most prominent organizers and great captains of the Red Army" (Berkhin 1958, 66), was also named to the RVS, along with Budenny, A. S. Bubnov, S. S. Kamenev, A. F. Miasnikov, G. K. Ordzhonikidze, N. S. Unshlikht, and Sh. Z. Eliava. Aleksandr Il'ich Egorov was added to the council in May.

Trotsky, in the face of these changes, had remained curiously in-active. In October 1923, he had gone hunting and gotten his feet wet. Subsequently, he developed a cryptogenic temperature, and his doc-tors ordered him to stay in bed. He remained there through the rest of the year. As his indisposition lingered into the new year, 1924, it was decided to send him to Sukhumi, where it was hoped the milder climate on the shores of the Black Sea would aid his recovery. On 21 January, while in Tbilisi en route to Sukhumi, he received a message from Stalin informing him that Lenin had died and that the funeral was to be on Saturday. Since Trotsky could not return in time, he was instructed to continue on to Sukhumi for his treatment. Later he found out that the funeral was held on Sunday and that he could have returned to Moscow in time (Trotsky 1930, 508). Adam Ulam, how-ever, observed that Trotsky was informed on Tuesday that the funeral would be on Saturday and that it was actually held on Sunday. The travel time from Tbilisi was three days by a regular train. Presumably Trotsky could have accelerated his return (Ulam 1973, 236).

Trotsky was visited at Sukhumi by a delegation of the Central Com-mittee, which included Frunze and Gusev. Its purpose was to coor-dinate the personnel changes in the Military and Naval Commis-sariat, but Trotsky considered the visit a farce—he felt that changes had been going on for some time behind his back. Trotsky particu-larly regretted that the man who had been his deputy since October 1918, Efraim Markovich Sklanskii, was being replaced by Frunze. Al-though he considered Frunze to be a serious person who had an out-standing record in the civil war, he deemed him far inferior to Sklan-skii as a military administrator. Sklanskii was transferred to economic work and died in a boating accident while on a business trip to the United States in August 1925. Trotsky also noted that a "talentless intriguer," Unshlikht, had been assigned to the Military and Naval Commissariat some months before in order to "uproot" Sklanskii and, in the future, Trotsky himself (Trotsky 1930, 511; SVE 7:372).

## MIKHAIL VASILEVICH FRUNZE AND THE MILITARY REFORMS

With Trotsky absent and now weakened politically, it fell to Mikhail Vasilevich Frunze to implement the reforms, the need for which was made so glaringly apparent by the various inspections and investigations. Frunze was probably the ideal candidate for the task. He was born in 1885 in Bishkek, the capital city of Kyrgyzstan, which was called Frunze during the Soviet period. He joined the Bolshevik Party in 1904 while a student in Saint Petersburg and was an active participant in the 1905 Revolution; he was arrested in 1907, and in 1909–10 he was twice sentenced to die. These sentences were eventually commuted to lifelong exile in Siberia. During World War I, he led the Bolshevik underground in Minsk, which had sections in the Third and Tenth Russian Armies. After playing an active role in the February and October Revolutions crushing counterrevolutionary outbreaks, he became a leader in the formation and development of the Red Army. In December 1918, he was designated commander of the Fourth Army of the Eastern *Front*. From July 1919 he commanded that *front* as it conquered the northern and central Ural region for the Bolsheviks. In August he completed the defeat of the southern wing of Kolchak's forces in Turkestan. After strengthening the Bolshevik hold on Turkestan, he again commanded the Southern *Front* in November 1920 as it successfully conquered the Crimean peninsula.

Following the civil war, Frunze was given command of the armed forces of the Ukraine and the Crimea as the Soviet state temporarily permitted national formations to exist within the Red Army. During this period Frunze on several occasions engaged Trotsky on the question of whether the Red Army should develop a unified military doctrine based on its experiences in the civil war. These somewhat scholastic exercises will be examined in more detail in the next chapter. Here it is necessary to mention only that Frunze took issue with Trotsky and thereby endeared himself to the anti-Trotsky faction, which was to eventually overwhelm the former "tribune of the revolution" (SVE 8:342–44). Frunze was an old Bolshevik, a tried and hardened revolutionary. He was not a military specialist; he was a self-taught, successful field commander during the civil war, and he had crossed pens with Trotsky, who nevertheless considered him a serious person.

## THE ESSENCE OF THE REFORMS

Both the size and the organizational makeup of the RKKA (including the fleet) were dictated to a large extent by the economic situation of the Soviet Union in 1924. In the concrete conditions of the 1920s, a regular *(kadrovaia)* army of 1.5 to 2 million men would have been desirable, but the Soviet state could not justify such a large army politically or economically. In fact, it could not support a 600,000-man armed force, and in the summer of 1924 it reduced the overall personnel ceiling to 562,000 due in part to a decline in the birth rate, which reflected the losses suffered in World War I and the civil war. At these levels the Red Army was 183,000 men smaller than the French Army.

One of the most important and decisive elements of the reforms of 1924–25 was the reorganization of the entire command and control system of the armed forces. The high command and its staffs, which had developed during the civil war, needed to be restructured in accordance with peacetime requirements. The central organs of the Ministry of the Army and Navy had grown to some 20,000 persons by the middle of 1921. Given the economic pressures facing the country, it was clear that one of the first orders of business was a serious reorganization of the high command. Initially, the staff of the RKKA, headed by P. P. Lebedev, a graduate of the Imperial General Staff Academy, was given both the operational and administrative functions, which had been divided between the Field Staff and the All Russian Main Staff during the civil war. It was reduced in size to 5,209 in 1922 and to 4,407 the next year, but these reductions served only to reduce its effectiveness. In any event, RKKA was found to be ineffective by the reformers of 1924.

To replace the staff of the RKKA, Frunze proposed three staffs. The first staff would be administrative and would be called the directorate of the Worker-Peasant Red Army. Its function would be to record all current processes with which the directorate was concerned and to serve the army's daily needs. The second staff would be the operational staff and would be similar in function to the old Russian General Staff and the Great German General Staff. This staff would be called the Staff RKKA. The third staff, called the Inspectorate of the RKKA, would be responsible for training the troops and would include all of the inspection functions for all arms and services (Zakharov 1989, 29, 30).

The supply function, which had been cited as catastrophic by the various inspecting bodies, was corrected by establishing a chief of supply as the senior director of all supply functions for the armed forces. All central directorates concerned with supply, including the technical services, would be subordinate to the supply chief in all of their aspects. Planning, including mobilization planning, was introduced into the supply system beginning at the central directorates and ending at the troop units. The chief of supply of the Red Army was the chairman of the Planning Commission of the Revolutionary Military Council. Similarly, chiefs of supply were appointed in each of the military districts.

Frunze, in addition to being deputy chairman of the RVS, was named the chief of Staff RKKA, with Tukhachevsky his first deputy. Sergei S. Kamenev, whose post as commander in chief was abolished as being unnecessary in peacetime, was named chief of the inspectorate. The directorate of the Red Army was headed by N. N. Petin, a military specialist who had fought with the Red Army during the civil war. The chief of supply was I. S. Unshlikht.

To provide the forces necessary to defend the country's frontiers and to train the annual conscription classes, it was decided to create a mixed army of regular and territorial units. The regular units would be stationed primarily in border military districts; the equipment and the cadre for the territorial units would be stationed in the most important political and economic centers of the country. Thus, for example, there were thirteen territorial divisions stationed in the Moscow Military District and only one in the Siberian Military District. In selecting the locations for territorial divisions, the considerations were the presence in the area of an adequate population of persons subject to the draft, communications infrastructure, and availability of barracks and remount horses. Tests conducted in early 1923 had established that for an infantry division a cadre of 1,607 was required to train a division of 12,656 (Berkhin 1958, 85, 97).

By 1925 the Red Army consisted of 77 infantry divisions—31 regular and 46 territorial. Of the 11 cavalry divisions and 8 brigades, only one division was territorial. The remainder of the cavalry divisions remained regular, but they were maintained at 60 percent of wartime strength. Corps artillery, artillery of special designation, and special and technical troops remained regular and were maintained at 80 percent of wartime strength (Berkhin 1958, 96). The territorial divisions were of three types depending on the size of the regular cadre that commanded and trained them. First-order divisions had a cadre of 2,400 for a division that totaled 13,081; second-order divisions were given a cadre of 604 for a division that was to total 12,354; third-order divisions were given a permanent cadre of 622 for a division that was to total 12,356. Finally, there were established "cells" *(iacheiki)* of possible future divisions with a cadre of 190 soldiers and officers. By April 1925 there were 28 first-order divisions, 16 second-order divisions, and 14 cells (Berkhin 1958, 98, 99).

The problem of *tekuchest* (turnover) was recognized and addressed as one requiring a multifaceted approach. As the army demobilized and units and entities were disbanded, accountability was lost, and individuals found that they could transfer to units closer to home without penalty. Some probably took advantage of the laxness in record keeping to leave permanently. To remedy this situation, units had to be assigned fixed tables of organization and equipment and given a stable command structure. The terms of service obligations were revised and fixed by law, and the entire system of registering, examining, and inducting those obliged to serve was reorganized. A decree of 21 March 1924 (which became a law on 18 September 1925) established that beginning in 1925 all individuals who had attained the age of twenty-one by 1 January would be eligible for active military service during that year. The term of service for the infantry, the largest branch of the armed services, would be two years; the term of service would vary for the other services—four years in the navy and some units of the OGPU (successor to the Cheka and predecessor of the NKVD) and three years in the air force. There would be one call-up a year during the fall. The new regulations replaced those of 1921, which had required eighteen months of service for infantrymen and two call-ups during a year. Service for those citizens considered hostile to Soviet power would be for two years in service commands (Berkhin 1958, 246, 247). Anti-Soviet elements would not be trusted to take up arms to defend the Soviet state but would perform noncombatant rear area duties.

To ensure the success of the annual call-up, the cooperation of local Party, Soviet, and social organizations was enlisted, accompanied by "broad and systematic agitational work conducted by the Bolshevik press." Barely three percent of those subject to the call failed to appear in 1925–26 (Berkhin 1958, 255). Eventually, the annual call-up would be depicted in the press as a happy occasion, as proud parents dispatched their sons to perform their patriotic duty, often with the accompaniment of a local band.

### EDINONACHALIE (ONE-MAN COMMAND)

One complaint that was woven into the lists of deficiencies that the reformers were determined to correct was that the command echelons throughout the armed forces were overladen with officers from the old army (the military specialists) and that there had been insufficient progress in replacing them with representatives of the proletariat and the peasantry. Despite their service in the civil war, the officers of the old army were still classified according to their pre-revolutionary social standing as being from the nobility *(dvorianstvo)* or the bourgeoisie *(meshchanstvo)*. To remove from the active officer corps what were described as "alien" elements, a review of command and administrative personnel was conducted during 1924. The result was that of the 2,598 former officers and military officials of the old army who were on duty on 1 June 1923, there were 397 on duty on 1 January 1925. During this period Soviet military schools were beginning to produce new commanders: 6,848 in 1924 and 9,193 in 1925. In 1924–25, the military academies graduated 258 officers.*

By the beginning of 1925, Frunze could write that 85 percent of the command staff of the army and the fleet were of peasant and worker origin and that this nucleus was firmly entrenched in all the command levels of the army and navy, including those posts demanding the maximum training and knowledge. He also noted that a solid cadre of officers had been developed for a Red General Staff (Berkhin 1958, 263). Frunze's reference to a Red General Staff when there was no such staff at the time reflects the ambivalence that ex-

---

*Soviet military academies should not be confused with U.S. military academies, which commission officers into the regular military services. Soviet military academies provide advanced training for officers at the middle and upper career levels.

isted in the Red Army toward the concept of a general staff. On the one hand, the advantages of a highly competent general staff were recognized, and there was a strong advocacy for establishing one in the Red Army. On the other hand, in Soviet and worldwide propaganda, the Great German General Staff was under attack for the part it had played in instigating and conducting the world war. For the Soviets the time was not ripe to establish a general staff even of workers and peasants (Zakharov 1989, 8, 9).

The conversion of the Red Army and Navy into a socially and politically homogeneous force raised the question of the role of the military commissars. During the civil war when the Bolsheviks, out of necessity, had to depend on thousands of former tsarist officers, the commissars had controlled their activities, countersigned their orders, and ensured that the will of the Party would be carried out. With the transformation of the political and social background of the officer corps, it was only a matter of time until the commissar would become redundant. This fact was recognized and acted upon as early as 1923. The RVS permitted the military districts to designate selected commanders, including some who were not Party members; they were one-man commanders *(edinonachal'niki)*—that is, they could function without a commissar looking over their shoulders.

In 1924, the new leadership of the RVS, while accepting the necessity of introducing one-man command, decided to delay full-scale introduction of the concept until the cleansing of unreliable and incapable elements from the officer corps had been completed. In the interim, the new RVS ordered that commanders become involved in political enlightenment work with the troops on a regular basis. It was not until late 1924 that practical steps to the introduction of one-man command were endorsed and disseminated by a plenary session of the Revolutionary Military Council. One senses an air of apology in the rationale that the council saw fit to provide for the steps: the introduction of one-man command was now possible because there had been a long selection of the best officers in a Soviet and military-political sense, and the numbers and roles of these elements within the army continued to grow.

At first there were to be two types of one-man commanders. In some cases the commander would be given full responsibility for the line aspects of his unit, including its administration without the former control of the commissar, but the commissar would retain control and responsibility for the political aspect of the unit and its morale. In some cases the one-man commander would also have responsibility for the political and morale aspects as well. The latter case was the most desirable, but at that moment it could not be widely adopted. According to Frunze, "This requires very special gifts and qualities, which are not always present in a commander who in all other respects stands at the height of his mission" (Berkhin 1958, 296).

Among the other factors slowing the tempo of conversion to one-man command was the large number of territorial divisions, the functioning of which required the closest liaison with the local Party, Soviet, and professional organizations. Maintaining such contact, it was believed, would complicate the command problems in such units; therefore, the guidance and assistance of a commissar would be neccessary. The fleet was also a special problem because of the high percentage of officers, especially senior officers, who had a noble or bourgeois background. It was therefore anticipated that, for the time being, the commissars would remain in the fleet and its supporting installations. As for the commissars who would become excess, independent administrative and economic posts would be found for these "most valuable" old Bolsheviks, and some would be transferred to the line after undergoing appropriate schooling (Berkhin 1958, 295–301). Iurii Petrov, the historian of the Party in the Soviet armed forces, reports that during the period of the reforms there was a "massive" shift of political workers to service in the line (Petrov 1968, 159).

One-man command lasted in the Soviet Army until 8 May 1937. Then, as the army was in the process of almost tripling in size in the next four years, the Party stratum became thinner and thinner, which became a matter of concern in the Soviet high command and eventually in the Central Committee. It may not have been accidental that the military commissars were reintroduced on the eve of the beginning of the great military purges, which began with the trial, conviction, and execution of Tukhachevsky and others in June 1937. The military commissars lasted until August 1940, when they were re-placed with one-man commanders. On this occasion, one-man command was declared to be total at command levels from the company to the corps, and its reintroduction was a recognition of the qualitative changes that had occurred in the officer corps of the army and the fleet. For those who had survived the purge of some 40,000 officers, there may have been some comfort in knowing that the quality of the officer corps had improved as a result. Here it should be noted that command at the army and *front* level remained collegial in the hands of the military council, which included a senior political officer who was a "member of the military council," as the position had been known in the civil war. The member's signature was required to validate all orders.

In July 1941, as the Soviet Army reeled back under the onslaught of the German Wehrmacht, military commissars were again introduced into the fighting forces as an extraordinary measure demanded by the huge losses in commanders suffered in the initial battles. In this critical situation, the commissar was expected to help the commander and strengthen his authority. According to Iurii Petrov, the degree of control that the commissar of the civil war exerted was not expected or authorized from the commissar during these critical days (Petrov 1968, 289). "Bourgeois historians," however, did not seem—or want—to recognize this difference, and they concluded that the introduction of military commissars implied that Stalin had lost confidence in his commanders (Petrov 1968, 289). Despite Petrov's protestations, the history of the introductions and withdrawals of the commissars seems to support the "bourgeois" view. When it became clear that the Soviet Army was going to defend Stalingrad successfully in the fall of 1942, the commissars were removed again and were not reinstituted during the remaining existence of the Soviet armed forces.

## THE REFORMS IN RETROSPECT

Voroshilov, writing in 1933, reminded his readers that the objective facts of the situation that the reformers found in the army in 1924 should dispel the "fairly widespread" legend that Trotsky was removed from his military posts because of his political opposition to the Politburo and its policies and not because of his poor performance in those posts. That Voroshilov felt constrained to make this point some eight years after Trotsky had resigned from his positions as chairman of the RVS and commissar for military and naval affairs (in January 1925), and four years after he had been exiled from the Soviet Union (to Turkey in February 1929), is an indication of the continuing fear that the Stalinists retained of the man and his ideas. Despite Stalin's efforts to expunge his name from the record of the revolution and the civil war, Trotsky and his opposition movement would be remembered as defendants in absentia in all of the great purge trials until Jaime Ramon Mercador del Rio stuck a pickax in Trotsky's skull on 20 August 1940. Trotsky died the next day (Payne 1977, 459–60).

The reforms themselves were hardly revolutionary. The regular-territorial army was a compromise between the economic realities of an exhausted country and the nervous fantasies of those who converted their ideological assumptions about a capitalist encirclement into a military threat. Which one of the powers that had almost bled one another to death in 1914–18 was prepared to open hostilities with the Soviet state in 1923–24?

The territorial system was already under trial in 1923, as was one-man command. What was needed was someone who was sufficiently interested and knowledgable to drive the reform process through the already stultifying bureaucracy. That man was Frunze—the embodiment of the one-man commander at the highest level. He had not been deeply involved in the various Stalin versus Trotsky controversies during the civil war and did not blame the situation he faced in early 1924 on Trotsky. Instead, he stressed that the reforms were due to the exigencies forced on the armed forces by the budget. As an example he reported that due to the shortage of funds, 100,000 members of the 1924 draft class were not called up (Osipov, ed. 1938, 62). He had a real understanding of the army's problems derived from his service as commander of the armed forces of the Ukraine and the Crimea. Delegating the various tasks to subcommittees, he was pushing the reforms through at the time of his death in a

Moscow hospital on 31 September 1925 while reluctantly undergoing an operation for stomach ulcers.

Frunze was succeeded as chairman of the Revolutionary Military Council and commissar for military and naval affairs by Kliment Voroshilov. The reforms instituted in 1924–25 guided the structuring of the Soviet armed forces for the next decade until the rising threats in the east and west required a modernization of the entire system to meet the new challenges.

# 7
# THE ARMY DEVELOPS A BRAIN

## ADDRESSING THE DEMAND FOR A "UNIFIED MILITARY DOCTRINE"

Even before the civil war drew to a close, freewheeling discussions began on the influence of the new social order, the political theories of Marxism, and the lessons to be derived from the Red Army's victories on Red Army doctrine and strategy. Trotsky, while seemingly standing aloof from the practical problems of force demobilization and restructuring, took an active part in these often heated debates, and he managed to have his point of view published before he lost his standing in the Party and the government.

The question of a new Red Army military doctrine was first raised in a "critical and impatient way" prior to the Tenth Party Congress (1921) by Frunze and Gusev in the form of theses that they attempted to "push through the Congress" (Trotsky 1925, vol. 3 book 2, 242). Mikhail Frunze at that time was the commander of Red Army forces in the Ukraine, and Sergei Gusev was the chief of the political directorate of the RKKA. Gusev was the reluctant political commissar who finally approved the order transferring the First Cavalry Army to the Western *Front* at the critical stage in the war with Poland in 1920. Klim Voroshilov, who was elected to the Party's Central Committee at the Tenth Congress, as might have been expected, was an active supporter of the concept, because the absence of such a doctrine was considered to be a shortcoming of Trotsky's administration of the People's Commissariat of Defense and Naval Affairs. Trotsky's opposition prevented the presentation of the theses to the congress (Erickson 1962, 120).

The next year at the Eleventh Party Congress, the theses appeared again, modified by the substitution of the word *mirovozrenie* (world view) for *doctrina* (doctrine) and the insertion of citations from Trotsky's own works in support of its various tenets. Trotsky again subjected the theses to a fierce attack. He questioned the attempt to somehow inject Marxist methods into the modernization of the field manuals of the old army. "Our [manuals] might be deficient but we will correct them based on our military experience. But how can we square them with a unified Marxist method?" (Trotsky 1925, vol. 3 book 2, 243–4). He explained that the Marxist method was a method of scientific thought, and he rejected the idea that there was a "military science." There were a number of sciences upon which military affairs were based, but the conduct of war was a practical art. Red Army field manuals were a collection of practical rules derived from experience.

In Frunze's theses, mobility was to be a cardinal consideration in the building of the new Red Army. Many of those supporting the concept of a unified military doctrine were veterans of the First Cavalry Army who wanted to universalize the "lessons" of the success of the Red cavalry during the civil war. Trotsky rebutted this thesis by recalling that the Red Army had been forced to imitate the success of such White cavalrymen as Mamontov, who had fewer peasants in his force and many more Cossacks (traditional horsemen). He also observed that the internal characteristics attributed to the Red Army— its revolutionary spirit, its combat élan, and the class nature of its proletarian commanding elements—could not be proven, and the claim smelled like bragging to him.

Similarly, some argued that the revolutionary Red Army should be trained and indoctrinated primarily as an offensive army. Trotsky observed that during the civil war the Soviet state had at times been under attack from all directions and that the Red Army could not counterattack on all fronts at the same time. In some areas Red Army units had been required to go on the defensive, and they very likely would have to do so in the future. He also recalled the Paris Commune of 1871—which Soviet historians would later call the "first proletarian revolution"—as an instance when the revolutionary forces had to defend positions inside a city, and he warned that the great cities in Western Europe might become the revolutionary battle-grounds of the future.

If there was one point on which there was agreement, it was that there would inevitably be a future conflict. According to Frunze's thesis number 5, either the Red Army would be called on to assist the revolution in a neighboring state, or the surrounding bourgeois states would renew their efforts to destroy the world's first proletarian dictatorship. For Trotsky, with his theory of "permanent revolution," a future conflict with the forces of capitalism was almost a certainty. But he argued that in the light of the country's current catastrophic economic situation, and to remain faithful to traditional Socialist teaching, a militia system would have to replace an expensive standing army. As early as 1919 he cited French Socialist Jean Juares, "despite his democratic utopianism," in support of his proposal. He continued to advocate such a system for the Red Army as late as October 1924 (Trotsky 1924, ix). Earlier he had cited the fact that all of the participants in the Great War, which had just ended, had used variations of a militia system to replenish their huge armies. One of his examples was the United States, which entered World War I with standing forces of 252,000 and eventually put 1,790,000 under arms (Trotsky 1924, vol. 2 book 2, 16). Trotsky had no way of knowing Gen. John J. Pershing's postwar judgment that if the U.S. Army had been at war strength (500,000) when the United States entered the war in April 1917, the war might have ended before the end of the year instead of dragging on until November 1918 (Pershing 1931, 9).

The Socialist concept of an armed people was immediately criticized by those advocating the maintenance of a standing army as a Menshevik conception that unrealistically adapted the mid-nineteenth-century ideas of Marx and Engels to the concrete reality of Soviet Russia facing a capitalist encirclement and a rebellious peasantry (Berkhin 1958, 28, 29). Menshevism was a label frequently attached to Trotsky's proposals by his opponents as they persistently recalled his longtime membership in that group.

Trotsky, as were Lenin and Stalin, was acutely conscious of the fact that the Workers and Peasants Army was made up of only 15 to 18 percent workers. Nevertheless he insisted that the workers retain their leadership role in the armed forces just as they were retaining it in the rest of the country (Trotsky 1924, vol. 2, book 2, 5). Budenny's successful career suggested to Trotsky that a gradual transition to one-man command was in the future for the proletarian officer corps.

In arguing against thesis number 5, Trotsky recalled that the army's composition (85 percent peasants) demanded that the reasons for a war must be understood by these broad masses. A "revolutionary war" would have little appeal to the peasants. Instead, Trotsky proposed that it would be far better to be able to tell the peasants of the concessions the Soviet government had taken to avoid war and that, in spite of those steps, the country was still being threatened by the imperialists and therefore the government was forced to keep older conscription classes under arms.

Observing that unit commissars had been singled out as prime targets of the White forces, Trotsky was an early proponent of the concept that Communists were not to surrender; he called the commissars a "new order of Samurais" (Trotsky 1924, vol. 2, book 2, 7). During World War II one of Stalin's civilian advisers, Lev Mekhlis, was to advocate expanding the concept to include all Red Army servicemen, with the tragic result that thousands of those who were surrounded and captured through no fault of their own in 1941 and 1942 were sent to the gulag in 1945 after spending years under subhuman conditions in German prisoner-of-war camps.

Since many of the veterans of the First Cavalry Army had also been with Voroshilov and Budenny when the former commanded the Tenth Army at Tsaritsyn, Trotsky could not resist recalling his struggle with the *partizanshchina* that existed there. Thus, in his discussion of the large peasant majority in the Red Army, he commented that, left to themselves, peasants could only create partisan detachments. He cited the troops loyal to anarchist Nestor Makhno as prime examples of the peasant mentality. He also questioned those now advocating a unified military doctrine who, while at Tsaritsyn, demanded the right to execute "good" orders and not execute "bad" orders. There could have been little doubt among Trotsky's listeners that he was referring to Voroshilov, who was now a strong advocate of a unified military doctrine (Trotsky 1925, vol. 3, book 2, 260).

In these sessions and in his written articles, Trotsky scored debating points. But it is not clear what he hoped to accomplish. It probably made sense to deflate some of the enthusiasm the Red Army commanders derived from their victories over the Whites and their foreign supporters. But, as Trotsky knew only too well, the country needed peace and not revolutionary war or any other kind of war. However, his attempts to convince the Red Army leaders that they should devote their attention to elementary soldiering and the creation of junior officers, squad leaders, and well-turned-out soldiers were not effective without morale-building praise for those who were still flush with enthusiasm for defending and spreading the revolution.

Trotsky's prescription for what the army would do if the country were attacked in spite of its concessionary policies was to delay the attacker by using the traditional Russian advantages of space and numbers while completing mobilization. Then, after holding the invader with an elastic defense, the army would counterattack and defeat him (Trotsky 1925, vol. 3, book 2, 256). Stalin, retrospectively, claimed that this was the strategy that he was following in 1941 and 1942.

Trotsky argued against the idea that the army should be trained and indoctrinated for the offensive and urged the victorious veterans of the civil war to concentrate on developing squad leaders. Because of such statements, he was soon accused of being a defensist who defamed the Red Army. Whatever his motives, he managed to turn the majority of the army's senior leadership against him. When the military reforms were installed in 1924 and 1925, his views were hardly considered.

### THE NOBLE REVOLUTIONARY'S DOCTRINE

Mikhail Nikolaevich Tukhachevsky was among those with whom Trotsky took issue in his efforts to temper the revolutionary enthusiasm of the Red commanders. In a collection of articles written between 1919 and 1920, the young hero of the civil war (he was twenty-five when he took command of the First Army in 1918) had argued for a standing army and against a militia system for the Red Army. He had also advocated the creation of a general staff by the Third Communist Internationale to calculate the forces and means available to the sides in a future civil war in countries still bound by capitalism (Tukhachevsky 1921, 140). Trotsky simply dismissed his proposal for an international general staff as "incorrect." Before such a general staff could be formed, there had to be national general staffs in several proletarian states. There were none to date. Trotsky considered Tukhachevsky's error and his theoretical attack on a militia system to be close to taking a stand in opposition to positions of the Third Communist Internationale. Trotsky also saw fit, in passing, to observe that baseless attacks were in general a weak side of Comrade Tukhachevsky, "one of our most gifted young military commanders" (Trotsky 1925, vol. 3, book 2, 235–36)—a remark that was more perspicacious than anyone probably thought at the time.

## TUKHACHEVSKY'S CONTRIBUTION

Literally everything that concerned the strengthening of the Soviet armed forces and the defensive capability of the country excited Tukhachevsky (Ivanov 1990, 223). This comment by one of Tukhachevsky's Soviet biographers, taken in conjunction with Trotsky's reference to his impetuosity, probably provides a fair characterization of Tukhachevsky's performance in twenty years of service to the Soviet state, from 1917 to 1937. From the very beginning of his active Red Army service with the Eastern *Front* in July 1918, he demonstrated an independence of judgment. Perhaps because of his Party status, which was unusual among the military specialists, he never hesitated to bring to the direct attention of his commander, and sometimes to the RVS of the Republic, his point of view and the reasons for his disagreement. It was not until his Fifth Army was subordinated to M. V. Frunze's southern group of the Eastern *Front* in March 1919 that Tukhachevsky at last had a commander whom he liked and respected and who apparently liked and respected him (V. M. Ivanov 1990, 89–94).

Tukhachevsky's opinion of Frunze was such that after two months serving as his subordinate, he recommended to the RVS of the Republic that Frunze was unusually talented and that if he were sent to the Southern *Front*—then retreating before Denikin's 1919 drive toward Moscow—the situation would quickly change (Ivanov 1990,

95). Tukhachevsky's recommendation was not accepted, and in the course of Tukhachevsky's and Frunze's service the two did not directly serve together again until 1924, when Tukhachevsky became deputy chief of the Red Army Staff under Frunze and helped him to propose and implement the military reforms. Subsequently, on Frunze's recommendation, Tukhachevsky became chief of the staff in November 1925. Frunze, unfortunately, died during an operation he underwent reluctantly on 31 October, and he was succeeded by Klim Voroshilov.

Voroshilov, who had been commander of the Moscow Military District, was appointed people's commissar for military and naval affairs* and chairman of the Revolutionary Military Council in November 1925. He remained at the head of the Soviet defense establishment for almost fifteen years, until May 1940, and as such bears a large share of the responsibility for the condition of the Soviet armed forces as they faced their sternest test in 1941. As Dmitrii Volkogonov observes, during the 1920s Voroshilov's fame was truly nationwide as Soviet propaganda applied such laudatory appellations to him as "leader of the world revolution," "the Bolshevik great captain *(polkovodets),*" and "the commander in chief from the lathe." A popular medallion signifying achievement in rifle marksmanship was named for him, and the designator for a heavy tank was given his initials—the KV. But Stalin, who was notoriously sensitive to the praise and adulation of his subordinates, seemed to be indifferent to Voroshilov's renown. Stalin knew, and those around him knew, that Voroshilov only executed the will of the leader, and that in the decisive moment Voroshilov, without hesitating, would support Stalin. Some considered this as evidence of their friendship, but in a true friendship, there can be no debtors, and Voroshilov was indebted to Stalin for his honor, his posts, his awards, and his position (Volkogonov 1989, 160).

---

*In 1934, the name of the commissariat was changed to the People's Commissariat of Defense. In 1946, the commissariat became the Ministry of the Armed Forces; in 1953, it became the Ministry of Defense, the title that it retained until the dissolution of the Soviet Union in 1991.

Despite Voroshilov's limitations as a military theoretician, because of his position he became the arbiter on many of the myriad details that are involved in the daily administration of the armed forces. Of course, on critical matters such as the disposition and composition of the armed forces, and its proclaimed doctrines and its senior leadership, he made no decisions without Stalin's approval.

Tukhachevsky served as chief of the Red Army Staff until May 1928, when he was relieved and assigned commander of the Leningrad Military District for reasons that are discussed more fully. Here it is sufficient to say that the demonstrated differences between the two men in intellectual level, social background, and independence of thought made it almost inevitable that they would have difficulty working together. Tukhachevsky remained in Leningrad until June 1931, when he was called to Moscow to head the Soviet rearmament effort as chief of armaments and later deputy commissar of defense. He remained there until May 1937, when he was "repressed," to use the Soviet euphemism for execution by being shot in the back of the head. Thus he was an early victim of the great purges.

Marshal of the Soviet Union Sergei Semenovich Biriuzov, chief of the Soviet General Staff from 1963 to 1964, in a foreword to a selection from Tukhachevsky's works, provided a summary of Tukhachevsky's contributions to Soviet military thought during his tragically foreshortened career. Biriuzov counted more than 120 works attributed to Tukhachevsky's pen on such subjects as strategy, operational art, tactics, and methods of schooling and training the troops. Tukhachevsky also participated in many of the intrawar exercises and maneuvers at which these theories were tested and perfected. Trotsky's political defeat also meant that his critique of the offense-minded advocates of a mobile warfare doctrine for the Red Army were left unrestrained. Tukhachevsky early recognized the promise that developments in engine technology implied for both overland and air mobility. The industrial commitment to produce the engines, the steel, and the aircraft that the Soviet state was making in the five year plans that began in 1928 was the concrete realization of his ideas and enthusiasms. The armed forces at that time had not more than a thousand aircraft and about two hundred tanks.

In 1929, the Central Committee of the Communist Party adopted a resolution that seemed to indicate to Tukhachevsky that he and the Party shared the same ideas about the future defense of the Soviet Union. The Party's announced goals were to modernize existing weapons and equipment, and in the next two years develop tested models of contemporary artillery, tanks, and armored cars and raise the quality of aviation to the level of the leading bourgeois countries (Ivanov 1990, 246).

Inspired by these goals for national defense, Tukhachevsky, then commander of the Leningrad Military District, in January 1930 proposed a sweeping reorganization of the armed forces on the basis of the latest technological achievements. His proposal was based on "the successes of our socialist construction . . . which place before us in its entirety the problem of reconstruction of the Armed Forces . . ." (Tukhachevsky 1964, I:12).

In addition to modernizing the equipment of the army, Tukhachevsky also proposed "new proportions" for the various arms and services. Here, one obvious change that the new technology demanded was a reduction in the number and size of the cavalry units in the army and an increase in the numbers of motorized, mechanized, armored, and aviation units. He also recommended an overall increase in the number of divisions the army should field. That change was bound to encounter the resistance of the First Cavalry Army veterans, led by Voroshilov and Budenny, who now had influential positions in the defense establishment.

In his enthusiasm for the possibilities presented by the new technological base for the army, Tukhachevsky saw the possibility of avoiding the former gruelingly difficult forms of battle for each center of enemy resistance and moving to new, more effective forms of battle by suppressing the entire depth of the enemy's position simultaneously (Isserson 1965, 36). Tukhachevsky was already thinking of a new form of offensive operation, which would become known as "deep battle" *(glubokii boi)* at the tactical level and "deep operations" *(glubokii operatsii)* at the operational level.

There was no immediate reaction to his proposal, and in April Tukhachevsky wrote to Stalin asking that he consider it. Stalin's reply was a harsh rejection, which was read by Voroshilov to an ex-

panded plenary session of the RVS of the Republic. Tukhachevsky
was accused of taking a non-Marxist approach to a problem by
proposing unreachable goals. Stalin also averred that Tukhachevsky's proposals would lead to the end of Socialist construction
and create a system of "Red militarism."

Tukhachevsky would not accept Stalin's rejection as final, believing that his proposal had not been accurately reported to Stalin. On
several occasions he requested that Stalin review his proposal, without result. He also began to feel himself isolated, because the interpretation placed on Stalin's letter barred him from even discussing
the subject with his peers. He was removed from his position as
leader of the strategy section of the Military Academy of the RKKA
(soon to become the Frunze Military Academy). Tukhachevsky's
protests were again not answered, but in June 1931 he was unexpectedly appointed deputy commissar to Voroshilov and chief of armaments of the RKKA. Stalin needed him to direct Soviet rearmament (Tukhachevsky 1964, I:12, 13).

From his post as chief of armaments, Tukhachevsky was in a much
more logical position to make recommendations on the employment
of the new weapons than he had been as a military district commander. At the end of 1931, he recommended that tanks be added
to the rifle and cavalry divisions. In 1934 he teamed with I. P. Uborevich to urge an increase in the number of aircraft in the forces. He
recommended that the Red Army should have 15,000 aircraft by
1935. In his enthusiasm for aviation, Tukhachevsky did not forget
that the Red Army was vulnerable to air attack, and he devoted attention to the development of antiaircraft weapons and to the in-
clusion of such weapons in the revised tables of organization and
equipment for the rifle division and corps. He also worked with the
Soviet Navy, participating with the Baltic Fleet in exercises testing his
ideas on the tactics of naval battles.

Tukhachevsky initiated the development of parachute troops in
the RKKA. After observing paradrops in the Leningrad Military District maneuvers in September 1934, he recognized the need to expand the size of the drops. In 1936, during the Kiev Military District
maneuvers, the size of the drops was truly massive. He also recognized early the need for the use of aviation to supply the airhead with

fuel, food, and ammunition. At the same time that he was concerned with the introduction of the latest technical achievements in armament into the RKKA, he did not overlook the need for specialists. He recommended the establishment of a number of academies to produce the officer specialists to lead the tank and mechanized units that would be created (Tukhachevsky 1964, I:13–17).

## THE DEVELOPMENT OF DEEP BATTLE AND DEEP OPERATIONS*

In the period between the wars, military thinkers throughout the world concerned themselves with the problems presented by the long sieges of trench warfare that characterized World War I, particularly on the western front. There, massed artillery could achieve a breakthrough of the enemy's forward positions, but the infantry could not continue to advance against the deeply echeloned secondary and tertiary positions and the enemy's reserves. Would the new technology—aircraft, faster and more reliable tanks, improved artillery, and mechanization and motorization—provide the capability to avoid a repetition of the grisly stalemate that had existed from 1914 until 1918? For Tukhachevsky, the answer was an enthusiastic yes. But he realized that conservative commanders in the various new arms and services would have to be taught to cooperate with one another, and the new concepts had to be tested in maneuvers and exercises.

At Tukhachevsky's instigation, these theories began to be tested as early as 1933. But their essence and significance was not immediately accepted. One who failed to grasp the importance of what

---

*In Soviet military thought of the period, deep battle (*glubokii boi*) would be conducted at the tactical level by units through the corps echelon. Deep operations (*glubokii operatsii*) would be conducted by operational formations—the field army or the *front*. These operations would involve divisions and supporting units of all arms and services, and they would be conducted over greater distances with larger numbers of troops than had been attempted previously. The direction and control of such operations would demand commanders and staffs of requisite capability and experience. The academic chair (*kafedra*) at the General Staff Academy charged with developing the theories and the commanders and staff officers for executing those theories was called the chair of operational art.

Tukhachevsky was trying to do was Klim Voroshilov, who criticized Tukhachevsky sharply before a plenary session of the RVS of the Republic. Tukhachevsky responded by writing a letter to Voroshilov, informing him that "after your speech at the plenum of the RVS many had the impression that notwithstanding the new weapons in the army, the old tactics must remain . . ." Tukhachevsky was writing because there was "uncertainty" in the minds of commanders. They were now talking about the refutation of the new forms of tactics and their development. This was contrary to what Voroshilov had said in the past, and Tukhachevsky took it upon himself to inform Voroshilov of the existing confusion (Tukhachevsky, 1964, I:18). Voroshilov corrected himself in 1934, and the development of deep battle and deep operations continued.

Although Biriuzov seemed to give Tukhachevsky almost sole credit for developing the theories of deep battle, Matvei V. Zakharov, also a former chief of the General Staff, gave much credit to Vladimir K. Triandafillov for the original concept. Triandafillov was killed in an air crash in 1931 while he was chief of the operations directorate of the staff of the RKKA (Zakharov 1989, 88). According to Zakharov, Triandafillov introduced the theory of deep battle to the staff of the RKKA in 1931, some months before his unfortunate death.

Zakharov attributed to Tukhachevsky an overemphasis on tanks. Tukhachevsky visualized tanks with three overlapping but different overall missions: tanks for direct support of infantry (NPP), tanks for distant support of infantry (DPP), and tanks for distant operations (DD). These would not necessarily be different types of tanks, but the training of their crews and units would be different. Tanks providing direct support for infantry might be slower and more heavily armored and would feature somewhat different armament than those for distant operations. It is more difficult to establish what, if any, difference there would be in the tanks designed for distant infantry support and distant operations. Tukhachevsky considered the combat support by artillery and aviation of the tank groups engaged in distant operations to be one of the most important missions that had to be accomplished if deep offensive operations were to be successful.

Zakharov reports that A. I. Egorov, then chief of the RKKA Staff, declared at a meeting of an expanded Military Council of the Commissariat of Defense in December 1934 that experience had shown that the infantry plays the deciding role and that all the new technology should be used to support the combat operations of the foot soldier. Egorov cited the same experience as proving the infeasibility and clumsiness of Tukhachevsky's differentiation of tanks into three categories and suggested that the idea of tanks in distant support of infantry be dropped (Zakharov 1989, 91). Characteristically, Tukhachevsky in his comments on the new Field Manual 36 *(Polevoi ustav 36)*, published in May 1937, the month before his death, gave his answer to Egorov.

> The failure to understand the role and significance of new fast-moving tanks armed with rapid-firing artillery is reflected also in that some comrades have not agreed to give tanks in contemporary battle a more decisive role than that which they had in 1918. . . . These comrades asserted that tanks are significant only as a means of direct support to the infantry. They don't see the possibility of organizing the cooperation of tanks and artillery in a new way. . . . For this reason they deny the capability of a breakthrough of tanks into the depth of the defensive position of the enemy for the seizure of the routes of his retreat (Tukhachevsky 1964, II:247).

The purges of 1937 and 1938 brought to a halt for a period the development of the theories and the practice of deep battle and operations. Since many of their proponents were declared "enemies of the people," the theories came under suspicion. The combat experience that some of the Soviet advisers brought back from the Spanish civil war also had a negative effect on the acceptance of the new ideas. From the reports of those experiences was drawn the "deeply erroneous, historically shortsighted conclusion" that the new combat systems only enhanced the capability to conduct contemporary attacks but did not change anything in their character and form. Mechanized corps were disbanded and the development of bomber aviation was cut back, depriving deep operations of some of the very weapons they needed to be effective (Isserson 1965, II:54, 55).

These cutbacks produced a temporary stagnation in the development of Soviet military theory, as did the "twilight war" along the

Franco-German border and the Soviet-Finnish war, which initially seemed to demonstrate the impregnability of fortified positions such as the Maginot and the Mannerheim lines. The rapid conclusion of the German conquest of Poland in 1939 seemed to demonstrate the feasibility of deep operations, but such a conclusion was suspect because of the overwhelming superiority of the German Army over the Polish in all measures of military capability. It took the German campaign in France and the Low Countries in 1940 to demonstrate conclusively that Soviet theories of deep operations were indeed on the correct path. The strategic outcome achieved by the German onslaught also exposed the character of operations that could be expected in the opening period of a modern war. But the latter lesson was overlooked at the highest levels of the Soviet state.

In some respects this gap was due to the rigid limitations that were placed on the fields of research of the Academy of the General Staff, which was reinstituted in the fall of 1936. The academy was reopened as the result of a perceived need to establish a special institution to master the art of conducting deep operations, and it provided a laboratory where even during the period of stagnation deep operations continued to be studied and developed and the officers to command them were trained. Limitations placed on the academy's curriculum from above had the negative effect of constraining the consideration of the implications of the German Army's operations. In May 1940, the Wehrmacht, in what was effectively the very outset of the war, achieved the strategic objective of defeating France and driving the British Army from the continent of Europe.

When the question arose of the scope that would be permitted the investigations of the academy before it opened, A. I. Egorov, then chief of the General Staff, put a clear demarcation on the areas that would be off-limits to the academic researchers: strategy, war plans, strategic deployment, and the conduct of war. "No one will permit you to do that, because that is the business of the General Staff" (Isserson 1965, II:50). The result was that the academy conducted its investigations without the context of the real events that were taking place in Western Europe. From what Egorov said, the assumption was that these topics were being addressed in the General Staff; actually, the most important of them were considered and decided in the mind of Stalin.

The draft field manual (PU-39) produced in the spring of 1941 was the last field manual to appear before the war. During the previous fifteen years, four versions of the manual were produced. The latest draft included the results of the continuing development of the theory of deep operations. It also included what Isserson referred to as certain propositions of a "declarative character" about the offensive conduct of war—that the Soviet Army would be an army on the offensive, and that the Soviet Army would immediately shift combat operations to the territory of the enemy. These propositions were imposed from above as immutable guiding directives. Although some of the instructors at the academy questioned their applicability in the light of what was happening in the west, they did so behind closed doors. The result was that the Soviet high command was confused in June 1941, unable to analyze events, impose its will, or gain the initiative. The situation that arose on the Soviet western borders required a completely different strategic orientation—a flexible frame of mind not restrained by such declarative policies, and one free to adopt the operational decisions considered appropriate to the existing situation. In addition, the older, more experienced commanders who had established and developed Soviet military theory and who knew how to put it into practice were gone, and the number of commanders capable of directing operations was grossly inadequate. "Thus the terrible drama which was played out in the summer of 1941 had deep causes of a political and a strategic nature connected with Stalin's personality cult. The consequences were extremely severe. They exacted huge sacrifices and caused enormous losses" (Isserson 1965, II:60, 61).

### THE FORMATION OF THE GENERAL STAFF AND THE DEVELOPMENT OF THE "BRAIN OF THE ARMY"

When Tukhachevsky asked to be relieved as chief of the Red Army Staff in 1928, it was because he had become convinced that the staffs created during the reforms of 1924–25 were not functioning properly and should be replaced with one single staff—a general staff. The 1925 reforms had created three staffs: operational functions were assigned to the staff of the Red Army, administrative functions to the main directorate *(glavnoe upravlenie)* of the Red Army, and troop training to the inspectorate of the Red Army. Such functions as political indoctrination, command and control of the air force, supply of the navy, research on the civil war, unified educational policy, and medical and veterinary affairs were entrusted to directorates, offices, and councils that reported directly to the RVS of the Republic (Berkhin 1958, 150–53). The direct cause of Tukhachevsky's resignation was the rejection of his recommendation that the functions of the staff, the inspectorate, and the main directorate be combined under one chief. His recommendation was opposed by several prominent civil war figures, including Budenny, N. S. Unshlikht, P. E. Dybenko, and A. I. Egorov, who signed a letter to Voroshilov accusing the staff of attempting to take the leading role in all questions affecting the structure and operations of the Red Army. They also took a direct slap at Tukhachevsky, writing that the Red Army high command problems could be solved by replacing the chief of staff with a person of greater organizational talent and greater experience in practical military affairs. One of the RVS conclusions on the recommendation expressed the fear that "there will be one rapporteur who plans, executes, and inspects, consequently, he will have in his hands all the criteria. In the hands of the leadership there will be almost nothing; agree and proceed under the reins of the staff" (Zakharov 1989, 33).

If these objections can be taken at their face value, it would seem that the protesters were anticipating the rise of a Bonaparte in the guise of chief of the Red Army Staff. Their assumption seemed to be that the leadership of the armed forces would be naive and ignorant of military affairs and would need a collegial body or bodies to provide competitive analysis and advice. Although this may have been the case with Voroshilov and, in 1928, perhaps Stalin, it is unlikely that either would have ever admitted to their lack of competence in military affairs. A more likely motivation for the opposition to Tukhachevsky's plan was a conservative fear of the man himself: his youth and vigor, his enthusiasm for the revolution, and his ideas for the modernization of the armed forces.

Tukhachevsky was succeeded as chief of the Red Army Staff by Boris Mikhailovich Shaposhnikov, then commander of the Moscow Military District. This was a surprising appointment inasmuch as Shaposhnikov was in the process of publishing a three-volume work entitled *Mozg armii* (the brain of the army), which was a historical treatment of the role and functions of a general staff developed against the experience of the Austrian General Staff prior to and during World War I. In the first volume, which appeared in 1927, Shaposhnikov advocated the creation of a Red Army General Staff. After his appointment, Shaposhnikov continued to press for more authority for the staff, and he achieved the assignment of all mobilization responsibilities to the staff before he was transferred to command of the Volga Military District in April 1931—a secondary command in the Soviet scheme of defense.

## BORIS MIKHAILOVICH SHAPOSHNIKOV

Boris Mikhailovich Shaposhnikov, the son of a distillery manager, was born in Zlatoust in the southern Urals in September 1882. After completing secondary school, he chose for economic reasons to enter the Moscow Military School, which he completed in 1903. He was then commissioned a *podporuchik* (second lieutenant) in the Russian Army. After service in Turkestan, he successfully took the competitive entrance examinations for the Academy of the General Staff; he graduated in 1910. During World War I, he served as a staff officer with troops and commanded a regiment. In December 1917, after the February and October Revolutions, he was elected commander of the Caucasian Grenadier Division. Due to an unspecified illness, he was hospitalized the next month and was eventually demobilized. He volunteered to serve in the Red Army and was accepted in April 1918. He served in the operations and intelligence directorates of the Supreme Military Council and the Field Staff and became chief of the operations directorate of the Field Staff in October 1919. As chief of this directorate during the war with Poland, he was directly involved in Soviet strategic decision making, including the drafting of the messages to Tukhachevsky and Egorov during the Warsaw-L'vov crisis in August 1920.

In 1924, after Tukhachevsky had given a series of lectures on the Polish war at the Military Academy of the RKKA, Shaposhnikov published a general critique of the Polish campaign. Originally intended as a review for the magazine *Voennyi vestnik* (Military herald),

Shaposhnikov's criticism grew into a book—*Na Visle* (On the Vistula). From his analysis of the Polish campaign and the strength of the two sides, Shaposhnikov concluded that even if the dispersion of the forces of the Western and Southwestern *Fronts* had not occurred, the Western *Front* could hardly have defeated the Poles. The Poles had already moved the ruling political party to Krakow, so that the seizure of Warsaw would not have ended Polish resistance. Even if Budenny's First Cavalry Army had begun to disengage from its advance toward L'vov on 8 August as envisioned by Tukhachevsky and the CINC, it could not have arrived in the area of Liublin in less than ten days—too late to prevent the Polish counterattack against Tukhachevsky's left flank. Shaposhnikov was also critical of other aspects of Tukhachevsky's conduct of the càmpaign (Shaposhnikov 1924, 29, 34, 201, 202).

From the historical record it is not clear whether the personal relationship between Tukhachevsky and Shaposhnikov was affected by Shaposhnikov's criticisms of the former's role in the Polish campaign. Lev Nikulin, a Soviet biographer of Tukhachevsky writing in the 1960s during the Khrushchev de-Stalinization campaign—after noting that Shaposhnikov took pains to claim that he was not criticizing for the sake of criticizing—observed that in 1924 Shaposhnikov was not yet under the influence of Stalin (Nikulin 1964, 123). In other words, Shaposhnikov may have been a dispassionate critic. In 1929, Shaposhnikov's negative reaction to Egorov's book on the campaign, and his advice to an officer considering an unfavorable review to use a pseudonym, made it clear that by then Shaposhnikov was at the least very wary of the dictator.

## THE BRAIN OF THE ARMY

Shaposhnikov completed the first volume of *Mozg armii* while serving as commander of the Leningrad Military District. It was published in 1927 in an edition of 5,000 copies. The metaphor (the brain of the army) referred to the General Staff of an army and was in common use in the armies of the world. A work in English published in 1895, *The Brain of the Army*, by Spenser Wilkinson, an influential British writer, was reportedly influential in the planning for a U.S. Army General Staff at the turn of the century (Bidwell

1986, 69). Although the Wilkinson work may have been available to Shaposhnikov in the military library of the Leningrad Military District, which at the time was the only one in the country where military literature was systematically collected, it was not acknowledged by the author as a source for either the title or the substance of *Mozg armii.*

Excerpts from the work were republished in 1974 and were taken from volumes 1 and 3 of what was planned to be a four-volume work. Volume 2 is concerned almost exclusively with the role of the various general staffs in the outbreak of World War I. Volume 4 was to address the role of the general staff in war planning, but it was never published. Whether or not it was ever written is not known.

To present his ideas on the role of a general staff, Shaposhnikov chose to describe the Austro-Hungarian General Staff, whose last chief, Franz Conrad von Hotzendorff, left a 3,000-page memoir of his service as chief of the General Staff from 1906 to 1911 and from 1912 until 1914, and as a commander in the field during World War I. Shaposhnikov did not limit himself to Conrad's work but drew on French, German, and Russian sources to provide a broader basis for his theories. He explained his choice of the Austrian General Staff, despite its record of failure, as being due to the fact that Conrad had left such a detailed record of the work of the General Staff in peacetime, on the eve of the war, and in the first operations of a war. The "humiliated and insulted" should not be forgotten, he wrote, using a Dostoyevsky title, because in their bitterness and sadness there is much that is instructive for the present and the future (Shaposhnikov 1927, 20). From a practical standpoint, the collapse of the Austro-Hungarian Empire made it possible to write freely about the staff, its personnel, and its policies without fear of diplomatic complications (Zakharov 1978, 60).

## THE GENERAL STAFF SYSTEM

Shaposhnikov, after asserting early in the first volume that no army can exist without a general staff, traces the development of the general staff system, frequently referring to the historical development of the German General Staff. The German system was created to permit the monarch and his noble relatives to be nominal field commanders while trained specialists of the General Staff conducted military operations in their name. This system suited a state such as imperial Germany, but would it be suitable for an army that had been conclusively freed from royal "superstitions" and that had young leaders in command? For the answer to this question, Shaposhnikov quoted the views of Col. Aleksandr Andreevich Svechin, another former tsarist officer who was serving in the Red Army.

> It does not follow that the General Staff is a survivor of feudalism . . . the commander in contemporary conditions of war must rely on an entire collection of selected assistants, capable of reliable work, deserving of complete trust. Such a collective is required for the regulation of the gigantic work of preparation for war. Only the *General Staff* [emphasis in the original] can coordinate and harmonize this preparation, a collection of people who have forged and tested their views in the same conditions and under the same leadership, selected meticulously, linked together by mutual responsibility and by vigorous performances achieving breakthroughs in military policy (Shaposhnikov 1927, 1:144),

Shaposhnikov took exception to that portion of Svechin's statement requiring that the staff be composed of people who by "vigorous performance" would achieve breakthroughs in doctrine, recalling that the "young Turks" of the French General Staff on the eve of World War I achieved a change in French military doctrine from a defensive attitude to an offensive one. Shaposhnikov saw such officers as the "demigods" and "intimate circles" who, in his view, were the negative aspect of European general staffs.

His critique of the German, French, Austrian, and Russian General Staffs focused on their tendency toward exclusivity. Being selected officers, dealing with the most sensitive secrets of the state, isolated from their fellow officers because of their training and for considerations of military secrecy, they were sarcastically called by such nicknames as the "black clergy" (in Russia), "demigods" (in Germany), "the brevetted ones" (in France), and "hierophants" (*zhretsy*—Shaposhnikov's own designation for the type). The operations sections of European general staffs were particularly vulnerable to these conceits.

> The operations section was the "holy of holies" of the staff, and its members were hierophants of the highest order not accessible to simple folk. Locked within themselves, giving the appearance of people burdened with the special importance of their work, striving to have contact with those surrounding them in the staff as little as possible, to say nothing of contact with the line, members of the operations section usually even dined at a special table as close as possible to high personages (Shaposhnikov 1927, 1:144).

Since Shaposhnikov had considerable experience in the operations sections of various staffs, he may have been recalling his own attitudes toward the other sections of the staff and those "unfortunates" who were in the line. Whether or not he was reflecting his personal experience, his mature conclusion was that staff officers who conducted themselves as if they were members of an exclusive club were reversing Count Alfred von Schlieffen's injunction that his subordinates "be more than they seem" and instead "seemed more than they were" (Shaposhnikov 1927, 1:37).*

### THE IDEAL GENERAL STAFF OFFICER

Shaposhnikov's warnings about the danger of exclusivity of certain elements of a staff was not included in the excerpts that were reprinted in 1974, possibly because the editors could not admit that such things could happen under Soviet conditions. But the injunction to general staff officers to be more than they seem was printed in 1974 with the emphasis that Shaposhnikov had given it. His ideas on the ideal general staff officer were also included. That officers

---

*Count Alfred von Schlieffen (1833–1912) was chief of the German General Staff from 1891 until 1905. The maxim has been attributed to one of his predecessors, the elder Helmuth von Moltke, by Walter Goerlitz in his *History of the German General Staff, 1657–1945* (New York: Praeger, 1953), p. 57.

would be selected carefully; be dedicated, well trained, and energetic, have initiative; be capable of working long hours; be independent in judgment and modest in communication.

The question of how much service with troops a general staff officer should have Shaposhnikov answered with the opinion that he should not have too much. He was opposed to such service if it was only for the sake of appearances, citing the case of the Austrian chief of staff, Conrad, who was proud of his long service with troops. Conrad's critics, however, objected that Conrad's service did not increase his understanding of the troops or their life. A knowledge of strategy was, of course, necessary for the future general staff officer, but it was impossible to understand strategy without a knowledge of tactics. Here again Shaposhnikov warned against specializing in any area of knowledge required of an officer, citing German general von Bülow, who commanded the German Second Army in the Marne operation in 1914. Bülow's credo was first tactics and then strategy. On the Marne he showed himself a good tactician but a poor strategist, so that his name was forever associated with the crucial first failure of the German Army.

Although general staff officers should at all times be abreast of the domestic politics of their own and foreign states and consider them fully in their planning, the general staff should never create its own politics. Politics in Shaposhnikov's view should be the business of other state organs and institutions, not the general staff. His comments on the role of the staff in politics both domestic and foreign were consistent with those of the Communist Party. He also commented that the conduct of political work in the armed forces should be the function of a special organ and not the general staff. This was also consistent with the practice of the Soviet Communist Party, which assigned political work in the armed forces to the Main Political Administration.

## THE INFLUENCE OF ECONOMICS
As did most of his contemporaries who had survived the cataclysm of the 1914–18 war, Shaposhnikov had a deep appreciation of the role of economics in modern warfare. He quoted with approval Svechin's

observation that the general staffs of all the states had prepared for a world war in the unshakable belief that it would be won with a strategy of annihilation *(sokrushenie)*—that is, that the war would be won in short order with the successful application of fire and maneuver to the battlefield. These staffs were incapable of reorienting their thought to the conditions of the war of attrition *(izmor)*, which developed during World War I (Shaposhnikov 1927, 242).

This misreading of the course of the war was attributed by Shaposhnikov to the cloudy impression prevalent in the staffs of "the level of achievement of the development of productive forces, of the accumulated economic power of the warring states and the level of influence this had on the war" (Shaposhnikov 1927, 243). From the vantage point of 1927, Shaposhnikov, while denying any claim to be a prophet, foresaw that the development of economic power would cause a future war to become an economic struggle in which rear areas would become military objectives as important as those at the front. He advised being prepared for a long and intense struggle employing new and more lethal weapons systems that would make a future conflict more deadly than previous ones. He also predicted that the resulting economic struggle would sharpen the class conflict and turn war into revolution (Shaposhnikov 1927, 244).

Preparation for such a war on the political and economic fronts should be the task of a special state institution and not the general staff. The staff would have its hands full with operational preparations. In making this recommendation, Shaposhnikov took issue with Svechin, who proposed the formation of an "economic general staff"—small in numbers but high in qualification.

Shaposhnikov saw preparation and defense of the military budget as an important function of the general staff. He warned that the military budget was not only a military matter but a political one and, above all, an economic one. He did not believe that the general staff should consider the economic capabilities of the country in formulating its requests because it was not the function of the staff to develop an economic or a financial basis for military plans. He did, however, recognize that if the general staff did not take into account the economic capabilities of the country, it might develop unrealistic budget requests (Shaposhnikov 1927, 257).

## THE INTEGRAL GREAT CAPTAIN

Shaposhnikov's conception of the general staff was one of an organization engaged in the military problem of preparing the country
for war. Where and when that war was to be fought was a matter to
be decided by the political authorities. Economic preparations for
war were the function of a separate body that would receive military
advice from but would not be part of the general staff. The chief of
the general staff, who might in time of war take command in the
field, would have the task of directing a unified staff—Shaposhnikov
was opposed to the creation of separate general staffs for the navy
and the air force—of highly qualified military specialists whose collective wisdom in combination with that of the political and economic specialists would direct what Shaposhnikov called the "integral great captain" *(integral'nyi polkovodets)* to achieve the strategy of
the state. Shaposhnikov considered the chief of staff, in wartime, to
be a high commander, "not in the old understanding, but only as a
statesman . . . as a member of a collective which directs the war"
(Shaposhnikov 1974, 113).

## MOBILIZATION

In Shaposhnikov's view, mobilization would be a more stressful and
lengthy phenomenon than it had been in 1914. Shaposhnikov was
assuming that there would be a general consensus among general
staffs that the war would be one of attrition. He recognized that no
matter how gradual and lengthy the mobilization period was, the first
forward echelon must be strong enough to avoid decisive defeat—
a defeat so crushing that it would be impossible to reestablish one's
forces and eventually achieve the numerical superiority for victory.
He cites Clausewitz for support on this point.

By the very nature of war it is impossible to achieve the complete simultaneous readiness of all forces for their commitment
to battle. Nevertheless, one must strive to make ready as large
a force as possible for the first battle even if that requires an
extreme effort. The reason is that a first failure is undesirable
and no one consciously wants to be exposed to one. It always
has a negative influence on the next battle, an influence that

becomes greater the greater the size of that failure (Shaposh-nikov 1929, 284).*

In the Clausewitzian manner, Shaposhnikov stressed that because war is conducted for the accomplishment of political goals, and those goals are reflected in war plans, there should be a direct relation-ship between war plans and the plans for mobilization. Depending on whether or not a war is to be fought on the main or a secondary front, mobilization may be either general or partial. The choice will be dictated by political motives. Here, Shaposhnikov was rehearsing the argument he used later when, as chief of the RKKA Staff, he achieved the transfer of the mobilization responsibility to the staff from the chief directorate.

Discussing the use of mobilization during crises, Shaposhnikov emphasized the negative effects of retaining reservists on active duty for long periods. He included in this category the Russian (and So-viet) practice of retaining a conscript contingent on active duty be-yond its term of service. Admitting that such measures—temporar-ily, at least—raise the combat readiness of the armed forces, he believed that they had the negative effect of lowering the morale of the army as a whole the longer the reserves had to stand and await a real war. Shaposhnikov was more inclined to risk awaiting an ac-tual mobilization and proceeding with a combat-ready organization rather than committing units that had lost their resilience from the prolonged military tension of waiting for a crisis to be resolved. He also touched on the question of how long a fully mobilized army could stand opposite another similarly prepared force without a spontaneous incident precipitating a war that neither side really wanted. He pointed out that mobilization raised the militancy of the forces to such an extent that mutual forays across the border, clashes of small units, and nervousness on both sides are almost unavoid-able. He recalled that the first wave of mobilization in 1914 was

---

*A slightly different translation (from the German) of this passage may be found in Michael Howard and Peter Paret's translation of *On War* (Princeton, New Jer-sey: Princeton Universtiy Press, 1976), p. 80.

marked by various border violations and rumors of violations that strained the already jangled nerves of border units. No matter what the military command might want, and more so the diplomats, the declaration of mobilization could create a situation in which the guns might begin to fire spontaneously.

Shaposhnikov also commented briefly on the impact of mobilization on the internal affairs of a state. He stressed that for bourgeois capitalist states there was always a worry about how the different classes in those states would accept a call to the colors. He recalled that the former minister of internal affairs of tsarist Russia signed the mobilization order with fear and a prediction of an unavoidable revolution. Shaposhnikov acknowledged that mobilization actually caused a patriotic upsurge inspired by the slogans that accompanied it, but that the enthusiasm soon cooled when the slogans were examined critically and the casualty lists arrived.

Looking into the future, Shaposhnikov foresaw that mobilization would be a forerunner to war, as it was in 1914, and he predicted that even before mobilization there would be the dispatch of diversionists. He also observed that the state that was best prepared to mobilize was also least likely to be concerned about the timing of the mobilization announcement and the actual beginning of hostilities. He did not contest the judgment that in his day mobilization would be conducted in phases, but he reasserted that those first called up must be sufficiently strong to withstand the initial enemy strikes and that the call-up must be rapid enough to continue the mobilization of succeeding echelons without concern for the early successes of the enemy.

Shaposhnikov ended his observations on mobilization with the following stark paragraph.

Mobilization in our days is the precursor of war, and the order of the government declaring mobilization is in fact a declaration of war. Diplomatically one can in many ways strive to justify war, publish any kind of white or any other colored books of documents, create broadcasting manifests, notes, and ultimatums, but reality always remains fact. MOBILIZATION IS WAR AND WE DO NOT CONSIDER ANY OTHER UN-

DERSTANDING [emphasis in the original] (Shaposhnikov 1929, 298).

Although the volume of *Mozg armii* in which Shaposhnikov intended to present his thoughts on war plans has never appeared, he did provide some general ideas on the subject in volume 3. Writing in the late 1920s, Shaposhnikov could recommend that war plans should be flexible and correspond to various political combinations and possibilities. Some of these could be foreseen. Therefore, the plans should include several variants for strategic deployment, and each variant must be adaptable to the political situation that exists on the external front at the moment of the declaration of war. The plan presented for approval to the government should designate the principal potential enemies, the main theater of war, the military objective, and a proposal on the means of achieving the military and political objectives of the war. Here Shaposhnikov had in mind whether the strategy should be that of annihilation or attrition. The plan should also allocate the forces to be used, establish the time by which they should be ready to begin operations, and provide the plans for the initial operations.

He tried to take a middle course on the question of which civilian members of the government should be privy to war plans. Although accepting the need for secrecy, he recognized that those conducting the foreign affairs of the state and those responsible for war preparations should be apprised of the plans and participate in judging their soundness. He even recommended this participation of the civilian ministries of bourgeois states in which ministers were more frequently changed. Rather than build a "Chinese wall" around the general staff, he suggested that unspecified other methods be used to preserve the secrecy of the plans (Shaposhnikov 1929, 272–74).

## THE INFLUENCE OF *MOZG ARMII* ON SOVIET MILITARY POLICY

*Mozg armii,* although it has retrospectively been acclaimed a classic by those Soviet officers who were to lead the Soviet forces in World War II, apparently had little influence on Stalin and Voroshilov. Shaposhnikov had sent the dictator an inscribed, specially bound copy of the three volumes in 1929. According to Ivan Stadniuk, an author who had access to Molotov in his retirement years, during the early dark days of the German invasion in 1941, while considering how to organize the country for war, Stalin reread Shaposhnikov's lines that he had underlined long ago: "Once that drama [war] is inevitable—you must be ready to act with full knowledge of your role, to invest in it all your being and only then can you count on success, on a decisive victory . . ." (Stadniuk 1981, 180). Stadniuk has Stalin comment that the work is worthwhile even though "grandpa" Shaposhnikov had been excessively coquettish and modest in addressing the enlightened military reader (Stadniuk 1981, 180).

Some of Shaposhnikov's recommendations were already in effect, at least as far as the economic preparation of the state for war. Integration of military and economic planning had been in progress since 1924. The Red Army Staff had begun work on the first five year plan for developing the army in 1927. In the spring of the same year, the question of an economic general staff had been decided, with the full restoration of the functions of the Council of Labor and Defense (*Sovet Truda i Oborony,* or STO). At the Fifteenth Party Congress in December 1927, Voroshilov reported that the STO was now meeting regularly "to decide all questions connected with defense," that mobilization sections had been established in all ministries, and that a special mobilization apparatus had been established in the National Economic Council and in Gosplan. Shaposhnikov's recommendation that a strong Red Army General Staff be created was only partially accepted when, in January 1930, the Red Army Staff was given responsibility for mobilization. His successor as chief of the Staff RKKA, A. I. Egorov, was on record as being opposed to the concentration of functions in the staff, and it is not at all clear that the change in name that occurred in 1935 when the staff became the General Staff of the RKKA was anything more than a cosmetic maneuver for foreign political consumption. A major reorganization of the high command in June 1934 concentrated more authority in the hands of Voroshilov, whom Stalin appears to have used as his spokesman on military matters and who was now to be called the people's commissar of defense. The Revolutionary Military Council (RVS), which made its decisions by majority vote, was dissolved. A

Commission of Defense, chaired by V. M. Molotov, was established in the Council of People's Commissars, which eventually became the Council of Ministers. The RVS was replaced by an eighty-man consultative body. It was also decided at this time to convert the army from a mixed territorial and regular army to an army in which the majority of the divisions were regular *(kadrovie)* divisions. Thus, if 74 percent of the divisions in the army were territorial until 1935, by the end of that year, 77 percent of the divisions were regular. The strength of the army that had stood at 885,000 in 1933 grew to 1,513,000 by 1 January 1938 (Zakharov 1968, 197, 198). Voroshilov, Stalin's creature, was in apparent sole command of the armed forces and was not likely to look with favor on the development of a powerful general staff. Although it seems clear that the work made little impression on the likes of Voroshilov, Budenny, and Shchadenko (if they read it at all), the younger officers and students at the military academies read it and eventually put some of Shaposhnikov's ideas into practice.

## EGOROV, CHIEF OF STAFF RKKA

When Aleksandr Il'ich Egorov returned to Moscow in April 1931 to be chief of Staff RKKA, he was forty-nine years old. Since the end of the civil war in 1920, he had commanded the Leningrad, Kiev, and Belorussian Military Districts, the Separate Caucasian Army, and the Western *Front.* In 1925 he had served a year in China, where he replaced Vasily Bliukher as senior military adviser to the Kuomintang and Chiang Kai-shek. When he returned to Moscow he was appointed deputy chairman of the military industrial directorate which later became the Military Industrial Commission, or VPK. While Egorov worked directly with Soviet industrial planners, a special directorate of the Red Army Staff coordinated the requirements of the forces and considered the infrastructure necessary to support a modernized army. The special directorate also assisted civilian factories engaged in military production by ordering selected graduates of military academies to duty at those enterprises. The military representatives were expected to ensure that the factory met the production schedule and maintained the required quality standards (Kalinovskii 1972, 67).

In the course of his duties, Egorov came into direct contact with the newest types of weapons as they were tested and produced. In his next assignment, commander of the Belorussian Military District, he had an early opportunity to experiment with the new weapons and equipment (Nenarokov 1973, 94–96). One of Egorov's first tasks on becoming chief of staff was to prepare a report for the Revolutionary Military Council on the tactics and strategy of the Red Army. The report attempted to anticipate the impact of modernization of the army and the development of an air force on the armed forces, particularly in the initial phase of a war. Modern technology, the report found, would convert the initial phase of a war from one in which the sides passively covered their mobilization to a period of active operations with far-reaching objectives. Large armored formations cooperating with massed cavalry, supported in the frontier battles by the infantry, would strike simultaneously over the entire depth of the enemy's defenses, attempting to suppress enemy artillery, divide his forces, and to disrupt the mobilization of the border military districts. The importance of communications to ensure control of the forces in both offensive and defensive operations was stressed. The report optimistically observed that the presence of water barriers such as the Dniester and a number of fortified regions made the threat to the deployment of the Red Army almost insignificant. And that threat could be further minimized by strengthening the garrisons of the fortified areas and the antitank defenses in peacetime. The "basic and only" threat to Soviet rail movement and deployment plans was enemy aviation. The guarantors of the uninterrupted execution of the mobilization and deployment plans would be a mighty air force, antiaircraft defenses, mechanized groups, and cavalry units, appropriately deployed in peacetime.

When the theses were published in 1963, the Soviet editors felt obliged to note that the role of the cavalry was overestimated and idealized as a combat arm and that in places attempts were made to transfer the experience of the civil war to modern conditions. In 1931, there were debates in all of the world's armies over the role of the cavalry in a future war. In the Soviet Union, the prominence accorded mounted units reflected the influence of Voroshilov and Budenny and their powerful protector—Stalin. But, unlike the other armies in the world, only in the Soviet Union would opposition to the idea of the continued usefulness of the cavalry on the battlefield be considered grounds for criminal indictment.*

The theses of Egorov's report were approved by the council in July 1932 and distributed widely throughout the Red Army. They were also used in developing "temporary instructions for the organization of deep battle," a subject on which the best military minds in the Red Army would continue to concentrate their attention in the years preceding World War II.

Isserson, in his discussion of the development of the theory of deep battle and deep operations, recalled Egorov's support of forward views on the character of contemporary military operations. This support was invaluable as the academies were attempting to blaze a new path against the opposition and skepticism of the older military specialists and the cavalry diehards. Some of the opposition was found in the operations section of the Red Army Staff, but it was overcome by Egorov's support, which he demonstrated by his presence and participation in a three-day war game in 1933 (Isserson 1965, 36, 41–43).

Maneuvers, exercises, and war games followed at which the new theory was tested and modifications were suggested. Subsequently, the modifications were presented for adoption at meetings before the expanded military council, where in December 1934 Egorov commented that it was a mistake to consider the tank as the critical element in the new offensive formations. Exercises had shown that the infantry retained the deciding role (Zakharov 1989, 91).

The work of an Austrian general, Ludwig Ritter von Eimansberger, seemed to reach a different conclusion on the significance of the tank. His book *Der Kampfwagen Krieg,* translated into Russian and published as *Tankovaia voina* (Tank War) in 1937, was considered a guide for Soviet tank troops. Eimansberger, after reviewing the occasions when tanks had been used during World War I, took as an example how armored and mechanized troops as conceived in the

---

*Budenny, one of the judges at the trial of Tukhachevsky in 1937, charged that to urge the formation of tank units while reducing the numbers and appropriations for cavalry units was vreditel'stvo (wrecking) (Viktorov, 1988, 3).

1930s might have been used in the battle of Amiens. He concluded that the tank was not a harmless scarecrow but a most important item for technological development—an all-terrain armored vehicle that would return the offensive spirit to the battlefield (Eimansberger 1937, 203).

The impact of Eimansberger's book on the Red Army was such that in May 1936 it was discussed at a meeting of senior commanders chaired by Tukhachevsky, then in charge of armaments. Egorov was also present when, after a series of favorable reports on the book, a young officer-engineer, N. Zavalishin, rose to present his calculation of the number of vehicles that would be required to supply the tanks with fuel, ammunition, and other services, including repairs and evacuation. At a subsequent meeting with Tukhachevsky and Egorov at the former's dacha, Zavalishin presented his calculation that the forces conceptualized by Eimansberger would require the support of 85,000 vehicles. This caused Egorov to order the *avtobronetankovoe upravlenie* (armor directorate) to work on the question and develop a supply and support system for the Red Army armored forces (Zavalishin 1963, 75).

## THE GERMAN CONNECTION

Soon after becoming chief of staff, Egorov met the future German field marshal, Erich von Manstein, who was accompanying General Adam, the chief of the *truppenamt*,* on an official visit to the Soviet Union. Von Manstein recalled that Egorov took great pains during a social function to assure him of the Red Army's friendship while painting a picture of a future brotherhood in arms against the common enemy—Poland. Von Manstein met and chatted with Egorov's wife, who spoke good French and was elegantly dressed and who later in the evening danced the *kazachok* and other national dances "with very charming vivacity" (Manstein 1958, 157).

Egorov's outpourings of the heart reflected real possibilities in 1931 and were probably officially inspired. Collaboration between

---

*The *truppenamt* was a post-Versailles device to avoid the restriction of the treaty that forbade Germany to have a general staff. It carried out the functions of a general staff.

the Red Army and the German Reichswehr had been under way since the early 1920s. It had taken the form of facilities in the Soviet Union where German military pilots and tank officers were given the opportunity to familiarize themselves with the construction and use of aircraft and tanks—weapons forbidden them under the Versailles Treaty. The Soviets, who considered themselves victims of the treaty almost as much as the Germans, and who in any case were not signatories to it, gained access to technical assistance in reconstructing their military industrial base and gained the opportunity to send selected officers to German military schools and to observe close up German staff work. The advent to power of Adolf Hitler and his virulent anticommunism in 1933 soon ended these arrangements. Both parties initially tried to give the impression that relations were cool and correct. In May 1933, however, the Soviets demanded that the Germans remove all of their installations and military personnel from the Soviet Union. They also refused to send any more officers to German military schools. The Soviets claimed that the Germans had revealed all the details of German-Soviet military cooperation to the French (Hilger and Meyer 1953, 196–98).

Within the Red Army, sympathy and goodwill toward the Reichswehr continued to be expressed for some time after the break. Tukhachevsky told a member of the German embassy staff in Moscow that it was politics that separated the armies, not the Red Army's attitude toward the Reichswehr, which continued to be sympathetic. In October 1935, Tukhachevsky again expressed regrets over the break, saying that if Germany and Soviet Russia were to march together, they could dictate peace to the entire world. If they were to clash, the Germans would find out that the Red Army had learned a lot in the meantime. Similar statements were attributed to Voroshilov and Egorov (Hilger and Meyer 1953, 193–96). In May 1936, during a visit to Moscow of the chiefs of staff of the three Baltic states, Egorov took aside Ernst Koestring, the veteran German military attaché, and in the course of the conversation told him that the stirring up of the German and Soviet peoples against each other could not go on, that "governments change, people remain . . ." Koestring assured Egorov that it was his mission to improve relations, but that Egorov, if he had read *Mein Kampf,* must understand how difficult it was. Egorov laughingly responded, "Don't bother me with that trash. It was written by Hitler in the bitterness of his Landsberg prison cell. We don't take it seriously" (Teske n.d., 85). Koestring goes on to say that he heard similar comments from Stalin.

United States recognition of the Soviet Union in 1933 raised hopes in the Soviet Union that diplomatic relations between the two countries would foster aid for Soviet economic and industrial development. Accordingly, the first official U.S. representatives were received warmly by the Soviets. Major Philip R. Faymonville, the first U.S. military attaché, was received by Egorov in August 1934. According to Faymonville's report of the meeting, Egorov found that the position of the United States and the Soviet Union was similar in that both were peaceful bystanders in a disordered world. Egorov compared Central Europe to an active volcano ready to erupt and warned against applying pressure from the outside. Commenting on the balance of power in the Pacific, Egorov remarked on the overwhelming strength of the U.S. fleet and expressed interest in U.S. projects for establishing bases in Alaska. He also commented on racial problems in Hawaii. He was probably referring to the large Japanese-American colony there. He believed that the Japanese were giving much thought to interrupting traffic through the Panama Canal (presumably in the event of war), and he congratulated the United States on the thoroughness with which countermeasures had been taken to defend the canal. He also praised the state of preparedness of the U.S. Army and its arrangements for utilizing the existing industrial base for war mobilization (Faymonville 1934, 2).

Faymonville's report suggests that Egorov was briefed carefully before the meeting to be friendly, not particularly forthcoming, and certainly not confrontational. If Egorov's appraisal of U.S. Army preparedness and its plans to use the existing industrial base for mobilization reflected Soviet intelligence estimates, it is clear that Soviet intelligence was overly sanguine about the readiness of the United States and its mobilization plans in 1934. Perhaps these comments were an attempt to flatter Faymonville, an ordnance officer who had received advanced training in military industrial production.

As the Soviet Union was probing for assistance in the West, Hitler was taking measures to demonstrate that his new orientation in foreign policy was to be backed with steel. On 18 March 1935, he announced plans for a new army of thirty-eight divisions based on compulsory military training accompanied by significant changes in military nomenclature, including the renaming of the *truppenamt* to the General Staff of the Army. All of these plans were in violation of the Treaty of Versailles (Goerlitz 1957, 291).

## THE BIRTH OF THE SOVIET GENERAL STAFF

The Soviet response to Hitler's defiance of France and Great Britain, the guarantors of Versailles, was to announce on 22 September 1935 that, henceforth, the staff of the RKKA would be known as the General Staff of the RKKA. On the same day, Egorov, along with Tukhachevsky, Voroshilov, Budenny, and Bliukher, was given the rank of marshal of the Soviet Union. Soviet historians attribute the change in name to the increased role and the complexity of the functions the staff was undertaking in guiding the growing Red Army in an atmosphere of international tension. Egorov remained as its chief and is credited with an important role in the process of establishing the General Staff as the center of strategic leadership in the Red Army. Egorov also consistently advocated organizational measures designed to make the staff and the high command capable of conversion to wartime operations without time-consuming delays in the event of the sudden outbreak of war. For some, the title of General Staff underlined the high competency and authority in military questions of the institution (Danilov 1978, 106).

It soon became apparent that merely changing the name of the staff did not create a general staff system. Trained officers were also required at the echelons below at the *front*, army, corps, and division staffs to make the system work. This became manifest in 1936, when Voroshilov discovered, while conducting a large exercise, that the high command lacked a unified approach to the solution of the most important operational and strategic problems. To remedy this shortcoming, he asked the Central Committee for permission to reestablish the Academy of the General Staff, which had not existed since 1921. The request was approved, and in April of the same year Egorov was ordered to establish and take control of the academy. A class of 137 officer students, selected under the "direct supervision of the Central Committee of the Communist Party," entered the academy on 1 November 1936 (Vasilevsky 1973, 90). All of those selected had long command experience and excellent service records. As a rule they had served in World War I and the civil war, had advanced military education, and were serving in high-level command and staff positions (Kulikov 1976, 48). Political reliability was undoubtedly also a selection factor. The students did not undergo written examinations, as had been the case in the tsarist academy (Sandalov 1970, 11).

The course was to last eighteen months, and a highly qualified faculty was assembled to conduct it. In addition, the students were frequently addressed by senior military officers such as Tukhachevsky and Egorov. Among the first group of students were three future chiefs of the General Staff—Vasilevsky, A. I. Antonov, and Zakharov—and four World War II *front* commanders. Designed to fill a recognized need in the senior ranks of the Soviet officer corps for commanders and staff officers to share a common view of high-level military problem solving, the academy epitomized the general staff concept. It was intended to instill in the senior officer corps habits and operational methods that allowed commanders and staffs at the higher echelons to grasp intuitively and execute the plans and designs of the commander in chief.

However, the experiences of the Finnish war and the German attack on the Soviet Union would submerge for a time the graduates of the academy, and the purges would bring into question the theories taught there. Instead, as will be seen, the old passions of the civil war would be reignited, and the old leaders would be called upon in the vain hope that they could halt the aggressors.

# 8
# THE MILITARY PURGES

The case of the so called *antisovetskoi trotskistskoi voennoi organizatsii v Krasnoi Armii* (antisoviet military organization in the Red Army) was addressed in issue number 4, 1989, of the journal *Izvestiia TsK KPSS*. The journal, published by the Central Committee of the Communist Party of the Soviet Union, resumed publication in January 1989 after a hiatus of seventy years. *Izvestiia TsK KPSS* had been a journal presenting documents and communications from the various agencies subordinate to the Central Committee and was therefore official and authoritative. The report had been prepared by a commission of the Politburo that reviewed the investigation during the Khrushchev years of the repressions that had occurred in the 1930s, 1940s, and early 1950s. The commission used materials from the archives of the Central Committee of the Communist Party, the KGB, and the Institute of Marxism-Leninism. This exposure of internal Party archives was a prime manifestation of the implementation of the policy of glasnost as practiced during the regime of Mikhail Gorbachev.

The commission began its review of the case by recalling the Soviet internal political situation in the second half of the 1930s. The intensification and broadening of Stalin's repressive measures aroused in the dictator apprehension as to the attitude of his senior military leaders. Since the civil war they had enjoyed the highest esteem and respect of people both in and out of uniform. Their professionalism, independence of judgment, and open criticism of some of Stalin's favorites such as Voroshilov, Budenny, Kulik, and

Shchadenko, who did not comprehend the urgency for establishing a modern army, were a source of irritation and suspicion in the paranoid mind of the dictator. Shchadenko, for example, called the idea of motorized war something dreamed up by the military specialists. The decisive role in a future war in the opinion of this veteran of the First Cavalry Army would still belong to the cavalry (Khorev 1988, 3). Budenny was to label the effort to reduce the number of cavalry divisions in the army as *vreditel'stvo* (sabotage or wrecking) (Ivanov 1990, 309). These professional military concerns were considered evidence of disloyalty and evoked in Stalin a definite fear that the army might hesitate to support his other policies. These policies included the forced collectivization of agriculture, during which gross violations of elementary rights had evoked in the army a substantial growth of sympathy for the peasants; accelerated industrialization, during which failure to meet production and quality goals was often attributed to sabotage; and the brutal elimination of all political opposition. Stalin's ascent to political supremacy was highlighted by a series of show trials featuring evidence from coerced witnesses. The decision to remove from the army those who were wavering and those about whom there was the slightest doubt in the minds of Stalin and his inner circle was attributed to these considerations (*Izvestiia TsK KPSS* 1989, no. 4, 43, 44).

This was not the first time that the army had been subject to repressions, but it was the first time that officers of high rank had been singled out. At the end of the 1920s there had been a purge of officers and political workers suspected of being in sympathy with the Trotsky opposition. In the early 1930s there had been a purge of former officers of the old army. In this case more than 3,000 officers were not only dismissed, but the victims were tried on the basis of falsified evidence. According to Voroshilov, a total of 47,000 officers were dismissed in these two purges, including 5,000 who were members of the Trotsky opposition (*Izvestiia TsK KPSS* 1989, no. 4, 43).

In mid-1936, arrests of Red Army commanders began again, based on the coerced testimony of three former factory directors who testified that there existed in the army a "military-Trotskyite organization." Their testimony incriminated the deputy commander of the Leningrad Military District, V. M. Primakov, and the Soviet military attaché in London, V. K. Putna. Primakov and Putna were arrested by the NKVD in August 1936. Both were accused of participating in a "Trotskyite-Zinovievite" organization; Putna was accused of maintaining ties with Trotsky. They both denied the charges until May 1937. Primakov, however, did admit that he had been a member of the Trotsky opposition until 1928 and that he had not severed his ties with that opposition completely. He also admitted saying hostile things about Voroshilov and Budenny.* He recalled that after he had returned from Japan in 1930 he had often met with Piatakov** but broke with him when he made some suspicious remarks. Putna also admitted that he participated in the Trotsky-Zinoviev opposition in 1926–27 and that he and Primakov had been members of the center of the Trotsky-Zinoviev Bloc but had broken with it at that time (*Izvestiia TsK KPSS* 1989, no. 4, 44, 45).

## THE FEBRUARY–MARCH 1937 PLENUM

During the February–March 1937 plenum of the Central Committee, Voroshilov and Ian Gamarnik, the head of the political directorate of the Red Army, spoke on the the political and morale situations in the army. From their evaluation there was no cause for alarm. Voroshilov declared that at the present time the army was

---

*Budenny had recommended that Primakov be tried during the civil war. In one of his letters to Stalin from prison, Primakov attributed his attitude toward Budenny and Voroshilov to the "unhealthy competition" that arose between the Cavalry Army and the Chervonyi Cossacks, whom Primakov commanded during the civil war. During the investigation, Primakov related that corps commander Kuibeshev, who was to die in 1938, had told him that Voroshilov's main interest was pistol marksmanship; he wanted around him lackeys or fools such as Kulik or ancients such as Shaposhnikov who would agree to anything; Voroshilov did not understand a modern army and did not comprehend the significance of modern technology (Khorev 1991, 4).

**Iurii Leonidovich Piatakov, a key deputy to Sergo Ordzhonikidze, the people's commissar for heavy industry and the driving force behind the second Five Year Plan, was tried, convicted, and executed in January 1937. Ordzhonikidze committed suicide or was shot in February of the same year.

combat ready and loyal to the Party and the state. The selection of people in the army was exceptional. "The country gives us the very best people" (*Izvestiia TsK KPSS* 1989, no. 4, 45).

The chairman of the Commission on Defense of the Council of People's Commissars, V. M. Molotov, was less sanguine about the loyalty of the army. Certain symptoms of sabotage had been exposed as well as spying-diversionary-Trotskyite work. Molotov believed that if, as the show trials had shown, there were saboteurs in all branches of the national economy, it would be absurd not to look for them in the military establishment. He wanted this to be checked carefully. For Voroshilov and the recently installed chief of the NKVD, Nikolai Ezhov, Molotov's words were taken as a directive to purge the army and to eliminate from its ranks all "enemies of the people" who were allegedly engaged in hostile activity. The NKVD was determined at all costs to beat out of arrested military leaders and some of their NKVD colleagues evidence of a military-Trotskyite organization in the army and evidence that at its head stood Mikhail Nikolaevich Tukhachevsky (*Izvestiia TsK KPSS* 1989, no. 4, 45).

## WHY TUKHACHEVSKY?

Tukhachevsky, seemingly a wise man, could not suffer fools gladly. His impression of Voroshilov, which dated from the civil war, was that he lacked the competence to head the military establishment of a state under the growing threat of two powerful neighbors such as Japan and Germany. One of the characteristics of Tukhachevsky's behavior, demonstrated frequently during the civil war, was that as a Party member he had the right and the duty to refer his proposals or complaints to the head of the state even if it meant bypassing his immediate superiors. Perhaps this trait derived from a naive understanding of his rights and duties as a member of the Communist Party, or an overblown conception of the importance of his proposals and ideas. These tendencies were particularly apparent in his decade-long struggle with Voroshilov, his immediate military superior from 1925 until 1937. As early as January 1926, when Tukhachevsky was chief of the Staff RKKA, he complained to Voroshilov, the commissar of military and naval affairs, that the staff was working in "abnormal conditions" that were making it impossible to do productive work. Tukhachevsky concluded that the staff was being systematically atrophied by the establishment of primitive mutual relations and being converted into an "apolitical organ" (Nikiforov 1993, 147). Here it is difficult to establish the precise nature of the complaint, but it would seem that it had to do with the perceived isolation of the staff from the policy makers of the state and the Soviet military establishment.

In a letter to Voroshilov dated 27 February 1927, Tukhachevsky reported insurmountable friction that had developed in the work of the staff. On 5 April 1928, Tukhachevsky wrote Voroshilov that the situation now seemed as if the commissar (Voroshilov) worked by himself and the staff worked by itself. He provided an example from the Odessa maneuvers. There the staff played no role in the development of Voroshilov's views on the preparation of the maneuver but served as a target for criticism from him and his guests at the maneuvers. Voroshilov, in preparing the critique of the exercise, had not solicited comments from the chief of Staff RKKA but from "a group of comrades who lived with you in the railroad cars" (probably the commissar's command train in which he could travel to the maneuvers in comfort). He also accused Voroshilov of discrediting the staff and undermining it in the eyes of other organs (possibly the main directorate and the inspectorate RKKA), with which it was already difficult enough to work. In a separate note, also dated 5 April, Tukhachevsky requested that, after that day's conversation with Voroshilov, he be relieved as chief of Staff RKKA (Nikoforov 1993, 147). Presumably the conversation between the two had not been pleasant. The next month Tukhachevsky was named commander of the Leningrad Military District.

While in Leningrad, Tukhachevsky apparently accepted as real the announced successes of the first Five Year Plan. In January 1930, he presented to Voroshilov a plan for reconstructing the armed forces, which the early achievements of the plan now made possible. Tukhachevsky recommended that the reconstructed RKKA include 260 rifle and cavalry divisions, 50 divisions of artillery in the reserve of the commander in chief plus large-caliber artillery and mortars, 225 machine-gun battalions, 40,000 aircraft, and 50,000 tanks.

Voroshilov referred the plan to the chief of Staff RKKA, Shaposh-nikov, for an estimate of its cost. The costs of Tukhachevsky's pro-posal were "stunning." Voroshilov then forwarded the plan and the cost estimate to Stalin, who made some negative marginalia on the document such as "mechanical approach," "he's off," and a sarcas-tic comment comparing Tukhachevsky's plan to that of a minor econ-omist who had forecast (correctly) that the collectivization of agri-culture would require coercion of the middle peasantry. Stalin also provided his general impression of the plan, which concluded that the adoption of the plan would be "worse than any counterrevolu-tion" (Nikiforov 1993, 148). Voroshilov dutifully passed Stalin's com-ments to Tukhachevsky.

Tukhachevsky continued to press his case, and in March 1931, af-ter a conversation with Stalin, he succeeded in gaining his approval for an increase in the number of rifle divisions to 150. He also continued to duel with Voroshilov, protesting what he saw as Voros-hilov's rebukes and openly challenging the commissar's ability to think broadly and perspectively. His attitude toward Voroshilov was reinforced by a letter he received from Stalin in 1932 admitting that the dictator had not fully understood Tukhachevsky's 1930 plan. Stalin's letter confirmed in Tukhachevsky's mind that Voroshilov had not presented the plan to Stalin accurately in the first place.

There was no relaxation of Tukhachevsky's pressure on Voroshilov in subsequent years. In 1933 he urged the creation of air, submarine, and torpedo boat forces to combat the threat of an "attacking" Japan-ese fleet in the Soviet Pacific waters. In 1934 he proposed improve-ments in the Mongolian rail system to enhance the ability of the So-viets to defend the country. Both of these recommendations were shrugged off by Voroshilov. In May 1936, according to Voroshilov, Tukhachevsky—in the presence of Stalin, Molotov, and others—had accused Voroshilov and Budenny of surrounding themselves with a small clique that determined the policies of the Military Commis-sariat. Subsequently, Tukhachevsky retracted the accusation. After this episode, Stalin directed that the matter be brought before the Politburo, where Tukhachevsky again retracted his accusations. Mat-ters in the military establishment remained unchanged. Again, ac-cording to Voroshilov before the Politburo, Iakir, Gamarnik, and

Uborevich conducted themselves in a hostile manner toward Voroshilov (Nikiforov 1993, 149).

If Voroshilov was correct, the Tukhachevsky affair had its origins in the May 1936 appearance of Tukhachevsky and other military leaders before the Politburo. The appearance, instigated by what Trotsky had noted long ago—an accusation by Tukhachevsky that he was not prepared to defend and was therefore considered baseless—resulted in Voroshilov's vindication. Voroshilov and Budenny, however, were not inclined to forgive and forget. In that same month one of the principal witnesses in the June 1937 trial—Primakov—was arrested and held while the dictator considered his next moves.

It is not clear just what plans Stalin and Ezhov had in the fall of 1936 with respect to a purge of the army. By the time of the February–March 1937 plenum, Stalin's fears of Trotsky's influence and the competence of the German, Japanese, and Polish intelligence services had overcome reason, and the NKVD was unleashed and ordered to find a plot.

## PREPARATION OF THE TRIAL

In January 1936, Tukhachevsky, despite his apparently ambiguous position in relation to Stalin and Voroshilov, was designated as the official Soviet representative to the funeral of King George V. On the return voyage he was permitted to visit Paris, where he was received by the chief of the French General Staff, Maurice Gustav Gamelin, visited a number of military installations, and dined with some of those who had shared his imprisonment at Ingolstadt during World War I, including Charles de Gaulle. The *Manchester Guardian*, commenting on the significance of Tukhachevsky's visit and the impression he made on a number of influential people, considered the possibility that it marked the beginning of a new period in Anglo-Soviet relations (Ivanov 1990, 300). Although the good impression that Tukhachevsky left abroad would not necessarily be received favorably by his paranoid masters at home—obsessed as they were with foreign spies and saboteurs—it was the opportunity to meet with a former subordinate that was ultimately to prove more damaging. Now the Soviet military attaché in London, V. K. Putna was called home and arrested the following May and would be accused along with Tukhachevsky of being part of the "Trotskyite plot."

In the spring of 1937, Tukhachevsky was again preparing to represent the Soviet state abroad, this time at the coronation of King George VI, when his trip was suddenly canceled. Soviet intelligence allegedly had learned that there was to be an attempt on his life during his voyage to London. His absence at the coronation was officially explained as due to his illness. Because it should have been possible to secure the life of such an important traveler on this voyage, it was clear that there was a greater threat to his well-being. This became more evident on 11 May, when he was informed of his relief as deputy commissar of defense and assigned to command the Volga Military District. When P. N. Kuliabko, the former member of the Central Executive Committee (TsIK) who had recommended Tukhachevsky for Party membership in 1918, learned of his transfer to the Ural Military District, he visited him in his quarters. He was told by Tukhachevsky that a girlfriend and a former aide were spies and had been arrested, and therefore Tukhachevsky had been transferred (*Izvestiia TsK KPSS* 1989, no. 4, fn. 50). The NKVD files included a report dating from 1924 accusing Tukhachevsky of "immoral conduct," suggesting that he may have occasionally strayed from the straight and narrow path. The 1924 report had been rejected outright by Mikhail Frunze, and there was no reference to Tukhachevsky's personal morals in the trial that was to come (Ivanov 1990, 298).

On 13 May, Tukhachevsky was granted a forty-five-minute audience with Stalin, with Voroshilov also present (Gor'kov 1995, 236). There was no record of their conversation. Tukhachevsky's sister, Mariia Nikolaevna, reported that as their last meeting was ending her brother told her that Stalin in saying good-bye to him had placed his hand on his shoulder and promised that he would soon be returning to Moscow (Ivanov 1990, 303).

Stalin kept his promise. On 22 May, less than two weeks after his exit interview, Tukhachevsky was arrested when his train reached Kuibeshev, searched in his compartment in the presence of his wife, and returned to Moscow. During the initial investigation, Tukhachevsky denied the charges against him. But he did not hold out for long. His interrogation was conducted personally by Ezhov. On 29 May, after face-to-face confrontations with his accusers— Primakov, Putna, and Fel'dman—Tukhachevsky confessed that as early as 1928 he had been drawn into an espionage organization by Enukidze, who had sponsored his entry into the Red Army in 1918. In 1934, he had been linked to the Germans by Bukharin, and in London, in 1936, Putna had arranged for him to meet with Trotsky's son. He also confessed to being part of the plot with numerous others, including S. S. Kamenev, the commander in chief during the civil war, who died in 1936. The commission investigating the circumstances surrounding the Tukhachevsky case found reddish-brown spots on the record of his confession that were subsequently identified as blood (*Izvestiia TsK KPSS* 1989, no. 4, fn. 50). But, in the record, in essence there is not one concrete, weighty, verified, proven-by-objective-evidence fact (Khorev 1991, 4).

Prior to the actual trial, Stalin and Voroshilov convened on 1 June an expanded session to the Military Council of the People's Commissariat of Defense attended by 116 military officers from the headquarters and the field. By that time 20 members of the military council were already under arrest. At the session, which lasted until 4 June, the participants were given an opportunity to examine the testimonies on Tukhachevsky, Iakir, and the other "plotters," which established the atmosphere of the meetings. Voroshilov and Stalin, using the false evidence obtained during the investigation, then laid out the case against the plotters. The political directors of the plot, according to Stalin, were Trotsky, Rykov, Bukharin, Rudzutak, Karakhan, Enukidze, and Iagoda, the former head of the NKVD. Trusting in the statements of Stalin and Voroshilov, some 42 of the participants gave statements of support after Voroshilov's presentation. Thirty-four plotters were soon arrested (*Izvestiia TsK KPSS* 1989, no. 4, 52–54).

On 5 June, Stalin, Molotov, Kaganovich, and the current NKVD chief, Ezhov, selected from a large group of the officers arrested in April and May 1937 those who would be tried with Tukhachevsky: I. E. Iakir, arrested while commander of the Leningrad Military District; A. I. Kork, arrested while head of the Frunze Military Academy; I. P. Uborevich, arrested while commander of the Central Asian Military District; R. P. Eideman, arrested while chairman of the Central Committee of *Osoaviakhim,* a mass organization of volunteers assisting the army by training workers in various military-related specialties; and B. M. Fel'dman, arrested while deputy commander of the Moscow Military District. Primakov and Putna were added to this group to give it an easily recognizable Trotskyite coloration, although they both had broken with Trotsky in 1927, ten years before.

On Stalin's initiative, a special military court was convened by the Supreme Court of the USSR to try the plotters. Its members included V. V. Ul'rikh, the chairman of the military collegium of the Supreme Court of the USSR; V. K. Bliukher, commander of the Far Eastern Army; S. M. Budenny, commander of the Moscow Military District; B. M. Shaposhnikov, chief of the General Staff; I. P. Belov, commander of the Belorussian Military District; P. E. Dybenko, commander of the Leningrad Military District; and N. D. Kashirin, commander of the North Caucasus Military District. Two substitute members, Ia. N. Alksnis and E. N. Goriachev, were added in case some member had to be replaced. The selection of the court was not accidental. They had all participated in the expanded military council held on 1–4 June, and all had contributed sharp denunciations of the accused as plotters after hearing Stalin and Voroshilov present the "facts" of the case.

## THE TRIAL

The closed trial was held on 11 June. Before the trial began, the accused were permitted to send repentant declarations to Stalin and Ezhov under the illusion that by repenting they might save their lives. The declarations have been preserved along with the contemptuous comments they evoked from Stalin and other members of the Politburo. The accused were accompanied to the trial by their NKVD interrogators, who had been ordered to convince their plotters to confirm their confessions in court. They remained with the accused in the waiting room and were in court during the trial. On the eve of the trial the accused had been warned that their fate depended on their conduct in the courtroom.

After the reading of the charges, all of the accused responded to Ul'rikh, the chairman of the court, by admitting to their guilt. Throughout the trial, the accused in general confirmed the evidence that was presented. However, when the members of the court asked the accused questions related to but not covered by their confessions, they could not answer. Tukhachevsky did not confirm some of the accusations against him, and Uborevich denied that he had engaged in sabotage and espionage. At that point the court adjourned for an hour; when it reconvened, the questioning on that point was not resumed. Chairman Ul'rikh pronounced the death sentence for all of the accused at 2335 that same day. The sentences were carried out the next day, and the victims were immediately cremated (Khorev 1991, 4). Given the haste with which the trial was conducted, the executions probably took place in the early hours of 12 June.

The forged documents with which Hitler and Himmler had attempted to prove that Tukhachevsky had been recruited for their service were apparently not introduced as evidence in the trial. Edvard Benes, the Czech president, had obtained the documents and he, in good faith, passed them to Stalin; they were probably in his hands at the time of the February–March plenum (Conquest 1990, 198, 199). The guilt of the plotters was established primarily by their coerced confessions.

On the day of the trial, Stalin had ordered the local Party committees throughout the country and in military units to organize meetings demanding the death penalty for all the accused. Stalin's order anticipated that the trial would be over that same day. The sentence was to be published on 12 June. Accordingly, Soviet public opinion was mobilized against the plotters, and Party organizations, especially those in the army, were misled as to the situation within the army. Ten days after the trial, 980 officers had been arrested, including 29 brigade commanders, 37 division commanders, 21 corps commanders, 16 regimental commissars, 17 brigade commissars, and 7 division commissars. These victims were treated to the same methods of physical coercion, blackmail, provocation, and fraud that were used in the Tukhachevsky case, with the same results. On 29 November 1938, Voroshilov could boast that the army had been cleansed of more than 40,000 officers—a number he was to call "stunning" (*Izvestiia TsK KPSS* 1989, no. 4, 59). The victims of this incredible bloody bacchanalia included 5 members of the court that had condemned Tukhachevsky. Only Ul'rikh, Budenny, and Shaposhnikov survived. By November 1938, of 108 members of the military council, only 10 survived. Stalin and Voroshilov were assisted in their endeavors by E. A. Shchadenko, the chief of the commanders' directorate of the Commissariat of Defense, and L. Z. Mekhlis, who succeeded Ian B. Gamarnik as head of the main political directorate after the latter's suicide in May 1937 when he believed he was to be arrested.

Soon after Tukhachevsky's arrest, his mother and older sister were arrested and exiled from Moscow, where they eventually died. His wife and two brothers, both holding the rank of brigade commander, were shot. Three other sisters spent seventeen years in the gulag and two years in exile before they returned to Moscow in 1956. His daughter was placed in a special children's home. When she reached maturity she was arrested; she remained in the gulag until her father was rehabilitated in 1956. She died in 1982 (V. M. Ivanov 1990, 311).

## THE OTHER TWO MARSHALS OF THE SOVIET UNION
When the composition of the court to try Tukhachevsky was announced, some observers considered it ominous that A. I. Egorov was not one of its members. Of the five serving marshals of the Soviet Union named in 1935, Voroshilov, as commissar of defense, was above the fray theoretically. Actually, he assisted in organizing the spectacle. Budenny and Bliukher were members of the court and Tukhachevsky was a defendant. Why was Egorov not included? One unlikely speculation had it that he had refused to sit in judgment of the plotters. Another possibility, more likely, was that he served as sergeant at arms for the court (U. S. Embassy Moscow telegrams 1937, 113, 114; Rapoport and Alexeev 1985, 8). Following the trial, Egorov continued to serve as a first deputy commissar of defense. A photograph exists of Voroshilov, Budenny, and Egorov with A. A. Zhdanov, the first secretary of the Leningrad Party committee, observing maneuvers near Leningrad in the fall of 1937. He was also elected to the Supreme Soviet. Soon after the first session of the Supreme Soviet in January 1938, he was ordered to take command of the Transcaucasian Military District, headquartered in Tbilisi (Nenarokov 1973, 103).

As we have seen, the sudden transfer of a potential victim to a new command was a favorite device employed by the NKVD, perhaps to isolate the suspect from any friends or potential allies. In Egorov's case, the transfer may also have been a trap to induce any other Georgians with treasonous intentions to contact Egorov who, of course, was under close surveillance. Egorov, it will be recalled, had served in Georgia both before and after the revolution and presumably still had friends there. An accusation *(donos)* sent to Stalin by an instructor at a military academy triggered the investigation of Egorov in 1937. According to the informant, when Egorov, the former Left Socialist Revolutionary, was chief of the General Staff, he had made a series of bad decisions that may have been sabotage. Stalin turned the matter over to Ezhov for investigation, and the transfer soon followed. Egorov had been in Tbilisi one month when he was ordered to return to Moscow, where, sometime in April 1938, he disapeared from his quarters and his family never heard from him again.

During the course of the investigation, another accusation was received by Voroshilov that in 1917 Egorov, then a member of the Socialist Revolutionary Party, had slandered Lenin. The accusation was signed by a Georgii Zhukov. Two prominent Russian authors writing in the 1990s, the late Dmitrii Volkogonov and Vladimir Karpov, mistakenly assumed that the signature was that of Georgii Konstantinovich Zhukov, the Soviet marshal. Actually, Georgii Konstantinovich at the time of the alleged slander had just been demobilized from the army and was making his way home. From this and other internal evidence in the accusation, it is clear that the Georgii Zhukov who signed the letter was not the Soviet marshal (Khor'kov 1992, 6).

Egorov was removed from the Central Committee of the Party (he was a candidate member) after a written canvass of its members was conducted by Stalin from 22 February to 2 March 1938. His removal was based on a face-to-face session with "arrested plotters" Belov, Graznov, Grin'ko, and Sediakin after which "Egorov turned out to be more politically stained than one could believe." Also, his wife, née Tseshkovskaia, with whom he lived "in perfect harmony," turned out to be a veteran Polish spy (Smetanin 1989, 4).

On 16 March 1939, the chairman of the Military Collegium of the

Soviet Supreme Court, Ul'rikh, "the sadly famous Stalinist execu-
tioner,"* reported to the dictator that between 21 February and 14
March the Military Collegium had heard the cases of 436 individuals, of whom 413 were sentenced to be shot. He also reported that
all of the condemned had confessed their guilt. Aleksandr Il'ich
Egorov was on that list. For some unknown reason, the sentence was
not carried out until 23 February 1939—Red Army Day. On that day
Stalin and Voroshilov took the Red Army oath accompanied by the
appropriate publicity while Egorov was executed. It is cruelly ironic
that Egorov, who contributed thirty-four years of service and much
blood to the defense of his country, including twenty-one years in
the Red Army, would die on the orders of two who seemed bent on
the army's dismemberment.

As was the case in the destruction of Tukhachevsky, there seemed
to have been no single proximate cause in Egorov's demise. The timing of his arrest and transfer to the Transcaucasian Military District
suggests that his connection with Avel Enukidze, the Georgian Bolshevik, may have made him suspect in Stalin's eyes. It will be recalled
that in 1918 Enukidze, as head of the Military Section of the Central Executive Committee, recognized Egorov's talent and guided his
early career in the Red Army. Enukidze was also responsible for the
early advancement of Tukhachevsky. Robert Conquest, in his mon-

*Aleksei Khorev, a special correspondent of *Krasnaia Zvezda,* who did a series
of major articles on the Tukhachevsky case, became intrigued with the persona
of Vladimir Vasil'evich Ul'rikh, the judge who had sent "so many innocent people to the other world." Khorev found that there was practically no public information available about him, and that only by consulting the pension records
was Khorev able to develop some facts about the judge. He apparently came
from a privileged stratum of prerevolutionary Russian society, was born in Riga,
joined the Party in 1910, served in the tsarist army, after the revolution served
as a finance officer in the Cheka and the NKVD, and in 1926 became chairman
of the Military Collegium of the Supreme Soviet. In that position he rose to the
rank of colonel general. In 1948 he was removed suddenly from that position
and reduced in rank to colonel. In that rank he served as the chief of the advanced training program at the Military Juridical Academy until his death from
a stroke in May 1951 at age sixty-two. There is no evidence that he ever received
any legal training. While serving as chairman of the Military Collegium he lived
in a luxury apartment in the Hotel Metropole (Khorev 1989, 4).

umental study, *The Great Terror,* speculates that Enukidze seemed to have become a special target for Stalin after 1935. He and others were tried as spies, bourgeois nationalists, and terrorists. On 16 December 1937, it was announced that they had confessed and had been executed. It was learned in the 1960s that Enukidze had been killed on 30 October. Whether or not there was a trial is not known. There is no explanation as to why Stalin felt it necessary to play this gruesome game (Conquest 1990, 245, 246).

It is also almost certain that the old antagonisms of the civil war were factors in Egorov's destruction even though he had generally supported Stalin in the controversies that followed. That Egorov was sent by Trotsky to correct the conditions prevailing in Tsaritsyn in 1919, and that he relieved Voroshilov as commander of the Tenth Army there, was an obvious source of resentment. That he bungled the Kiev operation in 1920, even if Stalin was equally responsible— thereby contributing to the failures before L'vov and Warsaw— would hardly have been forgotten. And, whether or not Egorov's actions were subsequently judged as being treasonous, they probably ensured that no one in the circle around Stalin spoke up when the case reached the dictator for final approval of the sentence.

In 1957, after Egorov had been rehabilitated, both of Egorov's sisters and his daughter each wrote to Voroshilov, then the chairman of the Presidium of the Supreme Soviet, asking if their brother (father) was still alive, and if he was how could they communicate with him. They had never been informed officially of his death. Voroshilov did not answer their letters (Smetanin 1989, 4).

## VASILY KONSTANTINOVICH BLIUKHER

Because much of his service was in the Soviet far east, Vasily Konstantinovich Bliukher has not often appeared in this account of Stalin's relations with his military lieutenants. Bliukher's service was nevertheless as eventful and significant as that of Tukhachevsky and Egorov, although it was performed on the far reaches of the Soviet state.

Unlike the latter, however, Bliukher's origins were above reproach from the point of view of a regime that purported to seize power and rule in the name of the proletariat and the poor peasants. Bliukher was born in 1890 to a poor peasant family in a village in Iaroslavl Guberniia. At the age of fourteen he was apprenticed by his father to a dry goods store in St. Petersburg. He later drifted through several jobs there, in Moscow, and on the Volga until he found employment in a railroad car shop on the outskirts of Moscow. There he became involved in the revolutionary movement. In 1910 he was arrested for calling for a strike, and he was sentenced to two years and eight months in prison. After his release from prison in 1913, he worked in Rybinsk and Moscow until the outbreak of World War I, when he was conscripted into the army. His service with the Southwestern *Front* was short—four months—before he was hospitalized with severe wounds. In March 1916, after more than a year in the hospital, he was discharged from the army with a first category pension. After a short stay at home, he worked as a mechanic at various places in the central Volga region and eventually joined the Bolshevik Party in 1916 (Dushen'kin 1966, 4–7).

Bliukher, according to several Soviet sources, became a noncommissioned officer and was awarded two crosses of St. George during his service with the tsarist army. However, a detailed search of the archives does not confirm either the promotion or the awards (Sharov and Vlodavets 1993, 14).

After the February Revolution, Bliukher was directed by the Samara Bolshevik city committee to volunteer for service in a local reserve regiment and spread revolutionary agitation among the soldiers. He managed to accomplish enlistment with difficulty because of his status as an invalid, but due to his determination and his combat record he was accepted. During the October seizure of power by the Bolsheviks, he is credited with leading the troops of his regiment to the support of the Bolsheviks. He subsequently became the commissar of the Samara garrison and the chief of the local security forces (Dushen'kin 1966, 7).

## CIVIL WAR SERVICE

Bliukher's active Red Army service in the civil war began with the command of a detachment *(otriad)* ordered from Samara to liquidate the forces of Ataman Dutov and the Orenburg Cossacks, who had surrounded and were threatening to capture Cheliabinsk. Bliukher's detachment of 500 men was the first Red Army help to reach the beleaguered city. Arriving on 20 November, they quickly dismissed the SR-Mensehvik city duma and established a military-revolutionary committee, which was soon chaired by Bliukher. With the aid of reinforcements from Petrograd, the Red detachments liberated Troitsk and in mid-December began operations against Orenburg, which was in the hands of the White Cossacks. By early January 1918, the Cossacks had been driven out of Orenburg.

The Czech revolt in May sharply changed the situations in the southern Urals. The Red detachments in Orenburg were surrounded, and the nearest Red Army units were 1,500 kilometers away. Bliukher led his partisans out of Orenburg and executed a raid along the Urals, which brought them into a series of battles with the Whites. This ended when contact was established with the Third Army in September.

On 20 September 1918, Bliukher's partisans were reorganized and incorporated into the 4th Ural Division, and Bliukher was given command. The division participated in the fall and winter campaign, helping to frustrate the White efforts to exploit their capture of Perm and to eventually drive them out of Perm. On 1 January 1919, Bliukher became deputy commander of the Third Army, and on 3 April he was given the additional duty of commander of the Viatka Fortified Region, which eventually became the 51st Rifle Division. With that division Bliukher pursued the beaten forces of Kolchak to Lake Baikal. In 1920 the 51st Division was moved to the Southern *Front*, where Bliukher was given command of the Kakhovka Fortified Region. It defeated one of the most powerful tank attacks of the civil war, which was mounted by Vrangel and his White Guards on 14 October 1920. Subsequently, in the decisive operations to clear the Crimea of Vrangel's troops, Bliukher and his troops became the heroes of the storm of the White Perekop and Ishun'skii positions.

In 1921, Bliukher was sent to the Russian far east, where at that time Lenin had decided to establish the Far Eastern Republic as a buffer state between the areas controlled by the Soviet state and the Japanese, who still occupied the Russian far east. Bliukher's mission was to liberate the Russian far east while at the same time avoiding the outbreak of war with Japan. Bliukher became the commander of the People's Revolutionary Army, which he reorganized, trained, and led against White Guards who were being used by the Japanese to consolidate their position. In February 1922, the People's Revolutionary Army stormed Volchaevka and seized Spassk. These were the last combat operations of the civil war.

Bliukher was recalled from the far east in 1922 and given command of the 1st Rifle Corps, stationed in Petrograd. He remained in that position until the end of 1923, when he was ordered to China as the chief military adviser to Sun Yat-sen and the National Revolutionary Army of China. This army had been formed as a counterweight to the regional warlords and their armies, which contributed to maintaining a fragmented China. After Sun Yat-sen died in 1925, Chiang Kai-shek became the leader of the right wing of Sun Yat-sen's Kuomintang Party and by 1927 was in a position to demand the removal of the Soviet military advisers from China. The removal occurred after Bliukher and his assistants had organized and helped lead the great northern campaign, a campaign fought largely with proclamations, posters, and newspapers (Fischer 1951, 663).

## THE CHINESE EASTERN RAILROAD
After returning from China, Bliukher served as deputy commander of the Ukrainian Military District until August 1929, when he was ordered to combine all of the forces serving in the far east into the Special Far Eastern Army. The problem facing the Special Far Eastern Army was the seizure in June of the Chinese Eastern Railroad by forces controlled by a Chinese warlord in Mukden, Chang So Lin, who was assisted by detachments of White Russian émigrés. In addition to arresting Soviet employees of the Chinese Eastern Railroad (it had been operated since 1924 by a joint Russian and Chinese staff), the Chinese also were very aggressive at various points along the twisting border, which stretches more than 2,400 kilometers from Manchouli to North Korea. The Chinese seemed to be considering a foray into Soviet territory, cutting the Trans-Siberian Railroad, the lifeline of the Soviet Maritime Province (Fischer 1951, 795–800). The Special Far Eastern Army and the Amur River flotilla launched their first attacks, striking the Chinese Sungari River

flotilla on 12 October and capturing the town of Lakhasusa. This attack was followed on 30 October with an attack supported by aviation along the river toward Fugdin. By the end of the next day, Fugdin had been captured and the entire Sungari River flotilla destroyed. From widely dispersed locations along the border, the Chinese continued to threaten both the Transbaikal and Maritime Provinces. The latter threat was defused by a cross-border attack on Mishan on 17 November. The threat to the Transbaikal section of the border was eliminated by an attack spearheaded by the 5th Kuban Cavalry Brigade, commanded by Konstantin Konstantinovich Rokossovsky. Operations in the Transbaikal were successfully completed with the capture of Khailar on 23 November (Dushen'kin 1964, 180–95). The Chinese soon after sued for peace, the Soviet captives were released, and the Chinese Eastern Railroad was restored to joint Chinese and Russian operation (Fischer 1951, 801–5). In May 1930, Bliukher was the first to be awarded the newly created Order of the Red Star.

## THE JAPANESE GROW RESTLESS

Japanese aggressive actions, beginning with the occupation of Manchuria in 1932 and the invasion of China in 1937, were accompanied by a sixfold increase in the size of the Kwantung Army and numerous border incidents. Under these circumstances, Bliukher, who became a marshal of the Soviet Union in 1935, because of his long and varied experience in the area, became the spokesman for the defense of the far east. When the initial plans for the strength of Soviet forces in the far east were made in 1938, the forces were to be increased by 10,000 men. Bliukher proposed that they be increased by 96,000 to 103,400 men. Voroshilov decided that the increase should be 23,500 men, saying that "V. K. Bliukher could not house such a number of people for a number of years" (Zakharov 1989, 134). Bliukher insisted that the matter be reviewed in his presence by the Main Military Council, where it was decided to increase the far eastern forces by 72,300 immediately and by 105,800 troops for the entire year 1938 and that capital expenditures on troop construction be doubled over the amount allocated in the previous year.

In June, the Far Eastern *Front* was established under Bliukher's command; it consisted of the First and Second Armies and the Khabarovsk group. As Zakharov, a future chief of the General Staff, commented, "The farsightedness of these proposals was confirmed by the entire course of subsequent events" (Zakharov 1989, 135). What Zakharov did not comment on was the effect that Bliukher's persistence had on the attitude of Stalin and Voroshilov toward someone who was defending a judgment about an area noted for its independence and self-reliance. Was Bliukher thinking of establishing a separate fiefdom in the far east?

The timeliness of Bliukher's warnings about Japan's aggressive intentions toward the Soviet far east was soon to be tested. During the month of July, the Japanese concentrated a war-strength infantry division on high ground along the border overlooking Lake Khasan. They chose an area in the most remote part of the Maritime Province, an area to which Soviet access was most difficult due to the absence of adequate infrastructure and swampy lowlands. The Japanese forces on the Manchurian side of the border had access to a rail line, and by fortifying the high ground they assured themselves a strong position from which to launch an attack.

On 15 and 20 July the Japanese demanded that the Soviets remove their border troops from the high ground west of Lake Khasan, saying that those heights were in Manchurian territory. The Soviets rejected the demand, and on the night of 29 July the Japanese launched an attack across the border. The Soviet command had reinforced one of the heights in question with an infantry regiment from the 40th Rifle Division and two companies of border troops. The First Army dispatched two additional reinforced battalions from the 40th Rifle Division, but by 31 July the Japanese had occupied two of the key heights on the Soviet side of the border. Uncoordinated Soviet counterattacks were unsuccessful, and the Japanese penetrated Soviet territory about four kilometers.

Late on 1 August, additional regiments of the 40th Rifle Division joined the battle after a 200-kilometer march, but of five artillery battalions only a few batteries had arrived. The commander of the 40th Rifle Division, without completing the necessary reconnaissance, ordered an attack at 0800 the next day. It failed due to a lack of artillery and mortar support, the inability of tanks to negotiate the swampy ground, and the overall lack of coordination. When the chief of the General Staff, B. M. Shaposhnikov, asked the commander of the 40th Rifle Division what his combat mission was, he responded that the division had received three missions: one each from corps, army, and *front* headquarters (Zakharov 1989, 137).

According to Zakharov, on 2 August the Politburo of the Central Committee, which at that time meant Stalin, ordered Bliukher to direct the combat actions in the area of Lake Khasan but not to move his command post without the knowledge of the commissar of defense (Voroshilov). The next day, after it had been decided to commit to the conflict the 39th Rifle Corps (which, in addition to the 40th Rifle Division, included the 32d Rifle Division and the 2d Mechanized Brigade), Bliukher was ordered to turn over the direction of the battle to the commander of the 39th Rifle Corps, who was to be Bliukher's chief of staff, G. M. Shtern. Shtern had recently conducted an inspection in the area of Lake Khasan.

On 4 August, Bliukher was ordered to bring the forces of the Far Eastern *Front* and the Transbaikal Military District to full combat readiness and to increase observation of the border—especially at night and during foggy or bad weather—to prevent further Japanese incursions. Bliukher and Shtern were also warned not to repeat the errors that had been committed on 2 August by the 40th Rifle Division (whose commander had been relieved). Shtern was also directed to organize the attack on the Japanese from both flanks. The boundaries of the 39th Rifle Corps were defined as extending from Lake Khasan to the Tumen'-Ula. After the ejection of the Japanese from the high ground, the Soviet troops were to return to the Soviet side of the border without delay. The operation, on 6–11 August, was successful—the Japanese were driven back over the border.

Matvei V. Zakharov, a member of the first group of students to attend the reestablished Academy of the General Staff in 1936, joined the General Staff as chief of the mobilization section in May 1938. Commenting on these changes to the command structure in the far east, he admitted that the selection of G. M. Shtern to command the 39th Rifle Corps had a certain logic if the goal was to place the operation in the hands of an experienced officer who enjoyed broad authority due to his former position on the Far Eastern *Front*. But the assignment significantly circumscribed the authority of the First Army commander, Kuz'ma Petrovich Podlas, and the *front* commander, Bliukher. The ambiguity of their place in the chain of command was further exacerbated by the authority given Shtern to report directly to the commissar of defense and the chief of the General Staff. Zakharov found Bliukher's position to be "difficult and isolated." On the one hand he was ordered to effect general leadership of the combat activities around Lake Khasan, but he was ordered not to leave his command post in Khabarovsk. He was also to command the entire Far Eastern *Front*, which had been brought to a status of full combat readiness; maintain close contact with the Pacific Fleet and local political authorities; supervise the rear services of the First Army (providing logistical support to the 39th Corps); and decide numerous other problems. As Zakharov observes, he could have coped with all of these functions if he was supported by a competent staff, but "that important organ of control . . . had been taken from him" (Zakharov 1989, 139, 140).

It had been taken from him in order to staff the 39th Rifle Corps. The purges had apparently affected the command and staff elements of the Far Eastern Military District. Another complication was the arrival at the corps headquarters of Lev Zakharovich Mekhlis, the chief of the Main Political Administration of the Soviet Army and Fleet, as Voroshilov's representative. According to Zakharov, Mekhlis did not understand the situation and did not improve the command and control of the troops. Reports to the General Staff were late, causing the chief of the General Staff to warn Shtern personally. Mekhlis was probably also sending other reports through his channels about the overall condition of the troops in the far east and their commander, Bliukher, which did not bode well for the latter.

Although the Soviet victory over the Japanese was widely proclaimed as a successful test against the Japanese Army, a much more serious opponent than the Chinese, it was obvious that there were problems with the command structure in the far east. Both G. M. Shtern and Bliukher were recalled to Moscow to report on the operation to the Main Military Council. After Shtern and Bliukher reported,* it was decided to disestablish the Far Eastern *Front* and replace it with two separate armies that would report directly to the commissar of defense: the 1st Separate Red Banner, to be commanded by G. M. Shtern, and the 2d Separate Red Banner, to be commanded by I. S. Konev. Bliukher was to remain in Moscow awaiting reassignment. The 57th Special Corps was to be deployed in Mongolia. The strength of the Soviet forces was increased by 167,200 men, so that by 1 January 1939, Soviet troop strength in the Far Eastern Military District rose to 470,000. Zakharov considered, in retrospect no doubt, the reorganization of the far eastern command structure to be baseless (Zakharov 1989, 141, 142).

## THE DEATH OF BLIUKHER

Bliukher was removed officially from his post on 4 September 1938 and placed at the disposal of the Main Military Council. While he was waiting a new assignment, he was offered the use of Voroshilov's dacha at Sochi. On the morning of 22 October, Bliukher was arrested and returned to Moscow. On 8 November 1938, after eighteen days of almost continuous questioning and torture, seven times by Lavrentii Pavlovich Beriia—the new head of the NKVD—Bliukher died. The Soviet Army now had just two marshals—Voroshilov and Budenny (Daines 1992, 5).

## THE EFFECT OF THE PURGES

Each time the history of the purges of the Red Army and Navy is reviewed and the specters reappear of the cold-blooded official mur-

---

*David Ortenberg, who was a deputy editor of *Krasnaia Zvezda* at the time, was present at the meeting of the Main Military Council at which G. M. Shtern reported on the operation at Lake Khasan. The meeting, held on 31 August, was attended by Stalin and Voroshilov. After Shtern had given his report, according to Ortenberg, Stalin took over the questioning of the rapporteur. Stalin's line of questioning took the form of a series of direct rebukes of Shtern—that the Japanese had been permitted to penetrate Soviet territory and take the high ground overlooking the lake. It was not easy for Ortenberg to listen, for he could not imagine that Stalin could be so infuriated. He thought to himself that even if Shtern was at fault, the high ground had been retaken and the Japanese had been driven back across the border, which was reported in his newspaper (Ortenberg 1995, 16, 17).

ders of literally thousands of experienced officers on the eve of the
country's life-and death-struggle with its declared enemies, one is
amazed by the communal madness of the entire enterprise and of
those who perpetrated it. As the international climate worsened on
both the Soviet eastern and western borders, it became obvious that
it would be necessary to increase the size and capability of the Soviet armed forces. The country's industrial capacity was expanding
and, despite the alleged damage to the economy caused by "wreck-
ers," it would meet the military demands. In 1940, the Red Army was
composed of 7 military districts and armies, 6 rifle corps, 22 rifle divisions, and 129 brigades and regiments. Also being formed were an
additional 9 mechanized corps, 20 tank divisions, and 20 tank
brigades. By 1941 it was planned to have 16 military districts, 1 *front*
headquarters, 20 field army headquarters, 62 rifle corps headquarters, 29 mechanized corps headquarters, and a total of 300 divisions
of ground troops (Gor'kov 1995, 47).

After the completion of the Tukhachevsky trial, subordinate commanders began to compete with one another in exposing "enemies
of the people" and reporting their achievements to the dictator. For
example, the commander of the Kiev Special Military District reported that 6.1 percent (1,834 officers) of the command element
had been relieved from duty, of whom 861 had been arrested, and
1,091 had been dismissed from the Party. Included were 7 corps commanders, 5 division commanders, 3 fortified-region commanders, 6
brigade commanders, and 21 regimental commanders. And there
were still several hundred more to be weeded out who were members of the bloc "of a military-Trotskyite and nationalist character."
The report was signed by army commander 2d rank Fed'ko and
corps commissar Shchadenko (Gor'kov 1995, 35). Ivan Fedorovich
Fed'ko was to be "suppressed" himself in 1939; Efim Afanas'evich
Shchadenko, a veteran of the First Cavalry Army, was to die a natural death in 1951 (SVE 7:265, 550).

By the end of November 1937, Nikolai Vladimirovich Kuibeshev,
commander of the Transcaucasus Military District and brother of the
deceased Bolshevik hero V. V. Kuibeshev, complained to the Main
Military Council that none of the commanders of the three divisions
in his district had ever commanded a unit larger than a company or

a battery (Gor'kov 1995, 49). Kuibeshev wondered how good division commanders could be expected to be developed without the experience of commanding lesser units. He was never to get an answer to his question. He was repressed in January 1938 (SVE 4:514).

Even the General Staff, the brain of the army, was treated as small change in Stalin's political game. The removal and destruction of Aleksandr Egorov in 1939 has already been noted. Egorov was the only officer in the Red Army who had the experience of commanding a large operational formation and who knew the complicated mechanism of the strategic leadership of the armed forces as a whole. The operations section (which became a directorate in October 1939) was the basic generator of ideas within the staff. In the six prewar years there were seven chiefs. There was a similar game of leapfrog played in the other sections and directorates of the staff. In the case of the General Staff, the problem was not so much that of losses as it was the absence of stability and the presence of tension engendered by the epidemic of unrestrained slander.

Where were the replacement officers for all these staffs to come from? Konstantin Simonov, in the second book of his novel *The Living and the Dead,* reminds us that "soldiers are not born." Neither are officers or commanders of regiments, brigades, corps, armies, and *fronts.* Fortunately, the situation was somewhat ameliorated by the expansion of the numbers of commissioning schools and academies that accompanied the enlargement of the armed forces. The Academy of the General Staff was reestablished in 1936. In late 1918, after the revolution, an academy had been established that functioned until 1921. Then, in connection with the reduction in the size of the Red Army, it was decided that the academy should offer more general instruction in command as well as staff officer skills. After the death of M. V. Frunze on 31 October 1925, the Military Academy of the RKKA was given the name of Frunze in his honor.

After a military strategic exercise in January 1936, which demonstrated that the senior leadership of the armed forces did not share a unified view on the solution of operational and strategic problems, it was decided to reopen the Academy of the General Staff. The first group of selected students, which entered the academy on 1 November 1936, consisted of 137 officers, several of whom would become *front* commanders but not until they had passed through the harsh school of combat experience. In mid-1938, the academy established five-month courses for chiefs of the staffs of divisions and larger units. The coures were modified over the years to provide advanced training for officers assigned to those positions who had not been schooled during their careers (Kulikov 1976, 48, 58). By 1940 there were more than 20,000 officer-students in the other 17 academies as opposed to more than 9,000 in 1937. Formally, the losses of commanders had been made up. Practically, the shortage of experienced, qualified commanders was catastrophic, as the war with Finland would soon show. And when the supreme test would come in 1941, the three *front* commanders who would command the units covering the three most important axes of the Wehrmacht's advance toward Leningrad, Kiev, and Moscow had never commanded any unit higher than a brigade.* The result was a military disaster that took almost two years and millions of casualties to correct.

*Zhukov, in 1944, commenting on a report on the status of the general officer corps of the Red Army, named eight officers who in the beginning of the war failed in one assignment "after another." His list included: Pavlov (Western *Front*); Kuznetsov (Northwestern *Front*); Popov (Leningrad *Front*); Budenny (Southwestern Axis); Cherevichenko (Ninth Army); Tiulenev (Southern *Front*); Riabyshev (8th Mechanized Corps); Timoshenko (Western Axis); and "others." Zhukov's comment was in a top secret (*sovershenno sekretno*)report. It is not believed that Zhukov ever publicly critized any of these officers. (Golikov 1944, 137).

# 9
# STALIN AND VOROSHILOV PREPARE TO MEET THE AXIS THREAT

Stalin seemed to be pursuing two contradictory policies during the late 1930s. On the one hand, the pace of the five year plans and the collectivization of agriculture required to support urban production centers were proceeding at what seemed breakneck speed to provide the industrial base for the modernization of the armed forces. On the other hand, the purges of 1937 and 1938 seemed to be intent on the decapitation of the very institutions for which the weapons and equipment were intended. Abroad, the impact of the military purges on the foreign perception of the Red Army's combat capabilities completely negated any positive impression that may have arisen from the expanding industrial base. Franz Halder, chief of staff of the German ground forces (1938–42), evaluated the Soviet officer corps as very poor and thought that it would take twenty years to return it to its former level of competence (Gor'kov 1995, 50).

Stalin, of course, did not measure the results of the purges with a military yardstick. He and his closest "military" lieutenants had long held suspicions about the loyalty and competence of the professional military, especially those military specialists who may have had some relationship with the former commissar of defense, Trotsky. They saw the military purges as a narrow escape from a Fascist-Trotskyite plot that, they claimed, they had not realized was so widespread and so deep and so rotten (*Izvestiia TsK CPSU* 1989, 59). It is unlikely that Stalin or his close associates ever regretted the decimation of the Soviet high command even when their armies were reeling back on Moscow in 1941. It is more likely that they shared the view of Joseph Davies, American ambassador to Moscow from 1936 to 1938; when

asked during World War II lectures whether there were fifth colum-
nists in Russia, Davies would respond jokingly, "There weren't any,
they shot them all." (Conquest 1990, 468).

## THE MILITARY FIVE YEAR PLANS

The Fifteenth Party Congress met in December 1927 to ratify the removal of Trotsky and his followers from the Party and other measures
of punishment. The congress also marked the end of the Lenin era
of communism. In approving the directives for the First Five Year
Plan, the delegates voted, most of them unwittingly, for Stalin's new
Russia. They voted to usher in the great national tragedy of forced
collectivization, which became the stage for almost ceaseless purge
and terror. The Russian people were pushed to the construction of
a mighty military base to provide a foundation for a despot whose
stature was to grow to superhuman proportions (Ulam 1973, 285).

Before the congress began in 1927,the staff of the Red Army began work on the first plan for "the construction of the Red Army and
Fleet." The goals of the plan were formulated by the Central Committee of the Party and the Council of People's Commissars and
passed to the Revolutionary Military Council of the Republic and the
commissar of defense in June 1929 (Ryzhakov 1968, 106). Fulfillment
of the plan was to ensure that in troop strength the Soviet forces
would not be less than that of probable enemies in the main theater
of war, and that in the area of arms and equipment the RKKA would
be superior to the probable enemy in the areas of aviation, artillery,
and armor. In July 1929, the goals were modified by adding the goal
that, in the next two years, contemporary types of artillery—in particular, battalion weapons of various calibers, large-caliber machine
guns, equipment for chemical defense, modern tanks, and armored
cars—would be introduced. And, as soon as possible, new types of aircraft and aircraft engines were to be placed in series production.

As a result of the achievements of the first year of the plan, the
goal for tank production for the next five year period was raised to
3,500, three times that envisioned in 1928 (Ryzhakov 1968, 106).

In November 1929, the position of chief of armaments was established. It was occupied by I. P. Uborevich until June 1931, when
Tukhachevsky was given the post. Three directorates were subordi-

nate to the chief of armaments: artillery, communications, and tele-mechanics, which was concerned with remote control devices. The chief of armaments worked closely with the Staff RKKA and its suc-cessor, the General Staff. Tukhachevsky is credited with playing a large role in the achievements of the 1st and 2d Military Five Year Plans. In 1936, Tukhachevsky was made a deputy commissar of de-fense and given responsibility for all combat training in the Red Army on the basis that the technical rearmament of the Red Army had been completed. The functions of the staff of the chief of ar-maments, were given to a newly created main directorate of arma-ments which was also given responsibility for mobilization planning, standardization, and inventions. Although the new main directorate was directly subordinate to the commissar of defense, it continued to work closely with the General Staff. It is instructive to note that although the process began in 1927, it was not until January 1931 that a firmly established comprehensive and scientifically based plan was in place. One can only imagine the bureaucratic battles that accompanied its development (Zakharov 1971, 3, 4).

To provide the command personnel required to use the new weapons effectively, the Commission of Defense in May 1932 ordered the creation of a number of special academies for training senior of-ficers for the RKKA: the Military Academy of Mechanization and Mo-torization, the Artillery Academy, and the Military Engineer, Military Chemical, Military Electrotechnical, and Military Transportation Academies. As a result of these measures, the network of higher level military educational institutions was almost doubled, and the num-ber of students increased from 3,200 in 1928 to 16,550 in 1932.

In 1932, a second five year plan of military construction was pre-pared for the period 1933–38. The goals set for the second plan were more ambitious than those for the first military five year plan. The plan called for superiority over the capitalist armies in all of the de-cisive weapons: aviation, tanks, and artillery. Upon completion of the second five year plan, the Red Army would be capable of defeating any coalition of capitalist states if they were to attack the USSR. In this period, much attention was devoted to the navy, the air force, and artillery armament.

## ORGANIZATIONAL AND COMMAND CHANGES

The growth of militarism and the deployment of mass armies in both the east and west and the sharpening of international tension caused the Party and the government to order a transition from 1935 to 1938 from the territorial system of organizing the army introduced in 1925 to a unified cadre (regular army) system. Mastery of the new and complex weapons systems and equipment that were being delivered to the forces could not be accomplished in short-term, after-work sessions. It required full-time, continuous, repetitive training (Zakharov 1971, 6). In May 1935, it was decided to increase the number of cadre divisions to 106 by 1 January 1938 and to increase the complement of permanent personnel in the remaining 35 territorial divisions. These increases raised the strength of the RKKA to 1,513,400 men by 1 January 1938, up from 885,000 in 1933.

The increase in the size and complexity of the armed forces was accompanied by changes in the organization of the high command. In 1934, the Revolutionary Military Council of the USSR was disbanded on the basis that its functions duplicated those of the Commission of Defense in the Council of People's Commissars, headed by V. M. Molotov. This was the official justification for disbanding the Revolutionary Military Council. The council, composed of uniformed military officers, was replaced by a body of largely civilian Party members, further concentrating control of the armed forces in the hands of Stalin and his trusted Party comrades.

On 22 September 1935, the staff of the RKKA became the General Staff of the RKKA, and A. I. Egorov remained its chief. In March 1938, the Main Military Council in the Commissariat of Defense was formed. Its chairman was Voroshilov and its members were Bliukher, Budenny, Kulik, Mekhlis, Stalin, Fed'ko, Shaposhnikov, and Shchadenko. Before the end of the year, Bliukher had been repressed; Fed'ko, who had been first deputy commissar of defense, met the same fate in February 1939. The surviving members of the Main Military Council were, with the exception of Shaposhnikov (who had replaced Egorov as chief of the General Staff), veterans of the defense of Tsaritsyn and were unlikely to oppose Stalin in any serious way.

On 30 December 1937, the Commissariat of the Navy was formed, and P. A. Smirnov was named commissar. Smirnov had acquired some naval experience as a onetime head of the political directorate of the Baltic Fleet, but most of his political work had been done with the army. He was repressed in 1938 and was succeeded in September by M. P. Frinovskii. Frinovskii had been a deputy commissar of the NKVD under Ezhov and had been very active in developing the Tukhachevsky case. Nikolai Gerasimovich Kuznetsov, who was eventually to become commissar of the navy, first met Frinovskii in December 1938 and found that he had only a foggy idea of naval affairs. Kuznetsov found it impossible to understand why Frinovskii had been placed in that post at a time when there was a major naval construction program under way (Kuznetsov 1966, 213). Kuznetsov, who was to experience his own vicissitudes in the Soviet system, probably could not conceive at that time that Stalin occasionally played games with people's careers and lives. Ezhov and his assistants had participated in the military and political purges of 1937 and 1938, and it was now time to replace them with Lavrentii Beriia and his associates. Frinovskii's short tour as naval commissar was ended in March 1939, when he was arrested. Ezhov, who had been given a similar incongruous appointment as commissar of water transport, was arrested on 19 April of the same year but was not executed until 1940. In all, some 150 of his followers were shot (Conquest 1990, 431, 432).

The creation of the Main Military Councils of the Army and the Navy and their respective commissariats was followed in May 1937 by an order creating military councils at the headquarters of fleets, armies, and military districts (many of which would become *front* headquarters in wartime). The councils were charged with the leadership of all combat and political training of the formations subordinate to their respective headquarters. The councils usually consisted of at least the commander, the chief of staff, and a political member who was known as "the member of the military council." The councils made their decisions on the basis of a majority vote. Any member not satisfied with a given decision had the right to appeal to the next higher headquarters. The councils were directly subordinate to the commissar of defense.

Stalin had occupied the position of member of the military council on several occasions during the civil war, and it was from this position during the war with Poland in 1920 that he had attempted to block the transfer of the First Cavalry Army to Tukhachevsky's Western *Front*, with disastrous consequences. The Party had prided itself on the creation of *edinonachal'niki* (one-man commanders) at the lower echelons. But the creation of the military councils at the military district, army, and fleet level meant that command at what the Soviets considered to be the operational and strategic echelons was to be collegial.

Commenting on the duties of "the member of the military council," David Ortenberg, who served as editor of *Krasnaia Zvezda* during World War II and who observed members of military councils as they performed their duties, came to the conclusion that "the position was to a large extent created by Stalin for control over the commanders and staffs of *fronts* and armies. The members, who were usually high ranking civilian Party members, such as L. Z. Mekhlis, A. A. Epishev and N. A. Bulganin, were to report to him everything that they saw in the forces which may have for a time been hidden in official reports" (Ortenberg 1995, 183).

## THE THIRD FIVE YEAR PLAN

After a thorough canvass of the military results of the first two five year plans, the third five year plan was inaugurated in 1938 for the period 1938–42. This plan sought to improve the strike capability and the maneuverability of the forces in the light of the possibility that the Soviet Union might be struck in the east and west simultaneously. Capital investment in the defense industry in 1938 was increased by 70 percent compared with 1937, and the production of ammunition, infantry weapons, and artillery was significantly increased. Five thousand young engineers were added to the defense enterprises. The productivity of these enterprises was also to be increased by the presence of uniformed military representatives at the plants. They were charged with overseeing the production runs to assure that completion schedules were met and that the end product was of the required quality. The institution of military representatives was given increased authority in 1939.

One of the assumptions of the plan was that there would not be a local, limited, or world war and that the development of the forces would proceed at an unforced tempo. The emphasis was to be on the improvement of the quality of Soviet armaments, organizational structures and command and control systems. In these conditions it was proposed to deploy ninety-five infantry divisions of four types: two types of reinforced cadre divisions; a cadre division that in case of war would deploy into three divisions; and a mountain division. The cavalry would be reduced by seven divisions to twenty-three cadre and mountain divisions, two Cossack divisions that would be territorial in structure, and five cavalry corps. The numbers of tank units and their strength would remain the same, but the overall number of assigned tanks would grow from 4,950 to 9,570. Artillery, which the RKKA divided into three types—troop artillery, artillery of the reserve of the commander in chief, and antiaircraft artillery—would be increased by adding to the division a second artillery regiment, a battalion of antitank rifles, and regimental mortar platoons. Two artillery regiments would be added to the twenty rifle corps. The numbers of weapons in troop artillery would increase from 6,810 to 8,900.

The air force would improve qualitatively and increase numerically from 9,385 to 11,049. Proportionally there would be 55 percent bombers, 34.7 percent fighters, and 9.9 percent reconnaissance aircraft. In the period from 1 January 1939 to 1 January 1943, the navy was to enjoy the most remarkable growth in battleships, from 3 to 19; in cruisers, from 7 to 20; and in submarines, from 221 to 341 (Zakharov 1970, 11). As Adam B. Ulam has observed, "Stalin had great ambitions for the Soviet navy. . . ." He did not believe that the day of the great surface vessels was over—he liked big things. He envied Britain and Japan. At the same time, naval personnel were cut down more piteously than were those in the army. Naval personnel, by the very nature of their duties, were more exposed to foreign contacts and, in the mind of the great paranoiac, more vulnerable to seditious ideas and espionage (Ulam 1973, 489).

## THE SPANISH CIVIL WAR

The outbreak of the Spanish civil war in 1936 provided an opportunity for the arms specialists of the European powers to test under combat conditions the effectiveness of the various new weapon systems that had been developed since the end of World War I. The Soviets, supporting the Republican government of Spain, claim to have delivered to the Republican forces more than 600 aircraft, 400 tanks and armored vehicles, 1,100 artillery pieces, 20,000 machine guns, and 500,000 rifles during the period 1936–39. The Soviet armed forces also permitted about 3,000 "volunteers" to advise and assist the Republican armed forces. Among these were two future marshals of the Soviet Union, R. Ia. Malinovskii and K. A. Meretskov, and a future admiral of the fleet, N. G. Kuznetsov. Unfortunately for the volunteers, their service in Spain occurred during the period when the paranoia of the military purges was at its zenith. Many of those who served with honor against the Franco-led Spanish nationalists and their Italian and German supporters were received with suspicion when they returned to the Soviet Union. After all, they had opportunities for unsupervised contacts with foreigners. Another ironic consequence of the Soviet military experience in Spain was that at least one of the specialist-advisers to the Republican forces drew the wrong conclusion from his encounters there with large tank formations. Dmitrii Grigor'evich Pavlov, who returned from Spain in 1937 to become chief of the armor directorate of the RKKA, argued against the retention of the tank corps in the order of battle of the RKKA. In his opinion, a tank corps was unsuitable for "raiding" the enemy's rear areas because it would not be possible to achieve a breakthrough of an enemy's position large enough to move a cumbersome tank formation through the breach. (In 1938, a tank corps was authorized to have 560 tanks and 12,710 troops.) The corps would have to be reinforced with infantry, artillery, and aviation, and the corps commander would not be able to command and control all of these supporting units (Ryzhakov 1968, 109). Pavlov's objections to including a tank corps in the menu of tank-heavy organizations authorized in the Soviet armored force were made in August 1939 before a committee of the Main Military Council, which was considering the organizational lessons of the Spanish experience. The committee did not accept Pavlov's recommendation, but in November 1939 the Main Military Council decided to disband the tank corps. By that time, the council had the benefit of the experience of the tank corps in the "liberating" campaigns in the western

Ukraine and Belorussia. There, the 15th Tank Corps of the Belorussian Military District and the 25th Tank Corps of the Kiev Military District had encountered great difficulty in controlling their subordinate tank brigades and had fallen behind even the cavalry divisions. The Main Military Council decided to disband the corps and form instead 15 motorized divisions: 8 in 1940 and 7 in 1941. Each division would have a total of 275 tanks. Of these, 258 would eventually be the new T-34 in place of the BT-7. By May 1940, 4 of these divisions had been formed (Ryzhakov 1968, 109, 110).

In May 1940, the German Wehrmacht demonstrated in France and the Low Countries how it intended to use its new armored forces. It was not going to use its tanks for "raids" but rather in conjunction with mechanized infantry and artillery supported by close support aviation to break through the enemy forward defenses, disrupt his rear areas, defeat his reserves, and—in the case of Holland, Belgium, and France—drive them out of the war. Although the Wehrmacht had demonstrated this capability in Poland in 1939, its significance had been dismissed because the Polish forces were considered inferior to the French and the British. It also should have been recognized as a Teutonic version of "deep operations," as a successful application of the theories of Tukhachevsky and Triandafillov. Unfortunately, Stalin and his close advisers were apparently still overoccupied with the problem of exposing traitors, spies, and saboteurs.

## DEVELOPING THE WEAPONS TO MEET THE THREAT

As the high command struggled with the complicated organizational questions of the proper mix of tanks, infantry, and artillery and the requirements for logistical support, a similar struggle was taking place among those responsible for developing and producing the weapons and equipment capable of defending against an aggressive foe possessing Europe's most highly developed military industrial complex. The problem was complicated by the fact that Stalin's personal authority in the Soviet state in all matters and especially in the area of national defense was absolute. In addition, he retained a predilection to appoint and retain in their positions mediocrities whose principal qualification was that they served with him during the defense of Tsaritsyn during the civil war. Voroshilov, whose limited capabilities have already been demonstrated to the reader, had no real authority but could be a significant roadblock as he conducted the daily business of the Commissariat of Defense. In May 1937, the *glavnoe artilleriskoe upravlenie* (GAU, or main artillery directorate) was entrusted to Grigorii Ivanovich Kulik, who became a marshal of the Soviet Union in 1940 and the dimensions of whose mediocrity remain to be explored. In November 1937, fresh from his volunteer service in Spain, Dmitrii Grigor'evich Pavlov was entrusted with the *avtobronetankovoe upravlenie* (ABTU, or armor directorate) of the RKKA. Pavlov, who was commissioned in the cavalry, had risen to command a mechanized brigade before going to Spain in 1936 where he also commanded a mechanized brigade (SVE 4:517; SVE 6:185). The GAU and the ABTU had the responsibility of establishing the requirements for the weapon systems, their characteristics, and the relationship between them needed for their respective branches. They were also responsible for testing and the eventual acceptance of the finished products furnished by the various defense production facilities.

## ONE DESIGNER'S EXPERIENCE

Vasilii Gavrilovich Grabin, who graduated from the Military Technical Academy named for Dzerzhinskii in the spring of 1930 at the age of thirty and who served throughout the period of the prewar rearmament program, has left an instructive memoir of the decision-making process, the decision makers, and the prevailing climate during the five year plans. His first assignment was to a government commission that was to inspect all artillery units in the Smolensk area for the condition of their weapons, ammunition, all associated instruments, and mobilization reserves. Each group of inspectors was to render a judgment as to whether the unit inspected was combat ready. This gave Grabin the opportunity to see for himself the extent to which Soviet artillery was still tsarist artillery and in urgent need of modernization. Following this assignment, Grabin joined a design bureau (GKB-38) located in Moscow and eventually led a group of twelve young designers to a bureau at a new factory, number 92, located at Privolzh'e, near Iaroslavl. Factory 92 was under the jurisdiction of the Commissariat for Heavy Industry, headed at that time by Sergo Ordzhonikidze.

The breakup of GKB-38 at the end of 1933 was caused by a decision of the then chief of armaments, Mikhail Nikolaevich Tukhachevsky, who became enamored with the possibilities of recoilless *(dinamoreaktivnaia)* artillery. Recoilless artillery, as Grabin recognized, has a number of advantages over conventional artillery for close support of infantry on the battlefield. A recoilless weapon is relatively lighter than a conventional weapon of the same caliber, and it is relatively easier to construct. Its disadvantages include the exposure of the weapon's position from the escaping gases through the rear ports after the gun is fired, a danger zone of twenty to thirty meters behind the weapon, and the large consumption of powder. These limitations weighed against its use as a tank weapon, an antitank weapon, and an antiaircraft weapon.

The GKB-38 was to be disbanded and its premises and equipment turned over to a new bureau devoted to the development of weapons based on the recoilless principle. Those members of GKB-38 who were engaged in the development of conventional artillery were authorized to offer their services to any other branch of industry.

Grabin, citing the situation in Germany that worsened each month after the appointment of Adolf Hitler as chancellor in January 1933, questioned why, when so much effort was being expended to rearm the country, a working center developing conventional artillery was disbanded. Was this an accident? Or had someone confused Tukhachevsky? (Grabin 1989, 52–56). One suspects that, had Grabin's memoir been written at an earlier time, the next question would have been "Or, was this sabotage?"

Before Grabin and his young colleagues could really begin to do what they had dreamed of doing at Factory 92, the factory director informed Grabin that he did not want the young designers to become engaged in experimental construction but instead wanted them to devote themselves to the factory's problems with series production. Therefore, the large number of designers in Grabin's bureau were not needed, and at least half of them should be transferred elsewhere.

Grabin wisely decided to play for time, saying that there was no need to hurry. After conferring with his young colleagues, he decided to use his next trip to Moscow to visit the main military mobilization directorate of the Ministry of Heavy Industry. There, he received authority to design and produce a new model of a division artillery piece. The decision was passed to his factory in the form of an order in which his name was not mentioned. The new model would be placed in competition with a "universal" model, the design of which was already under way. A universal gun was one that could, in theory, perform as an antiaircraft, an antitank, or a general support weapon. The concept was being explored by many foreign armies at the time, and the main artillery directorate had ordered a Soviet design bureau to produce a similar weapon.

In Grabin's opinion, the universal gun could not meet the requirement for a new division weapon. Its muzzle velocity would be less than that needed for an effective antiaircraft gun. Although it would not be a bad antitank weapon, it would be too heavy to have the battlefield mobility required of a weapon that would be towed by horses or trucks and manhandled in and out of position (Grabin 1989, 77). As the principal artillery support weapon of a division, its importance to the RKKA cannot be overestimated, both its battlefield function and in terms of the numbers of such weapons that would be required to supply the divisions that the Soviets would eventually field.

The 76mm division gun F-22 was accepted for the RKKA in 1936 after a series of field tests and only after Stalin personally made a decision on 14 June 1935 against further consideration of the universal gun (Grabin 1989, 138). Stalin's role in the development of this weapon is remarkable. In addition to making the decision against the development of the universal gun, he was present on three other occasions when decisions were made concerning the F-22. These included a meeting in the Kremlin in May 1936, when those involved in the gun's development were decorated (Grabin 1989, 113–76). On the indoor occasions, Stalin would pace around the hall, smoking his pipe, commenting occasionally, calming the rapporteur if he had been rudely interrupted by Voroshilov or Molotov, and playing the role of the calm, all-knowing, confident chief. For those who did not experience his rages, it is hardly surprising that, during the purges, many assumed that he was unaware of what his subordinates were doing.

## DESIGNING TANK GUNS

Grabin became involved in the design of tank guns after a chance meeting at Sochi in the summer of 1937 with a young engineer, P. E. Sorkin, from the main artillery directorate (GAU), who was concerned that insufficient attention was being given to the tank guns being designed and developed for new Soviet tanks. As a result, a gun designed by the Kirov factory, the L-11, was to be used in the new medium and heavy tanks despite its relatively low muzzle velocity and an organic defect in its recoil system that would take the weapon out of action after a certain number of firings. The young engineer had brought his concerns to the attention of the chief of the GAU, Kulik, without result. Nevertheless, Sorkin urged Grabin to design a more powerful and reliable gun for the new tanks on an initiative basis, and he eventually produced an order authorizing Grabin's design bureau to develop a new 76mm tank gun.

Prior to initiating work on the new gun, Grabin visited the ABTU and its chief, corps commander D. G. Pavlov, hoping to receive some guidance on the directorate's ideas for the parameters of the new gun. There he found that the directorate and Pavlov were content with the prospect that the new tank would be equipped with the L-11 and that they did not foresee a need for a new gun. He also determined that he and his design bureau had views on the combat role of the tank that did not coincide with those prevailing in the tank directorate.

Grabin and his colleagues believed that a tank was primarily a gun platform. Pavlov and the ABTU considered the tank to be the vehicle for mechanized cavalry and were far more concerned that the tank be light and speedy. They rejected as a secondary consideration not deserving much attention Grabin's contention that a tank needed firepower. Grabin suggested that if speed was such an important consideration, a more powerful engine should be developed. Pavlov responded that a more powerful engine could not always be procured. He also objected that a more powerful gun would have to have a long barrel, which would be dangerous for a tank in the passage of ditches and tank traps in which a long barrel might hit the ground and become plugged or otherwise impede the tank's mobility. Pavlov closed the conversation by repeating that speed was the most important characteristic for a tank, enabling it to change position rapidly, use the terrain for cover, and burst on the enemy's position without overly exposing itself to hostile fire (Grabin 1989, 341, 342).

Despite the discouraging reception at the ABTU of the idea of a new tank gun, Grabin and his bureau designed and tested a new gun, the F-32, a 76mm gun that eventually became the main armament for the KV heavy tank. The L-11, as Grabin and Sorkin had expected, failed its field tests. In the opinion of Grabin, a 76mm gun was still not powerful enough for a heavy tank. This shortcoming was obvious in the fall of 1939 when word was received that the French had armed a heavy tank with a 155mm gun. The French gun was five and a half times more powerful than the F-32.

In this atmosphere, Grabin's design bureau began work on a gun for the new medium tank, the T-34. Again, Grabin looked in vain to the GAU and the ABTU for guidance as to the desirable characteristics of the new weapon. The ABTU refused to give Grabin any information, saying that the new tank already had a gun selected for it. The design bureau developed its own characteristics and proceeded to fabricate the 76mm F-34. Because of the experience gained from the design of the F-32, the F-34 was built in six months. The gun as originally designed had a barrel that was one and a half meters longer than that of the F-32. When the ABTU was informed of the length of the barrel, it insisted it be shortened by ten calibers— 762mm. That reduced the gun's power by 35 percent. Even shortened, the F-34 was considerably more powerful than the gun that the ABTU had planned for the T-34. And, as was to be determined, the power of the F-34 was eight times that of the German medium tank, the T-3 (Grabin 1989, 358, 359).

The first factory tests of the F-34 coincided with the start of the war with Finland in late November 1939. The gun was mounted on the light tank, the BT-7, which was normally equipped with a 45mm gun. The BT-7 weighed 13.8 tons and could be moved either on its wheels or on tracks. Its top speed on tracks was 53.4 kilometers (33 miles) per hour. The gun passed the tests with flying colors, but no tank needed it. The T-34 had undergone its factory testing with the 76mm gun, the L-11, in spite of the shortcomings of that gun's recoil system. The tank's designers, however, were not satisfied with the L-11 and were surprised and pleased that another gun was available. The F-34 was soon mounted in the T-34, and the new tank was sent to the Finnish *front* for what was in effect the ultimate field test. Surprisingly, Grabin and his design bureau never received the results of the test against the Finns. Nor could the GAU or the ABTU give an account of how the tank and the gun had performed. Finally, Grabin persuaded the director of his factory to proceed with series production of the F-34, even though he was told by the new head of the ABTU, Iakov Nikolaevich Fedorenko, that, as far as his directorate was concerned, the T-34 already had a gun and did not need another one (Grabin 1989, 382).

It was not until sometime in 1941, after the tank and the gun had been in combat service against the Germans, during a session of the State Committee of Defense (GKO), that Grabin was able to get recognition for the F-34. He explained that the gun had never received official acceptance, that his factory had proceeded to put the gun into series production without authorization, and that the tank and the gun were performing successfully in the field. After hearing Grabin's story, Stalin ordered Ia. N. Fedorenko, the head of the ABTU, to conduct the necessary acceptance tests on the F-34. The tests, which included firing 1,000 rounds with the main armament, were completed successfully in five days (and nights), and the F-34 was officially accepted as the main armament for the T-34 tank (Grabin 1989, 384, 385).

## ARMAMENT FOR THE HEAVY TANK

Selection and development of the main armament for a new heavy tank involved a similar tortuous, subjective, and unscientific process. As has been noted, Grabin and his design bureau were at odds with the ABTU over the concept of increasing the power of the guns for each class of tank. They believed that the gun on a heavy tank should be more powerful than the gun on a medium tank. They did not believe that the 76mm F-32 was an appropriate gun for the KV-1 and proceeded to work on an 85mm and a 107mm model. These projects were put aside during the development of the F-32 and F-34. Their opponents resisted the development of more powerful weapons because those weapons would require longer barrels (Grabin 1989, 478). They were also against a more powerful gun because they thought such guns would require a larger fighting compartment to accommodate the recoil and would thus spoil the silhouette of the tank— making it taller or broader or both and hence more vulnerable.

The matter came to a head in early 1941 when Marshal Kulik became convinced from intelligence reporting that the German Army was rearming its armored force with tanks with increased armor and guns of more than 100mm caliber. Kulik was convinced that all Soviet artillery from 45mm to 76mm caliber would shortly become ineffective. Kulik was therefore proposing to cease production of all artillery pieces from 45mm to 76mm in caliber and converting their productive capacity to 107mm, the majority of which would be tank guns. Kulik made this proposal to B. L. Vannikov, the commissar of armaments, who paid little attention to it because Kulik was known for his effusiveness and his predilection to believe all manner of rumors.

Kulik, however, received support "from above" and within several days was visiting the various plants producing artillery weapons to canvass their capability to produce the 107mm guns. After Kulik made his survey, Vannikov was contacted by Stalin and asked why he was opposed to Kulik's proposal. Vannikov responded that the Commissariat of Armaments was aware that as late as 1940, the largest gun on a German tank was 75mm, and that since, as a rule, the armor of a tank was roughly equal to the caliber of its gun, the Soviet arsenal was capable of defending against German armored forces. It was also doubtful that the Germans could improve their forces to the extent that the intelligence report indicated in less than a year. If it was necessary to improve the armor-defeating capability of Soviet tank weapons, Vannikov favored improving the 76mm gun and then considering converting the 85mm antiaircraft gun to tank and antitank use. He also opposed halting the production of other artillery pieces in favor of the 107mm gun.

At this point, A. A. Zhdanov entered the room, and Stalin said to him, "Vannikov doesn't want to make 107mm guns for the Leningrad [the new heavy] tanks. And these guns are very good, I know them from the Civil War." Zhdanov answered, "Vannikov is always opposed to everything—that is his style of work."

Stalin then appointed Zhdanov to head a commission including Vannikov, Kulik, and others to investigate the matter and provide a recommendation. Stalin ended the session by repeating that he considered the 107mm gun to be a good gun; he was referring to a field gun of the civil war that had nothing in common with the gun that would be needed for the new heavy tank. Vannikov observed that one of Stalin's casual remarks usually decided the matter, and that this case was no exception (Vannikov 1962, 79–81).

Grabin did not become aware of these conversations until much later. He had been surprised by a visit from Kulik to his design bureau. The marshal had been particularly interested in whether the 107mm gun could be installed on a heavy tank. And he had been startled while in Leningrad to receive a call from Stalin during which the dictator raised the same question and asked him to come to Moscow the next day.

By the time Grabin reached Moscow, Zhdanov's commission had had one meeting and was disbanded when Zhdanov accused Vannikov of sabotaging the armament effort because he did not permit the representatives of the armament industry to express their opinions. Vannikov, in turn, accused Zhdanov of disarming the army on the eve of a war. Zhdanov said he would report Vannikov to Stalin, then he closed the meeting.

When Grabin joined Zhdanov's commission, it consisted of Fedorenko, representing the ABTU; representatives of the plant constructing the tank; and Grabin, representing the artillery constructors and designers. During the discussions, Grabin was opposed by Fedorenko and the representatives of the tank plant. Their position remained unchanged; for them, the most important features of the tank were its armor and maneuverability. The discussions, which lasted two days, concluded with a dispute over the time allowed to produce the tank and the gun. Grabin was ready to agree to produce the gun in forty-five days. Zhdanov and the others tried to laugh Grabin out of the room. When Zhdanov saw that he was serious, he accepted his promise but told him he could have more time if he wanted it. The decision to arm the new tank with a 107mm gun was approved on 6 April 1941. Stalin informed Vannikov of the decision and told him to inform all plant directors to cease production of 45mm and 76mm guns and to take all equipment from the shops not needed for the production of 107mm guns.

In early June 1941, Vannikov was arrested and was being held in solitary confinement when the war started. From the first days of the war it was clear that an unforgivable error had been committed. The German armored forces were equipped with a variety of tanks, and they were by no means first class. They included a number of captured French tanks and 926 of the obsolete German models T-I and T-II armed with a 20mm gun, which the Wehrmacht had not planned to use against the Red Army (Vannikov 1962, 81).

As the Soviet forces retreated, they lost large numbers of their field guns and ammunition, production of which had been halted. A crash program was instituted to restore the production of 45mm and 76mm guns at the plants were they had formerly been produced. Orders to produce these weapons were also given to other military and civilian plants. Some of these plants were equipped to handle much larger guns and equipment leading to what Vannikov called "technological barbarism." Through these efforts the production of 76mm guns began to level out in six months, and in 1942 it began to exceed that of the second half of 1941 (Vannikov 1962, 81, 82).

Grabin's design bureau proceeded to design a 107mm tank gun, the F-42, which was based on the 107mm field gun, the M-6. The first round was fired by the new gun on 14 May 1941, one day earlier than promised. But the new heavy tank was not ready for the gun. The gun was nevertheless put into series production, which was eventually brought to a halt because of the delay in producing the tank. But a halt was not ordered until 800 powerful new guns were produced. These guns were fated to be shipped to an open-hearth furnace and melted down. As 107mm guns, they were never used against the enemy. When the new heavy tank, the IS-1, appeared in 1943, it was armed initially with an 85mm gun, but in December a

122mm gun became the main armament. The harsh experience of combat had proven Grabin right.

It is probably true that in the haste and confusion of the unexpected outbreak of the war, there were similar cases of waste in all of the wartime production of the major arms manufacturers. The causes could range from mistaken priorities to bureaucratic infighting. What seems remarkable about the case of the 107mm gun was that the man who caused the problem was clearly identifiable and that he apparently suffered no consequences. Instead, shortly after the war broke out, he was sent on a critical assignment in which he accomplished no recognizable good. How many casualties the Soviet Army suffered because of the absence of antitank guns in the summer of 1941 will never be known.

## THE SKIRMISHING INTENSIFIES

While the Soviet arms industry was struggling with the problems of rearmament, and the General Staff was striving to develop the proper organizational forms to ensure that the new weapons would be effectivly employed, and the Soviet dictator was continuing to assure himself that his army was loyal, events in Europe and Asia continued to move to their cataclysmic conclusion. In 1936, German troops entered the Rhineland, Italian forces entered Abyssinia, and Japan joined the AntiCommintern Pact. In January 1937, Hitler withdrew Germany's signature from the Treaty of Versailles. In November of that year, Hitler decided to use armed force against Austria and Czechoslovakia. The Anschluss with Austria was accomplished on 11–12 March 1938, and in the next month Hitler began to discuss openly the fate of the 300,000 Sudeten Germans in Czechoslovakia. By September, Prime Minister Chamberlain of Great Britain was in Berchtesgaden arranging for the secession of the Sudeten areas to Germany. Their loss deprived the Czechs of their mountain barrier and its fortifications. The country was left defenseless before the rearming Germans. At Munich on 29–30 September, the transaction was completed.

The Soviet response to these events was to bring sixty rifle and ten cavalry divisions, three tank corps, twenty-two separate tank brigades, and seventeen aviation brigades to combat readiness. These steps required the call-up of 330,000 reservists and the retention on active duty of tens of thousands of conscripts who had completed their term of service. The fact of these measures was communicated to the French military attaché in Moscow. The problem was that the Soviet Union did not have a common border with Czechoslovakia in 1938, and the Poles would not permit the passage of Soviet troops through their territory. In addition, the Poles had their designs on a portion of Czech territory, which they realized in March 1939 when Germany completed the destruction of Czechoslovakia (Zakharov 1989, 115, 116). Following these events, Litvinov was removed from his post as People's Commissar of Foreign Affairs and replaced by Molotov in May 1939. A sharp change was coming in Soviet foreign policy.

## HALHIN GOL—STALIN FINDS A COMBAT LEADER

Hitler now turned his attention to Poland. His initial demands were the return of Danzig, a superhighway, and a rail line with extraterritorial rights across the Polish corridor. The Japanese chose this moment to attempt another test of Soviet resolve in the (Soviet) far east, this time along the border between Manchuria and Mongolia, with whom the Soviets were bound by a mutual aid pact dating from March 1936. The initial Japanese probe by about 2,500 troops was beaten back by a Soviet Mongolian force on 28 May. In early July a second attempt by a larger Japanese force enabled it to establish a position on the right bank of the Halhin Gol north of the Bain Tsagan Mountains. The Soviet troops involved in these actions were units of the 57th Corps, commanded by N. V. Feklenko. According to M. V. Zakharov, who was present during a conversation between Voroshilov and Shaposhnikov on 1 June, Voroshilov gave as his opinion that Feklenko should be replaced with a good cavalry officer. Zakharov recommended corps commander Zhukov, whom he had known during his service in the Belorussian Military District. Zhukov was now inspector of a horse cavalry–mechanized group in the Belorussian Military District. The next day Zhukov was in Moscow.

## GEORGII KONSTANTINOVICH ZHUKOV

Georgii Konstantinovich Zhukov was forty-three years old when he arrived in Moscow on 2 June 1939. He was the son of an impoverished shoemaker peasant and a physically powerful woman who at times lifted 180-pound sacks of grain to supplement the family income. Georgii completed the village three-year parochial school with praise at the age of ten and was apprenticed to his uncle, a successful Moscow furrier, at the age of eleven. At the age of fifteen he became a submaster furrier. During World War I he was conscripted into the Russian Army, where he was wounded and decorated and became a noncommissioned officer. After the February Revolution, he became a Bolshevik sympathizer and, in March 1919, he became a Party member. During the civil war, he served as a cavalryman, rising to the command of a cavalry squadron by the end of the war in 1920.

Zhukov remained in the Red Army after the war, and by 1937 he was given command of a cavalry corps. As a corps commander, a *komkor* in the system of ranks then employed by the Red Army, Zhukov was in one of the most vulnerable personnel categories during the purges of 1937–38. By the end of 1938, thirty-three Red Army corps were without commanders and sixty of the sixty-seven *komkor* had been repressed (S. P. Ivanov 1990, 27, 28). That Zhukov escaped was due in no small measure to his personal courage in standing up to his accusers. Even so, when Zhukov was ordered to report to Moscow on 2 June 1939, he and his family feared that he would be arrested there.

In Moscow, he was briefed on the situation in Mongolia, ordered to go there, and, if necessary, to take command of the Soviet and Mongolian troops who were confronting the Japanese. On arriving at Tamsag Bulag, the headquarters of the 57th Corps, 120 kilometers from the scene of the action, he found that the corps commander had not visited the area. This suggests that the corps commander may have been under a restriction from Moscow similar to the one placed on Bliukher at Lake Khasan in 1938 not to leave his headquarters. Zhukov, who was under no such restriction, after a personal reconnaissance recommended that the Soviet-Mongolian troops continue to hold their positions on the right (east) bank of the Halhin Gol while a force was assembled behind the west bank of the river to drive the Japanese back over the border. The force that Zhukov recommended for the west bank was to include additional aviation, three infantry divisions, artillery reinforcements, and one tank brigade. He also volunteered to take command of the Soviet forces.

Zhukov's recommendations were approved. He was initially placed in command of the 57th Corps, which was to become the First Army Group* on 15 July. While awaiting the arrival of reinforcements, Zhukov was confronted with the problem of an unauthorized directive issued by then army commander of the first rank Kulik, still head of the main artillery directorate, who was in the area to instruct Soviet artillery units committed to the operation. Kulik, exceeding his authority, ordered the bulk of the 57th Corps to withdraw to the west bank of the Halhin Gol to be reorganized, reinforced, and refitted. Zhukov, who disagreed with Kulik's order, appealed to Moscow. Kulik was overruled, rebuked for exceeding his authority, and, on 20 July, ordered to return to Moscow. Although Kulik's orders were promptly countermanded, the Japanese managed to occupy two important terrain features in the confusion of the partial withdrawal.

When Kulik returned to Moscow, he immediately obtained an audience with Voroshilov at which he recommended that five to seven divisions be sent to Halhin Gol. Otherwise the Japanese would soon be in Chita. Voroshilov rejected Kulik's recommendations and rebuked him because of his panic-stricken reaction (Zakharov 1989, 154, 155).

The first reinforcements to arrive were the air elements, in time to contest a Japanese attempt to gain air superiority over the incursion area. In these air battles, which lasted from 22 to 26 June. the Japanese lost 64 planes. After that, the air conflict continued daily but on a reduced scale. In early July, the Japanese managed to insert what Zhukov claimed were 10,000 troops, around 100 artillery pieces, and 60 antitank guns across the Halhin Gol to take up posi-

---

*The Soviet designation should not be confused with a U.S. Army Group, which is a group of armies. The Soviet equivalent of a U.S. Army Group was a *front*. An *armeiskaia gruppa* in the Soviet Army was a temporary combined arms unit formed to accomplish a particular mission. Such groups were often called operational groups during World War II.

tions on the Bain Tsagan Mountains. They moved this force through the Mongolian cavalry division responsible for the security of the right flank of the Soviet-Mongolian position. The incursion was discovered during a routine check of the Mongolian position. Zhukov reacted immediately before the Japanese could complete their digging in. The penetration was wiped out in the course of two days of hard fighting and heavy Japanese losses due to the immediate availability of a Soviet tank brigade and a mechanized brigade plus a Mongolian armored battalion armed with 45mm guns. The Japanese infiltrators had no armor (Zhukov 1990, I:244–46). After this catastrophe, except for an attack by a reinforced regiment on 12 August, which had some success against one of the Mongolian divisions, the Japanese limited themselves primarily to reconnaissance patrols.

Zhukov makes no attempt to explain how, in the relatively narrow confines of the Halhin Gol battlefield, the Japanese could have infiltrated 10,000 armed troops with supporting weapons through the Mongolian troops and across the Halhin Gol. The episode suggests that liaison with the Mongolians at that time was poor or nonexistent or that a massive defection or collapse of the Mongolian cavalry had occurred. If Kulik knew of this episode, it may explain to some extent his "panicky" appraisal of the Soviet position at Halhin Gol.

The Soviets, taking pains to convince the Japanese that they were maintaining a defensive posture, managed a buildup of fuel, food, and ammunition to support an offensive that was scheduled to begin on 20 August. Concentration of strike forces on the east side of the Halhin Gol was accomplished mainly under the cover of night. Night sounds of the movement of tank and mechanized units were covered with sounds of aircraft engines, artillery, mortars, machine guns, and rifle fire controlled to coincide with planned movements.

Some of the Japanese commanders were absent on leave when the Soviet-Mongolian attack began at 0615 on Sunday, 20 August 1939. The initial artillery targets were Japanese antiaircraft guns and machine guns. Marking rounds were fired to locate targets for the 153 bombers and almost 100 fighters that soon appeared over the Japanese positions. At 0845, Soviet artillery and mortars switched to ground targets, and by 0900 the troops moved in to attack. During the next two days the attack continued. Japanese resistance in the area of Bol'shie Pesky (Big Sands) was particularly fierce. By 26 August, Soviet-Mongolian armored units on the flanks had completed the encirclement of the Japanese troops (Zhukov refers to them as the Sixth Army). After that day, the remainder of the operations consisted of liquidating small groups of the enemy who continued to fight to the last man.

Zhukov had executed a Cannae, a successful double envelopment, on the dry steppes of Mongolia on a battlefield 74 kilometers wide and 20 kilometers deep almost 2,000 years after Hannibal destroyed the Roman army of Terentius Varro. The form and sweep of the operation was dictated by political considerations. Stalin rejected the idea of pursuing the Japanese beyond Mongolian territory and risking a wider war. Zhukov, in addition to these considerations, accomplished the feat, despite being 750 kilometers from his sources of supply and evacuation, despite the gratuitous advice of G. M. Kulik and G. M. Shtern,* and despite the poor performance of some of his troops.**

Early in September, the Japanese made another attempt to invade Mongolia; they were defeated by the First Army Group. After the second attempt the Japanese requested an armistice, and combat operations ceased as of 16 September. Japanese losses were assessed at more than 60,000. Soviet-Mongolian losses were more than 18,500 killed and wounded.

At the end of October, the headquarters of the First Army Group moved to Ulan Bator where Zhukov was given command of the Soviet troops in Mongolia. He remained there until May 1940, when he was promoted to general of the army and given command of the Kiev Special Military District. He remained there barely six months when Stalin brought him to Moscow as chief of the General Staff. Stalin had found a general.

---

*As commander of the Transbaikal Military District, G. M. Shtern had responsibility for the logistical support of the First Army Group. During the Soviet-Mongolian offensive he became concerned with the number of casualties the Soviet

## THE WAR WITH FINLAND

When Zhukov returned from Ulan Bator in May 1940, although neither he nor Stalin realized it, the scene was almost set for the final act in Hitler's Gotterdammerung—the German invasion of Russia. During his first face-to-face meeting with the Soviet dictator, Zhukov asked for his views on the German war with the French and British, which had started on 1 September 1939. The war had diverted world attention from his victory at Halhin Gol.

The dictator's response was to the effect that France and England did not wish to become involved seriously in a war with Germany. They were still hoping to push Germany into a war with the Soviet Union. In 1939, by refusing to enter into a pact against Hitler with the Soviet Union, they had demonstrated their desire to encourage him to move against Russia. He also predicted that the French and British would pay for their shortsightedness. Stalin thus gave Zhukov the short version of his rationale for the German-Soviet nonaggression pact, which he had signed on 23 August 1939, freeing Hitler to conquer Poland.

Stalin blamed Voroshilov for the poor performance of the army in the opening phase of the war with Finland. He told Zhukov that Voroshilov had headed the army for a long time and that it had not been prepared to fight as it should have been. Voroshilov had been replaced by Timoshenko, who had a better grasp of military matters than his predecessor (Zhukov 1990, 1:272).

Stalin, of course, did not tell Zhukov of his own role in the decision to solve his problems with Finland by the force of arms. The 23

---

troops were incurring. On the third day of the offensive he proposed that Zhukov halt temporarily to allow a reorganization of the attacking troops. Zhukov rejected his proposal, saying that to halt the offensive would increase the losses ten times. Shtern, after determining that he had no operational authority over Zhukov, withdrew his proposal (Simonov 1987, 53).

**For example, the 82d Rifle Division was a territorial division that broke and ran when it came under Japanese artillery fire for the first time. The episode at Bain Tsagan suggests that the Mongolian troops also left something to be desired (Simonov 1987, 53).

August pact with Germany, as even official Soviet commentators were later to admit, did not enhance the security of the Soviet Union; rather it heightened the danger. The country was now isolated, and the pact pushed the Soviet government to moves that were not thoroughly considered.

In this atmosphere, the strengthening of the defenses of Leningrad became a subject of constant concern. Although there was in existence a nonaggression pact between Finland and the Soviet Union, the Finns seemed to the Soviets to be pursuing a policy of improving their relations with Germany. There were also nationalistic forces in Finland, advocates of the idea of a "Greater Finland" created with territory torn from the Soviet Karelia and the Leningrad area. How realistic these ambitions were and how powerful their advocates were in the Finnish body politic remains a question, but it is not surprising that the suspicious, insecure Stalin, in these circumstances, felt it necessary to have additional guarantees protecting his Finnish border from a potential attack.

In March 1939, the Soviets proposed that the Finns rent them some islands in the Gulf of Finland for strengthening the approaches to Leningrad. They also proposed moving the border along the Karelian Isthmus farther to the north to take Leningrad out of the range of long-range artillery in exchange for territory to be given the Finns elsewhere. The Finns rejected both of these proposals, having in mind the recent Soviet participation in the division of Poland and the forced entry of Soviet troops into the Baltic States followed by their "request" to join the Soviet Union. The Finns also began military preparations and allegedly intensified their military contacts with Germany, England, and Sweden.

In the summer of 1939, the Main Military Council considered a plan for war against Finland developed by the General Staff and its chief, B. M. Shaposhnikov. In the plan, which considered it possible that Finland would be supported by some outside power, it was observed that defeating Finland in a short time would not be easy, and it called for the Leningrad Military District to be given reinforcements for the task. In the General Staff plan the main effort would be a drive across the Karelian Isthmus toward Vyborg and Helsinki. Stalin rejected the General Staff plan on the grounds that it overestimated the capabilities of the Finnish armed forces. He turned over the preparation of the plan and its execution to the Leningrad Military District and its commander, K. A. Meretskov.

## KIRILL AFANAS'EVICH MERETSKOV

Kirill Afanas'evich Meretskov was the forty-two-year-old commander of the Leningrad Military District when he was given the task of bending the Finns to Stalin's will. The firstborn of poor peasants, he began to help his father with the plowing at the age of seven. He learned to read and write during two winters of instruction from a retired sergeant who had served in the Russo-Turkish War and during four winters at the village elementary school. He was sent off to Moscow as an apprentice at the age of fifteen to learn the machinist's trade. By the age of eighteen he was employed in a factory engaged in war production, which enabled him to avoid conscription. He was not inclined, he admits, to "offer his stomach for the 'father-tsar.'" After participating in a wartime strike, he fled to Sudogda, a city 200 kilometers east of Moscow, where he found another war production job. It was here that he experienced the heady days of the February Revolution. He joined the local Social Democratic Revolutionary Party and was appointed chief of staff of the local detachment of Red Guards. To overcome his lack of military training, he would often take a pistol and go off into the forest early in the morning to practice marksmanship.

After the October Revolution, the Red Guard detachment assumed the responsibility of protecting the Sudogda Soviet from anti-Soviet elements in surrounding communities. Meretskov became the detachment's military commissar responsible for recruitment and training. In early July 1918, he saw his first action of the civil war when he accompanied a detachment of Red Guards sent to prevent the capture of Murom by the Whites. He did not recall that even one round whistled over his head. In early September, in the Red effort to retake Kazan, the twenty-one-year-old commissar was knocked unconscious by a blow of a rifle butt to the back of the head. It put him out of action for almost two months.

When he recovered, his request that he return to the active army was denied, and he was sent to be a student at what remained of the

Nikolaevskii General Staff Academy now in Moscow. He was to remain there for parts of almost three years; he finished in the fall of 1921. Part of these years were spent as a staff officer in units fighting Denikin and the Don Cossacks, in the course of which he was wounded again this time in the shin. While his comrades held him, the bullet was removed by a local *fel'dsher* (aid man) with a hook that had been sterilized by fire. Meretskov was hospitalized until autumn, when he resumed his studies at the General Staff Academy.

The outbreak of the Polish war in April 1920 and the threat from Vrangel's White Guards in the Crimea caused a new levy on the academy for officers. Meretskov joined the First Cavalry Army in Uman on the eve of the counteroffensive that was to retake Kiev from the Poles. En route he had his first meeting with Stalin (who was concerned that the young officer knew how to handle a horse), Budenny, and Voroshilov. Meretskov was eventually assigned as an intelligence officer with the 4th Cavalry Division. He was wounded in the leg at Korosten, and after a week of hospitalization he caught up with the army at Rovno. As the army was closing in on L'vov, Meretskov was recalled to Moscow to resume his studies at the General Staff Academy, thus missing the controversial failure of the First Cavalry Army to join Tukhachevsky and the Western *Front.*

Following the civil war, Meretskov served in various command and staff positions in the Petrograd Military District, the North Caucasus Military District, and under Voroshilov's command in the Moscow Military District. He then became military commissar following the death of Frunze. In 1928, Uborevich took command of the district. Eighteen months later Uborevich was given command of the Belorussian Military District. Meretskov, who was an admirer of Uborevich, was not able to rejoin him there until April 1932. In the meantime Meretskov had a tour of duty as commander of the 14th Rifle Division and a brief unsatisfactory tour in the Moscow Military District with A. I. Kork, whom he did not like. Meretskov became Uborevich's chief of staff and remained so until January 1935, when he was unexpectedly transferred to the same position with the Special Red Banner Far Eastern Army, commanded by V. K. Bliukher, who had been in command since 1929. Meretskov found Bliukher much like Uborevich in his speech but not as dry or penetrating.

Meretskov was given the opportunity to acquaint himself with the Soviet far east as a potential theater of military operations. He determined that the area was in need of barracks, training facilities, airfields, and roads. Eventually, he and Bliukher took their concerns
to Moscow as the international situation continued to worsen. During that visit to Moscow, Meretskov was hospitalized with persistent
tonsillitis. He did not return to the far east until 1945.

## MERETSKOV IN SPAIN

Meretskov arrived in Spain in the fall of 1936 as Franco was closing
in on Madrid. He did not relate or speculate on the reason that he
was selected for this assignment, but it may have had to do with his
extensive experience as a staff officer. The Republican government
had been left without an organized military structure when the majority of the officer corps had defected to the nationalists. The immediate task was the defense of Madrid.

After reporting to Ian Karlovich Berzin, the former chief of the
intelligence directorate of the RKKA, now the senior Soviet military
adviser in Spain, Meretskov was given the task of stiffening the defenses of the city. By early November the government was forced to
evacuate to Valencia, but shortly after this episode the Republicans
were encouraged by the arrival of the first unit of Soviet tanks to join
the defenders, a company of T-26 tanks led by an officer whom
Meretskov had known in the Belorussian Military District. Aided by
the Soviet tanks and D. G. Pavlov's tank brigade, the Republican
forces, formed and trained by Meretskov, frustrated nationalist attempts to isolate Madrid from Valencia. In early March, the Italian
Expeditionary Force, which was heavily armored, was concentrated
north of Guadalajara, a provincial capital fifty kilometers north of
Madrid. The Republicans beat off the Italians, inflicting heavy losses
in a series of battles climaxed by a counterattack led by Pavlov's tanks
that began on 19 March. By 21 March the operation had ended.

The Italian defeat, in addition to its impact on the morale of the
Italian armed forces, also had an effect on the perception of European general staffs of the effectiveness of mechanized forces on the
battlefield. The Italians had intended to demonstrate how they
could execute modern techniques of war. Instead, as Hugh Thomas

concludes, the battle was an object lesson of how a mechanized attack should not be conducted. Many tanks were left immobilized for lack of fuel. The Italians had not maintained contact with the Republican forces; they tried to operate without air cover or anti-aircraft protection. The Italian commander had only a commercial road map to aid him in directing operations, while his battalion commanders had no maps at all (Thomas 1977, 603, 604). Of the European general staffs, the French and the Soviet seemed to take the "lessons" of Guadalajara most seriously. As we have seen, the Soviets, as a result of a one-sided interpretation of the unique and limited character of the combat actions in Spain, concluded that large armored units would not be effective on the modern battlefield. The postaction reports of the battle from Pavlov and Meretskov must have influenced the decision. The four mechanized corps that the Red Army had prior to 1939 were disbanded, only to be hastily reconstituted in 1940 after the successes of the Wehrmacht in Poland and France. The Germans had been restrained from drawing this conclusion by their contempt for the Italians as soldiers (Thomas 1977, 604).

**COMMANDER OF THE LENINGRAD MILITARY DISTRICT**
The battle of Guadalajara was Meretskov's last battle on Spanish soil. On 1 June 1937, he crossed the border of the Soviet Union and the next day he was in Moscow. Shortly after arriving there, he was invited to the Commissariat of Defense. There, along with other senior officers, he was shown the materials that incriminated Tukhachevsky and the others, including Uborevich. In a few days he was in the Kremlin, where the case was discussed and some of those in attendance spoke of their suspicions of one or the other of the accused. When Meretskov was given the floor, he began to talk about his experiences in Spain, only to be challenged to speak about the important thing—did he suspect Uborevich, with whom he had worked for many years? He answered that he had trusted him and had not observed any misconduct on his part. Meretskov also commented that many of those who had spoken here of their suspicions had been silent up to now. Stalin then said, "We also trusted him and I understand you correctly" (Meretskov 1970, 167). Stalin assured

Meretskov that his service in Spain was appreciated, that the experience he had acquired there would not be wasted, and that he would soon receive a higher post.

Soon thereafter Meretskov was appointed deputy chief of the General Staff, a post he held until late 1938, when he was given command of the Volga Military District. He remained there only until February 1939, when he was transferred to command the Leningrad Military District. Although Meretskov does not mention it, these frequent changes of assignment were the result of the personnel turbulence caused by the purges. Meretskov was the third person to command the Volga Military District since Tukhachevsky had commanded it, nominally at least, in May 1937.

## PREPARING FOR THE FINNISH WAR

En route to Leningrad, Meretskov stopped off in Moscow to see commissar of defense Voroshilov, who instructed him to study the Leningrad Military District as a possible theater of military operations. The commissar warned that Stalin and the Politburo were concerned that the Finns were growing closer to the large "imperialist" states and that he would soon be asked to report on his observations (Meretskov 1970, 171).

Soon after assuming command of the district, Meretskov reviewed the district's operations plans and found that they were somewhat out of date, particularly as they applied to Finland and how it might be used by the "main enemies of socialism"—Germany, England, France, and the United States. Military intelligence in Moscow was asked for additional information, which would be predominantly economic and political in nature. Military intelligence on the Finns was sparse, especially on the so-called Mannerheim line. Meretskov also made an extensive personnel reconnaissance of the district, which stretched from Estonia along the Finnish border some 1,200 kilometers to the Barents Sea. He knew that the border at that time was only 32 kilometers from Leningrad, within range of long-range artillery fire. Inspecting the various regions of the district, sometimes accompanied by the first secretary of the Leningrad Oblast Party committee, A. A. Zhdanov, Meretskov was soon convinced that a huge effort to improve the district's infrastructure would be required. It would also be nec-

**THE RUSSO–FINNISH WAR 1939-1940**

NORWAY

Atlantic Ocean

Petsamo

Murmansk

Kandalaksha

Salla

Kemijaervi

SWEDEN

Tornea

Kem

Suomussalmi

Kajaani

SOVIET

Gulf of Bothnia

Vaasa

FINLAND

Lake Onega

Tampere

Lake Ladoga

UNION

Vyborg

Abo

Gulf of Finland

Hango

Leningrad

Stockholm

Tallin

Baltic Sea

ESTONIA

0          100
Miles

LATVIA

Occupied by Russia in October 1939

Russian attacks on Finland in November 1939

The Mannerheim Line defences, broken by Russian assaults by land, sea and air

Finnish territory ceded to Russia by the Treaty of Moscow

Russia granted access to the Norwegian border by Finland

Russia given a thirty-year lease on the strategic Hangö Peninsula essary to train and equip its troops for operations in a forested, swampy area, possibly in winter conditions. There followed a proposal to Moscow to embark on a program of road, airfield, and fortified area construction in the spring of 1939. The proposal was supported fully by Zhdanov and approved by Moscow; its implementation was followed closely by Stalin in the second half of 1939 (Meretskov 1970, 171–74).

From Meretskov's point of view, the construction was not completed fast enough. According to Meretskov, the reckless Finnish leaders of that time continued their political game, and in the fall of 1939 they punctuated their rejection of Soviet proposals with shots across the border. The Finns, he continued, had no hope of defeating the Soviets alone but were counting on the promises of aid from the "imperialist" powers to support them with troops and equipment. And, in the event that their "offensive on Leningrad" failed, they were counting on the strength of the Mannerheim line, built with foreign money under the control of foreign engineers. Curiously, for all the alleged involvement of foreigners and the possibilities of gaining information from them, the Mannerheim line was a mystery to Soviet intelligence, some of whose analysts considered the line to be nothing but propaganda. That, according to Meretskov, turned out to be a "crude miscalculation" (Meretskov 1970, 176, 177). It was not the only one.

Meretskov's recollection of how the plans to meet the Finnish "offensive" evolved acknowledged the military farsightedness of Shaposhnikov's plan. That plan was based on the assumption that the Finns might receive assistance from abroad and that any subjugation of the Finns would not be an easy task. It called for the creation of a *front* that would drive through the Mannerheim line to Vyborg and, if necessary, on to Helsinki. Stalin and his colleagues rejected it out of hand and turned the problem over to Meretskov and the Leningrad Military District. It is not clear whether there were other plans to deal with the Finns. If there were, Stalin considered them separately with different groups of people. They were not presented to the Main Military Council. Meretskov claims that in all questions dealing with the counterattack, he called Stalin directly, and he reported to Stalin personally on all matters related to Finnish affairs.

On two or three occasions Voroshilov was there and on the last occasion Mekhlis and the finance commissar, A. G. Zverev, were in attendance.

The plan that Meretskov produced called for the Finns to be subdued in twelve to fifteen days and the Mannerheim line to be enveloped by the Soviet Eighth Army attacking northeast of Lake Ladoga. The Red Army would use its 30:1 superiority in tanks, 2:1 superiority in manpower, and 5:1 superiority in aviation and artillery without considering the problem of using massed tanks in the Finnish theater with its woods and swamps and without considering the character of the Finnish defense (Portugal'skii 1994, 93).

## THE FINNISH WAR

On 26 November, Meretskov received an urgent report from the border that the Finns had opened artillery fire on Soviet border troops near the village of Mainila, killing four and wounding nine troopers. He immediately "took control" of the entire border and reported the incident to Moscow. He was ordered to prepare to counterattack. In the counterattack plan these preparations were allotted one week, but because Finnish detachments and diversionary groups were already crossing the border, the period was reduced to four days. On 30 November, regular units of the Red Army moved out with the mission of liquidating the Finnish "bridgehead" on the Karelian Isthmus (Meretskov 1970, 182).

It is noteworthy that Meretskov immediately took control of the border without driving the thirty kilometers or so to investigate the incident in person or sending a staff officer to do so. The border guards under normal circumstances are under the operational control of the state security organs. Only under extraordinary circumstances would the military district commander take control. The sequence of events, as outlined by Meretskov, suggests that the incident was preplanned, as was the "counterattack." The Finns investigated the incident immediately and determined that their border units had logged the fact that seven probable artillery rounds had been heard exploding at the time of the reported incident on the Soviet side of the border. There was no Finnish artillery within range of the explosions (Tanner 1992, 86).

It took the Red Army almost two weeks to move through the Finnish security zone, which was heavily mined and fortified—circumstances that did not suggest that the Finns had serious offensive plans. After a five day artillery preparation, the Soviet Seventh Army continued to attack the main fortifications but was unable to move forward. After reporting to Stalin in Moscow, Meretskov returned with instructions to conduct a reconnaissance in force to determine the number and construction of the Finnish strongpoints, which seemed impervious to Soviet light artillery fire.

Meretskov admits that it was only after increased aerial reconnaissance during the month of January that maps showing the location of all the strongpoints became available. It was also determined that the strongpoints were constructed of one and a half to two meters of high-quality reinforced concrete covered with two to three meters of compacted earth. Their embrasures were reinforced with several layers of armor plate. Grabin was correct in his recommendation that Soviet tanks and self-propelled guns needed more powerful main armament to neutralize such obstacles. One solution to this problem was the KV-2, hastily armed with a 152mm howitzer. As Grabin describes this vehicle, it was not designed to perfection. The overall silhouette of the tank was vertical, making it a perfect target for antitank gunners. But it performed its tactical mission successfully. Its successor, the SU-152, had a lower profile and played the role of a firing battering ram in the tank battles of World War II (Grabin 1989, 389).

By the end of December, it had become obvious to Stalin that Meretskov and the forces available to the Leningrad Military District were not capable of winning a quick decision. Newsreel audiences around the world were being shown clips of Finnish ski troops in white camouflage scooting through the snowy forests around the wrecks of Soviet military equipment and groups of bedraggled Soviet prisoners of war. The Finnish resistance was also inspiring the British and French publics to do more than just applaud Finnish grit and skill but to pressure their governments to send aid to the Finns. The Soviet Union after all had been at least the silent partner of the Nazis in the fourth partition of Poland. Stalin, realizing the dangers of a prolonged war and the damage the Soviet image was suffering, decided to put the Shaposhnikov plan into effect. Semen Konstantinovich Timoshenko, then commanding the Kiev Military District, volunteered for command of the newly created Northwest *Front* (Portugal'skii, 1994, 96). Meretskov remained in command of a reinforced Seventh Army. The month of January was used to train the entire force on how to fight under the conditions of the Winter War.

On 11 February, after a heavy artillery preparation, the Red Army attacked, and after six days the Seventh Army had penetrated the main belt of the Finnish defenses. Two more weeks were required to reduce the second and third belts to reach the two-belt defensive system around Vyborg. Here the Red Army faced the complication that the spring thaw would enable the Finns to flood the entire area before the city. The Soviets were fortunate in that the thaw was late in 1940. The ice held and they were able to storm the city. The Finns sued for peace, and the war ended on 13 March 1940 (Meretskov 1970, 175–89).

In early June, Meretskov was promoted to the new rank of general of the army as the Red Army introduced general officer ranks. In the summer of 1940, after Timoshenko became commissar of defense, replacing Voroshilov, Meretskov was named deputy commissar in charge of combat training and the higher military schools. In this position, Meretskov accompanied Timoshenko on visits to the Moscow, Leningrad, Belorussian, and Kiev Military Districts to observe training exercises at the division level. The type of exercise that was stressed was that of an infantry division in the attack of an enemy in a prepared position with combat firing. In Belorussia, they conducted a staff exercise with two tank corps. Meretskov and Timoshenko agreed after these visits that the level of proficiency of the rifle units was better than that of the tank units. Meretskov held the opinion that there were still too few tank units and that their level of proficiency was unsatisfactory.

In the course of reporting these findings to Stalin in August 1940, the participants were invited to his quarters for supper. Meretskov was surprised to be nominated and appointed chief of the General Staff, replacing Shaposhnikov. At the time, Stalin told those present that Shaposhnikov was in failing health and had to be replaced (Meretskov 1970, 195).

The dictator told Shaposhnikov that he was being relieved because, although he had been right about Finland, only he and Stalin knew that and the world would not understand if the chief of the General Staff were allowed to continue in office while the commissar of defense was dismissed. Everyone knew that the commissar and the chief of staff worked closely together and that by relieving both, enemies of the Soviet Union would understand that the lessons of the Finnish War had been thoroughly absorbed. Shaposhnikov responded to Stalin's contrived logic by saying he was ready to serve wherever he was assigned. Stalin made him a deputy commissar of defense in charge of the construction of the fortified areas in the newly annexed territories on the western borders of the Soviet Union (Vasilevsky 1973, 107).

By that time the Soviets, under a new leader—Timoshenko—were engaged in correcting the deficiencies in the armed forces that had been exposed in the Finnish campaign.

# 10
# TIMOSHENKO TRIES TO ANSWER THE FINNISH WAKE-UP CALL

## REPERCUSSIONS OF THE FINNISH WAR

The end of the Finnish war was followed almost immediately by a series of meetings at the upper levels of the Soviet state. The results and lessons of the war were examined during the March plenary session of the Central Committee of the Party. If for no other reason, the tremendous number of casualties suffered by the Red Army demanded drastic action: an estimated 48,745 killed and 158,863 wounded and frostbitten. (According to the last chief of the Soviet General Staff, M. Moiseev, the number killed was an appalling 67,000 [Moiseev 1990, 213].) Even Voroshilov abandoned *shapkozakidatel'stvo* and admitted that neither he nor the General Staff nor the Leningrad Military District had imagined all of the peculiarities and difficulties involved with the Finnish war. Timoshenko, who also spoke at the plenum, focused on the shortcomings in the Soviet theory and practice of troop training and supply. He proposed proceeding immediately to correct the Red Army's inability to keep pace with the progress in military affairs (Portugal'skii 1994, 105). The next month in northern France, the extent to which the Red Army had fallen behind would be vividly demonstrated by the rapidity with which the Wehrmacht overran what was considered to be the strongest army in Europe.

A meeting of an expanded session of the Main Military Council from 14 to 17 April, described by Timoshenko as the most businesslike that he had attended in many years, worked out the specifics of the corrective measures that would be necessary to overcome the deficiencies exposed by the war. Stalin, speaking to the council, admitted that the combat experience gained in the civil war was no longer relevant for coping with the problems presented by contemporary warfare and that anyone who did not understand that would be a casualty on the modern battlefield. He called for the training and promotion of a new, younger generation of leaders (Portugal'skii 1994, 106); thus, he seemed to provide an ex post facto rationale for the purges.

The council's deliberations produced a resolution entitled "On measures for combat training, organization and structure of the Red Army based on the experience of the war with Finland and the combat experience of recent years." The resolution became the guide for the theoretical and practical measures that were to be taken to overcome the Red Army's deficiencies.

Major personnel shifts soon followed. On 8 May, it was announced that Timoshenko had been promoted to marshal of the Soviet Union and that he was to become the people's commissar of defense. Zhukov would replace him as the Kiev Military District commander. Despite the army's miserable performance, Klim Voroshilov retained his high rank while apparently being kicked upstairs to the chairmanship of the Committee of Defense in the Council of People's Commissars. In August, Meretskov, who was initially appointed first deputy commissar of defense for combat training, replaced Shaposhnikov as chief of the General Staff. Budenny remained a deputy commissar of defense; he became the first deputy when Meretskov became chief of the General Staff.

The Main Military Council was revamped, and Timoshenko was to be its chairman. Its members included the chief of the General Staff at that time, Shaposhnikov; Budenny and Meretskov, deputy commissars of defense; Malenkov and Zhdanov, secretaries of the Central Committee; L. Z. Mekhlis, head of the main political directorate; the commanders of the Western and Kiev Special Military Districts, D. G. Pavlov and G. K. Zhukov; the chief of the main artillery directorate, G. I. Kulik, who was promoted to marshal of the Soviet Union for no apparent reason; and the chief of the air force directorate, Ia. V. Smushkevich.

Prior to assuming his new duties, Voroshilov and Timoshenko, assisted by Zhdanov, Malenkov, and Voznesensky, completed what was, in effect, an inventory of the Commissariat of Defense. It was not an inventory of physical property but of the presence or absence of formulated plans and policies to guide the institution charged with national defense in carrying out its functions.

Timoshenko soon discovered that his inheritance was a meager one. The document that formalized the assumption of the office of commissar listed as deficiencies, among other things, the absence of a war plan; no specific information on how the state borders were to be defended in the event of war; absence of firm views on the employment of tanks, airpower, and air assaults; and the preparation of potential theaters of military operations. Timoshenko also noted serious shortcomings in mobilization preparations and in the condition of the various arms and services. In short, fifteen years of Voroshilov's management of the Soviet defense establishment had left the country poorly prepared from a managerial standpoint to meet the challenges that were rising on both the eastern and western borders. The name of Stalin does not appear in the document. It was as if he had been on another planet while his trusted but unsupervised and uninstructed comrade had commanded the Red Army (Moiseev 1990, 215).

In early June, the central newspapers published the names and photographs of more than a thousand officers who were given the new ranks of general and admiral. During the April session of the Main Military Council, it had been recommended that the traditional officer and noncommissioned officer ranks be introduced as a measure to strengthen command authority. However, publication of such an extensive listing, with photographs, of the senior staff of the armed forces was highly unusual in Soviet practice, and it was a boon to foreign order of battle intelligence. It was apparently intended to demonstrate to the Soviet public and the world at large that, despite the extensive losses of 1937 and 1938, adequate replacements had been found. By reintroducing the old system of ranks, the new generals could be easily distinguished from those comdivs, comcors, and comandarms of the old system who had turned out to be traitors and spies. The listings also served to reintroduce some of the officers who had been falsely accused and imprisoned during the *ezhovshchina*. After Ezhov's trial, more than a quarter of the officers he had arrested were released and returned to duty, including the former commander of the 5th Cavalry Corps, K. K. Rokossovsky. At about this time, Timoshenko, the new commissar of defense, who had experienced the acute shortage of experienced senior officers while he was commander of the Kiev Military District, submitted to Stalin a list of about 300 officers who had been repressed in 1937 and 1938 and whom he had known in his service; he requested that their cases be reviewed. Prior to doing so, he consulted both Voroshilov and Budenny for their reaction to the list; they both opposed the idea. Unexpectedly, Stalin approved the review, and a number of officers were released. Apparently, Stalin also recognized that there was a shortage of senior officers (Portugal'skii 1994, 129).

The listing of the generals of 1940 also was clear evidence that Stalin's remark at the April 1940 plenum of the Central Committee had had an effect. Young officers were being trained and brought into positions of influence. The names, the new ranks, and the pictures could also be taken as signs that the purges were over and that the Red Army, under a reinvigorated leadership, was preparing to meet the challenges of the Third Reich in the west and the Rising Sun in the east.

## THE PURGES CONTINUE

Although the massive repressions of 1937 and 1938 were over, Ezhov's successor, Lavrentii Beriia, continued to campaign against the so-called "military plot" that targeted officers in the high command. Pavel Vasilevich Rychagov, who in August 1940 was appointed chief of the main directorate of the air force, was transferred ostensibly to the Academy of the General Staff in April 1941. He had flown against the Axis in Spain, the Japanese in China, and the Finns in 1940. But, as a thirty-nine-year-old two star (general-lieutenant), he had the temerity to tell Stalin during a discussion in the Main Military Council of the frequency of aviation accidents that the accident rate would continue to be high because "you are making us fly in coffins." The remark caused the room to become deadly silent. Stalin, who had been pacing up and down, halted for an instant, then resumed pacing and finally turned to Rychagov and said, "You should not have said that." After another turn around the room, Stalin faced Rychagov again, repeated what he had just said, and closed the meeting. Within a week Rychagov disappeared and was never seen again (Simonov 1988, 73).

Although Stalin devoted considerable attention to the air force and considered himself to be the patron of that service, senior air force officers were at considerable risk during this period. On the same day that Rychagov disappeared, the head of long-range aviation was arrested. Later, in 1941 and early 1942, the chief of staff of the air force, the head of Air Force Schools, and the head of the Air Force Academy were all arrested and shot.

G. M. Shtern, who was involved in the events at Halhin Gol, subsequently commanded the Eighth Army in the Finnish war and, after the war, the Far Eastern *Front*. He was called to Moscow in February 1941 to become chief of the main antiaircraft directorate, which had been established in December 1940. In March 1941, Timoshenko was given a report purporting to show that Shtern had been a Trotskyite since 1923. The report contained numerous citations from the "confessions" of previously repressed participants in the military Fascist plot. The commissar of defense ordered further investigations of Shtern, which resulted in his arrest in June. He was shot, without a trial, on 28 October 1941.

Aleksandr Dmitrievich Loktionov was also shot on 28 October as the Germans closed in on Moscow. He had commanded the Baltic Special Military District from 1940 until he was called to Moscow in February 1941; he never returned. The Baltic Military District, which was formed on 11 July 1940, was designated a "special" military district—one that was supposed to have more and stronger military units and priority in regard to personnel, new weapons, and equipment and supplies. The Belorussian (later to be named the Western) and the Kiev Military Districts were so designated in 1938. The problems that must have faced the new Baltic Military District commander, Fedor Isidorovich Kuznetsov, when he took command of the district in February 1941 can only be imagined. That he would have been able to solve them and fulfill the mission of a "special" military district by the time the war broke out four months later would have been a military miracle.

## IMPROVING DISCIPLINE AND TRAINING

As Timoshenko took over the Commissariat of Defense, he was advised by Stalin that he should give first priority to instilling in the army *tverdost* (hardness, firmness, resoluteness). Stalin told Timoshenko to focus on discipline and troop training and not to be concerned with the fact that as a member of the Council of People's Commissars he would be called on to make government-level decisions. He would become a statesman in time. In the meantime, "we will support you" (Portugal'skii 1994, 109). Timoshenko may not have realized that when Voroshilov was commissar, Stalin did the thinking about matters of state for both of them.

One of the shortcomings that was noted when Timoshenko assumed command of the Soviet defense establishment was that discipline was at a low level. During the Finnish war there had been cases of self-inflicted wounds, desertion of soldiers and junior officers, and refusals to carry out orders. After the war, absence without leave became widespread, sentries were sleeping on their posts, and drunkenness and other misdemeanors were tolerated. Within a month after Timoshenko became commissar, he forwarded a report to the Politburo designed to demonstrate that the penalties for military offenses authorized by the criminal code of the Russian republic were too lenient and did not promote discipline in the Red Army. The reaction was immediate: on 30 July a draft of a new law governing military offenses was issued. A series of other measures included a new disciplinary manual issued on 1 December 1940, which included the proposition that discipline in the Red Army must be severer and harsher than the discipline based on class subordination found in other armies. The defense of a Socialist state demanded the application of the severest measures of coercion to the violators of that discipline. These exhortations to severity led to a sharp increase in the perversion of disciplinary practice, including episodes of seniors using their hands and fists on their subordinates—a practice almost always associated with the tsarist army in Soviet literature. The relationship between junior and senior in the Red Army was supposed to be based on comradeship, and Timoshenko devoted some attention to restoring a balance between the drive to improve discipline and the instillation of political conviction in the

SOVIET ANNEXATIONS 1939–1940

FINLIND

Petrozavodsk

0    150
Miles

Helsinki

Vyborg

Leningrad

Tallin
(Reval)

Pskov

Riga

BALTIC SEA

Memel

RUSSIA

Kaunas
(Kovno)

Konigsberg

Vilna

EAST
PRUSSIA

Grodno

Minsk

Belostok

Warsaw

Brest

Pinsk

POLAND

Lublin

Kiev

Tarnov

Zhitomir

Lvov

Przemysl

CZECHOSLOVAKIA

Uzhgorod

Kamenets-
Podolsk

Balta

HUNGARY

Jassy

Kishinev

Odessa

Occupied by Russia Between
October 1939 and December 1940

RUMANIA

BLACK
SEA

still largely peasant masses of the Red Army (Portugal'skii 1994, 131–35).

The restoration of one-man command at the tactical level and the renaming of the main political directorate of the RKKA as the main directorate of political propaganda led to a noticeable slackening of the influence of political work in the armed forces. The new disciplinary manual, the political officers believed, led to a sharp increase in the number of disciplinary penalties. Some of the officers who had served in the old army tried to idealize the relationship between the soldiers and their officers that existed in the tsarist army, but they underestimated the effectiveness of conviction in strengthening discipline. In April 1941, the main directorate of political propaganda reported to the Central Committee that in some units there was massive use of the military court system in place of detailed educational work. Also, limiting the role of the political officers to political education and enlightenment had restricted criticism and self-criticism—"the most important means of overcoming shortcomings" (Petrov 1964, 334, 335).

While the new disciplinary measures were being introduced and absorbed by the forces, the General Staff devised and directed an extensive training program designed to teach the troops what they required for war. A rigorous, even brutal, program of tactical training for the summer months was set forth in Timoshenko's order of 16 May 1940. A former infantry officer, training in Tashkent at that time, recalled the 100-kilometer marches in the blazing Central Asian sun, entrenching drills, draconian discipline, and the suicides of several classmates. Soviet tactical training was strongly influenced by the Mannerheim line. The theme of many of the exercises in 1940 was the breakthrough of a solidly fortified defense—training that did little to prepare the Red Army for the onslaught it was to face the next summer (Tarleton 1991, 86, 92, 93).

In late June, Timoshenko, accompanied by Khrushchev, was able to visit his birthplace in the village of Furmanka in Bessarabia as that region was reincorporated into the Soviet Union. The area had been made part of Romania in 1918 while Soviet Russia was engaged in the civil war. The Soviet Union had never recognized that the territory belonged to Romania and had often raised the Bessarabian question in the interwar years. In the summer of 1940, the preoccupation of Great Britain, France, and Germany with the new situation in Europe created by the defeat of France and the removal of the British Expeditionary Force from Europe presented the opportunity for the Soviet Union to unilaterally rearrange its western border and launch what it described as a liberation campaign in Bessarabia. The northern part of the former Austrian territory of Bukovina was occupied at the same time. The campaign was conducted by the Southern *Front,* commanded by Georgii Konstantinovich Zhukov, drawn from the Kiev Special Military District. The combination of the various "liberation" campaigns against Finland, the Baltic States, Poland, and Romania had moved the Soviet borders some 200 to 300 kilometers to the west.

## RELOCATING THE FORTIFIED AREAS

At first blush it seemed that the Soviet strategic position in the west had improved markedly. If, as Soviet doctrine proclaimed, the Soviet Army was going to take the offensive and fight the war on the territory of the aggressors—Germany and its allies—Soviet troops in their start positions were 200 to 300 kilometers closer to Berlin. But, after the defeat of Poland and the fall of France, only a nonaggression pact stood between the Red Army and the victorious Wehrmacht. And because the Germans were still at war with the British, they could reasonably claim that they were using eastern Poland as a training ground as they concentrated their troops beyond the range of British bombers.

The new territories also required improvements in their military infrastructure. Roads, airfields, barracks, communications, and fortifications had to be built. A belt of fortified areas had been under construction based on the old state borders. They consisted of belts of field fortifications prepared for lengthy defense by specially trained troops cooperating with combined arms units. Each area was defined by the length and depth of the defensive belt. In the period 1929–38, 13 fortified areas had been constructed. These belts included 3,196 defensive structures including 409 structures for artillery. The garrison for these belts was 25 machine-gun battalions with an overall strength of 18,000 troops. In 1938 and 1939 an additional 8 fortified areas were started, of which some 60 percent had been completed when construction was halted due to changes in the state border. Were they now to be completed, or should a new belt be constructed to defend the new border? The Finnish war had demonstrated that such fortifications could be an important factor in the initial phase of a war. That the Maginot line had been ineffective against the Wehrmacht was attributed to flaws in the French program.

In February 1940, the chief of the General Staff, B. M. Shaposhnikov, directed the Kiev and Western Special Military Districts to maintain the old fortified areas in combat readiness until new fortified areas were built along the new state border. Subsequently, the order was given that, with the exception of three areas, the fortified areas should be placed in storage and their equipment removed and stored so that it could be put back in action if necessary. A commission that inspected the Minsk fortified area in September 1940 found that no one had been given responsibility for the equipment removed from the fortified areas and stored. Portions of the equipment were rusting and spoiling. Security for the area and its equipment was almost nonexistent.

As the international situation worsened in 1940 and 1941, twenty new fortified areas were begun along the new state borders. At the end of 1940, this defensive construction was considered to be proceeding slowly, and only a small percentage of the work had been completed. The main military engineer directorate of the Red Army informed the chairman of the Defense Committee that the plan of defensive construction for 1941 called for the completion of all the works started in 1940 and that all important axes on the border would be covered by emplacements made of concrete reinforced with either steel, rock, or wood. In the spring of 1941 in the three special military districts, 136,000 laborers were engaged in the construction of fortified areas. But, despite the assurances of the main military engineer directorate that the necessary materials were at hand to complete the task, in some areas the materials, transport, and equipment were not available. By the beginning of the war, the construction of even the first belt of fortified areas was not completed. On the majority of the axes of the German advance, the fortified areas were overcome from the march (Khor'kov 1987, 47–54).

## THE MECHANIZED CORPS RETURNS

During a conversation with Shaposhnikov in late May 1940, Stalin asked why there were no mechanized and tank corps in the Red Army. Citing the experience of the Wehrmacht in Poland and France, he demanded that the question be reexamined and that several corps should be organized having 1,000 to 1,200 tanks. When the problem was passed to M. V. Zakharov, then on the General Staff, he recalled that there was in existence a table of organization for a mechanized corps. He was told that Stalin had been very specific— the corps should have two tank divisions and one motorized division. The origin of Stalin's idea for the structure of the new corps is not known. What was known was that Stalin wanted a quick response, and he did not want to hear that such large tank formations were too clumsy and difficult to control. It was proposed to confer with D. G. Pavlov, the chief of the armored directorate, who the previous year, working in a commission chaired by G. I. Kulik, had endorsed the opinion that the tank corps was clumsy and impractical. On 9 June 1940, the commissar of defense approved a plan to deploy eight mechanized corps and two separate tank divisions. The mechanized corps was to consist of two tank divisions and one motorized division. Each tank division would have 375 tanks and the motorized division would have 275 tanks. The corps would have a total of 1,031 tanks.

Commenting on the organization, Zakharov observed that the corps, which also included a number of corps-level units, was in reality clumsy and heavy. Commanding such a formation was complicated by the absence at that time of reliable communications and mobile supply and support services. A considerable period of time was required to develop the highly qualified commanders and staffs for these units (Zakharov 1989, 187, 188).

## STRATEGIC DEPLOYMENT

Aleksander Mikhailovich Vasilevsky, who after the end of the Finnish war became first deputy to the chief of the operations directorate of the General Staff, in mid-April 1940 began work on the plan for repelling possible aggression. The broad outlines of the plan were drawn by the chief of the General Staff, B. M. Shaposhnikov. Vasilevsky and others provided the details and put the plan in a form to be briefed for Stalin and the Politburo. In September the plan for 1941 was ready for presentation. Although there had been a change in the chief of the General Staff (Meretskov had replaced Shaposhnikov), the plan was essentially unchanged. Shaposhnikov considered that the most advantageous deployment for the Wehrmacht would be to the north of the mouth of the river San; consequently, the plan called for the deployment of the main forces of the Soviet Army from the Baltic Sea to the Pripyat Marshes (Polesie). The Northwest and Western *Fronts,* which had the largest share of the force, would be stationed there. The plan envisioned that the Germans could deploy on the Soviet western borders in ten to fifteen days, but there was no prediction as to when the war might begin.

Stalin speculated that the most likely axis of the German main effort would be to the southwest, to the south of the Pripyat Marshes. The dictator reasoned that Hitler would want to seize the rich industrial, raw material, and agricultural regions in the Ukraine and the Donbass first before proceeding to subdue the rest of the country. The General Staff was directed to rework the plan to place the main body of the defenders on the southwest axis.

The new plan was to be ready by 15 December. This involved coordinating the change with the railroads and also the various military districts so that all affected could work on their own plans by 1 January 1941 (Vasilevsky 1973, 110).

The General Staff was also concerned with the development of the infrastructure in the new territories acquired by the "liberation campaigns." In addition to the fortified areas, it was necessary to develop the road and rail nets in the new territories and to provide communications and everything necessary to rapidly concentrate and deploy the troops and lead them in combat against potential aggressors.

In February 1941, the commander of the Western Special Military District since June 1940, D. G. Pavlov, had submitted an extensive list of infrastructure improvements, which he urged be completed in 1941. He estimated the cost at more than 1.5 billion rubles. He also recommended that the entire population of the Soviet Union, including students above the tenth grade (excluding servicemen who would continue their training), be organized into work units to provide the manpower for these projects. Stalin directed that Pavlov be informed that although his suggestions were justified, it was not possible to satisfy his "fantastic" proposal (Zhukov 1990, 313, 314).

Proposals to build airfields close to the border and to locate supply, ammunition, and fuel dumps there were opposed by Vasilevsky and others. The General Staff and those directly involved with supply in the Commissariat of Defense recommended placing these vital installations along the line of the Volga. This was categorically opposed by G. I. Kulik, L. Z. Mekhlis, and E. A. Shchadenko. They argued that the aggressor would be quickly turned back and that the war would be fought on the enemy's territory. If that were the case, then why move the supply dumps to the rear? Their argument prevailed (Vasilevsky 1973, 113).

Possibly the most serious shortcoming in the equipment of the Red Army on 22 June 1941 was the shortage of contemporary means of communication and the absence of mobilization and emergency supplies of communications equipment. In particular there were shortages of radios in the special military districts that varied from 73 percent in the Western Special Military District to 70 percent in the Kiev Special Military District to 40 percent in the Baltic Special Military District. Even the General Staff had only 39 percent of its requirements for a particular type of radio. In the event of war, it was planned to use the regular telephone and telegraph lines of the civilian communications system and the high-frequency system of the NKVD. The result was an overdependence on highly vulnerable land lines and a shortage of personnel capable of using radio communications at the division, corps, and army level. This lack of competence led to a lack of confidence in the radio as a means of communication and a preference for wire systems. Stalin, according to G. K. Zhukov, did not appreciate the role of radio in contemporary maneuver warfare, and it proved impossible to convince him of the need to upgrade military radio technology and to provide for its mass production. This should have been done long before the war. It was not, and the forces suffered throughout the initial phases as a result (Zhukov 1990, 1:315).

## CADRES DECIDE EVERYTHING

One of the slogans of the Five Year Plans was "Cadres decide everything." The implication was that if the proper people are selected, almost any problem can be solved. One wonders how the cadres' directorates could stay abreast of the bewildering number of command and staff changes in the days of handwritten paper records considering the personnel changes caused by expansion, usually promotions; by the repression of 40,000 officers, many from the pinnacle of the rank pyramid; by combat losses at Halhin Gol and in the war with Finland; by the return of some of those who had been arrested; and by Beriia's continuing search for Trotskyite members of the military-Fascist plot. The expansion of the forces in itself would have overwhelmed the most experienced personnel specialists: by 22 June 1941, there were 170 divisions and 2 brigades (2.9 million men) concentrated in the western border military districts. As it was, the specialists were not immune from the purges; witness the presence of Boris Mironovich Fel'dman in the first group of victims. Fel'dman was the chief of the command cadres directorate of the RKKA.

The 4,500-kilometer-long border was also defended by 100,000 border guards and 11 regiments of operational troops of the NKVD (Zakharov 1968, 252). As we have seen during the war with Finland, the operational command of this mass of troops and equipment would become the responsibility of the commander of the military district in which the troops were located. In that case the military district commander with his staff would form a *front* headquarters.

By his expectation that the German main effort would be south of the Pripyat Marshes, Stalin had assigned the main defensive task to the Kiev Special Military District. Mikhail Petrovich Kirponos, who replaced Zhukov as commander of the district in January 1940, had distinguished himself in the last days of the Finnish war. He had led his 70th Rifle Division in a six-day passage across the weakening ice in the Gulf of Finland to take the Finns in the rear by surprise and facilitate the capture of Vyborg. This bold deed had attracted the attention of Meretskov, the Seventh Army commander, and after the war Kirponos became Meretskov's deputy. When Meretskov moved on to Moscow in the summer of 1940, Kirponos became the Leningrad Military District commander. Six months later Kirponos was commanding what Stalin thought would be a critical military district if the Germans were to attack.

### MIKHAIL PETROVICH KIRPONOS

In an autobiographical sketch written in October 1938, presumably to verify his political reliability, Kirponos described himself as the son of a poor peasant; he was born in January 1892 in a Ukrainian village about 100 kilometers north of Kiev. To supplement the family income, his father worked in the village tearoom. After his father died in 1917, his mother worked for more prosperous peasants (kulaks) in the village. Kirponos received about three years of formal education at the local parochial and zemstvo schools and began to work at the age of nine. In September 1915, when he was conscripted into the Imperial Army, he was working as a supervisor in a forest nursery, receiving twelve rubles a month. While in the tsarist army he completed a military aidman *(fel'dsher)* course, which was the only event in his service he saw fit to record.

Following his return from the Romanian front in February 1918, he organized and led several partisan detachments and eventually joined the 1st Soviet Division, where he served in various positions, including division commander. In the summer of 1919 he participated with Shchadenko in the liquidation of a group of Ukrainian partisans. In 1923 he was sent to the academy, which eventually became known as the Frunze Military Academy. After completing his courses in 1927, he served in various infantry divisions until 1934, when he was assigned the job of chief and commissar of the Kazan Infantry School. In 1938, this was one of seventy-five such schools that were developing junior officers for the Soviet armed forces.

In the course of his autobiographical sketch, Kirponos was careful to include all of the anti-Party oppositioners that he had exposed and to note that he had maintained close contact with the counterintelligence and internal security "organs." His second wife's brother had emigrated to Poland in 1924 or 1925, but neither he nor his wife had had any contact with him. His wife's father was exiled to Alma

Ata in 1930, but neither Kirponos nor his wife knew where he was currently living or even whether he was still alive. They were not interested in his fate. Why he was exiled they did not know, but his wife understood that he had obviously deserved it. His wife never had any sympathy for him.

From Kirponos's own testimony it is clear that he wanted to be known as a true believer. What was missing from the account was any hint of the military qualifications, such as advanced military education or field experience at the level of military district command, that might be reasonably required of the future commander of a critical region of the nation's defense.

With the outbreak of the Finnish war, Kirponos volunteered for combat duty. He was motivated, he said, by a desire to acquire combat experience in order to be able to pass on to his future students the demands on a commander in modern warfare (Khorev 1995, 4). Being the head of an officers' training school would ordinarily not be considered adequate preparation for the command of a division in the type of combat experienced in the Winter War. Nevertheless, Kirponos succeeded, and the 70th Rifle Division was awarded the Orders of Lenin and the Red Banner. At the end of the war, he fully expected to return to developing young officers armed with his combat experiences.

Probably because of the impression he made on Meretskov, Kirponos moved rapidly up to the rank of colonel general *(general polkovnik)* and into command of the Kiev Special Military District. Before going to Kiev, he had an interview with Stalin. In the course of their conversation, Stalin sought his views on the shortcomings of the current Red Army field manuals. Kirponos was bold enough to tell Stalin that the field commander should be given more independence in combat and be able to make his own decisions on tactical maneuvers and retreats. Stalin rejected this proposal firmly.

Kirponos did not share with Stalin that he had sincere doubts about his competence to be the Kiev Special Military District commander. He wondered whether he could be a worthy successor to such previous military district commanders as Egorov, Frunze, Iakir, Timoshenko, and Zhukov. From a psychological point of view, he was not ready to continue the list of such brilliant and popular names with his own—which was barely known in the country.

Despite his self-doubt, he attacked his new duties vigorously. Two additional armies had to be located in the military district. Rifle and mechanized troops had to be moved into the zone along the border, and all this had to be accomplished without causing a conflict with the Germans. Stalin was convinced that some incident on the border might provoke Hitler into an invasion of Russia. Stalin's conviction was so strong that, according to Zhukov, the NKVD in the border areas was directed by Beriia to report any provocative movements by Soviet troops! In early June 1941, Stalin was informed that the commander of the fortified areas on the Ukrainian border had moved troops into the forward defensive area *(predpol'e)*. If this was so, Stalin wanted the order rescinded and the issuer punished (Zhukov 1990, 1:368). Given that the special border military districts were receiving almost daily reports of the German buildup in Poland and were the frequent victims of German cross-border operations of one type or another to obtain current information about the Soviet forces opposite them, those charged with defending the borders as far forward as possible were placed in an unenviable situation. For the Kiev Special Military District, these restrictions complicated the already difficult problem of defending an 800-kilometer section of the border.

## DMITRII GRIGOR'EVICH PAVLOV

Dmitrii Grigor'evich Pavlov's lackluster performance as chief of the armored directorate has been described. As an officer trained in armored warfare (a skill that he never fully mastered), it was not surprising that he was on the Karelian Isthmus during the last months of the Finnish war. That he then was given command of the Western Special Military District seems to exemplify the acute shortage of experienced senior officers in the Red Army in 1940.

Pavlov was born in what is now Kostroma Oblast on 4 November 1897. Like many of his fellow Soviet generals, he was the child of a peasant family. He rose to the rank of noncommissioned officer during World War I, joined the Communist Party in 1919, and entered the Red Army the same year. He graduated from the Omsk Cavalry Officers School in 1922 and the Frunze Military Academy in 1928. After completion of the academy, he commanded cavalry and then mechanized regiments. From 1934 until 1936 he commanded a mechanized brigade. In 1936 and 1937 he commanded a tank brigade in Spain. From 1937 until the start of the Finnish war, he was the chief of the armored directorate of the RKKA. During the last phase of the Finnish war, he commanded a "reserve group of the Stavka," consisting of three rifle divisions, a tank brigade, and a cavalry corps with reinforcements. As part of the February assault on the Mannerheim line, Pavlov's group was to attempt to cross over the ice in the Gulf of Finland and operate in the deep rear of the Finnish position. There is no evidence that this operation was ever attempted, possibly because of the condition of the ice in the Gulf (Pospelov 1961 vol. 1, 266).

In June 1940, Pavlov was given command of the Belorussian Special Military District, which became the Western Special Military District on 11 July 1940, when the troops in Smolensk Oblast were included in that military district. Pavlov, who had never really commanded anything more than a brigade and whose performance as chief of the armored directorate left something to be desired, was now charged with the defense of a 450-kilometer sector of the Soviet border that included the shortest overland route to Moscow.

## FEDOR ISIDOROVICH KUZNETSOV

Fedor Isidorovich Kuznetsov was born in 1898 to a peasant family in a village in Mogilev Oblast in Belorussia. He was conscripted into the tsarist army in the summer of 1916 and chosen to attend warrant officers' *(praporshchiki)* school. The October Revolution found him in the hospital recovering from his second wound. After demobilization he returned to his native village, where he organized local detachments to fight counterrevolution. In the summer of 1918, he joined the Red Army; he rose to the command of a regiment during the civil war. In 1923 he entered what became known as the Frunze Military Academy. In 1930, after line service, he was assigned to the Moscow Infantry School and in 1935 was the director of the chair of tactics at the Frunze Military Academy. There he joined the Communist Party. In December 1940, he was given command of the Baltic Special Military District, which was created after the Baltic States were incorporated into the Soviet Union. The district was charged with defending the 300-kilometer border with East Prussia with the Eighth and Eleventh Armies. The defense of the Baltic littoral from Tallin to Liepaia was the task of two rifle divisions. Two of the offshore islands were defended by a separate rifle brigade.

## THE DEFENSIVE ROLE OF THE LENINGRAD AND ODESSA MILITARY DISTRICTS

The 1,200-kilometer stretch of the border from the Gulf of Finland to the Rybachii Peninsula was to be defended by the three armies of the Leningrad Military District. The military district commander was Markian Mikhailovich Popov, a thirty-nine-year-old lieutenant general who was a soldier in the civil war; he remained in the Red Army after completing infantry command courses in 1921 and the Frunze Military Academy in 1936. In July 1939 he was appointed commander of the First Separate Red Banner Army in the far east; in January 1941 he was made commander of the Leningrad Military District. Since the start of the Finnish war in December 1939, Popov was the fourth commander of the Leningrad Military District.

The Odessa Military District, formed on 11 October 1939, included the territory of Bessarabia, which had recently been annexed. By the end of the year it had eleven rifle, two tank, one motorized, and two cavalry divisions. In the second half of 1940, the Odessa Military District was ordered to reconnoiter the locations for three fortified areas along the new state border. In the event of war, the military district headquarters was to form the Ninth Army headquarters. It was not until some days after the war had started that the Ninth Army learned that it was to be part of the Southern *Front*. The *front* headquarters was formed from the headquarters of the Moscow Military District. As far as the Ninth Army could determine, no one from the Moscow Military District had ever contacted the army or had attempted to coordinate a subsequent relationship. The Ninth Army first heard about the arrival of the Southern *Front* headquarters in the theater when the *front* commander, Ivan Vasilevich Tiulenov, called and requested a map showing the current situation (Zakharov 1989, 190, 280).

Tiulenov was a cavalry officer who had served in the tsarist army since 1913, been decorated in World War I, and been elected a member of his unit committees in the period between the February and

October Revolutions. During the civil war he had served in staff and command positions, including the command of a brigade. From 1922 until 1931 he had commanded a separate cavalry brigade and a cavalry division. From 1932 he had served in the inspectorate of cavalry of the RKKA. From February 1938 he had commanded the Caucasus Military District and from August 1940, the Moscow Military District.

## THE BORDER'S DEFENDERS

A Soviet soldier's oath required him to defend his motherland courageously and skillfully with worthiness and honor, not sparing his blood or even his life (SVE 1978, 547). Before the Finnish war, commanders had been selected on the basis of their class background and their participation in the ritual denunciation of colleagues. After the war there was a strong movement to institute a merit-review system independent of the chain of command and to eliminate the collegial command system. However, in the selection of the officers to lead the special military districts, no clear trend is visible with the exception of Kirponos; he took pains to inform his superiors of his participation in the denunciation game yet seems to have been advanced rapidly in recognition of his performance. Pavlov's advancement, on the other hand, does not seem to be related to any specific conspicuous performance. The Finnish lessons had not been fully absorbed.

# 11
# STALIN'S LIEUTENANTS

**SOVIET INTELLIGENCE AND THE OUTBREAK OF THE WAR**
In July 1940, Filip Ivanovich Golikov, who would prove to be one of
Stalin's most loyal lieutenants, became chief of the main intelligence
directorate (*glavnoe razvedivatel'noe upravlenie,* or GRU). He replaced
Gen. Lt. I. Iv. Proskurov, a thirty-three-year-old air force officer.
Proskurov was a former favorite of Stalin's who had been awarded
the gold star of a Hero of the Soviet Union for his exploits in Spain
(Akhmedov 1984, 127). Proskurov was one of the last of what Beriia
referred to as "the band of Berzin" in a report to Stalin written on
the eve of the German attack. Ian Karlovich Berzin, who had headed
the GRU for eleven years, had also been the chief Soviet military adviser to the Spanish Republican Army in 1936 and 1937. He returned
to head the GRU again from July until he was repressed in November 1937 (SVE 1976, no.6, 453). There followed a series of arrests
that removed the experienced leadership of the GRU as the Soviet
Union prepared to face its sternest tests.

The substance of Beriia's report to Stalin was that Golikov was
complaining about the Soviet ambassador to Berlin and one of his
military attachés who was reporting that Hitler had concentrated 170
divisions on the Soviet western border. Beriia added that he and his
people constantly kept in mind Stalin's wise forecast that Hitler
would not attack the Soviet Union in 1941 (Portugal'skii 1994, 141).

Golikov, who was forty years old at the time, was born in a village
in Kurgan Oblast in western Siberia. He joined the Red Army in
1918 and attended a military-agitators course in Petrograd. Most of
his early career in the Red Army was spent in political officer as-

signments. In 1931, he transferred to command duties, commanding a rifle regiment, a rifle division, a separate mechanized brigade, and a mechanized corps. In 1938, during the purges, he was appointed the member of the Military Council of the Belorussian Military District.

As the member of the military council, Golikov investigated the political reliability of corps commander Georgii K. Zhukov in what Zhukov interpreted to be a hostile manner. Zhukov later considered his assignment to Halhin Gol in 1939 to have been an escape from the threat of more drastic action against him by Golikov and the NKVD (Simonov 1987, no. 6, 54). In November 1938 through 1939, Golikov commanded army-sized formations in the Kiev Special Military District; in 1939 he participated in the "liberation" of the western Ukraine (SVE 2, 585).

Considering Golikov's more than ten years of service as a political officer—instructing in the dogmas of Marxism, Leninism, and Stalinism—and his devotion to Stalin and his lack of intelligence experience, Golikov would appear to have been a poor choice for an intelligence officer at the highest state level. During this period, Golikov often reported directly to Stalin over Timoshenko's head even though the GRU was directly subordinate to the commissar of defense. His reporting reinforced Stalin's conviction that Hitler would not attack in 1941 because he had not settled accounts with England. For example, on 20 March 1941, Golikov sent Stalin an intelligence report that discussed three variations of a possible German attack on the Soviet Union, one of which was similar to the German plan for Operation Barbarossa. Golikov drew the conclusion that the document must be considered as *dezinformatsiia* (disinformation) disseminated by either British or German intelligence because the Germans would not attack until after they defeated Great Britain. Golikov, when questioned about the document after the war, admitted that he had doubts about the correctness of his conclusions but, because the conclusions squared with those of Stalin, he was afraid to give voice to his doubts (Anfilov 1992, 4).

On 13 June, Timoshenko and Zhukov, alarmed by the continuing German buildup in Poland, asked Stalin for permission to order the troops in the western military districts into full combat readiness.

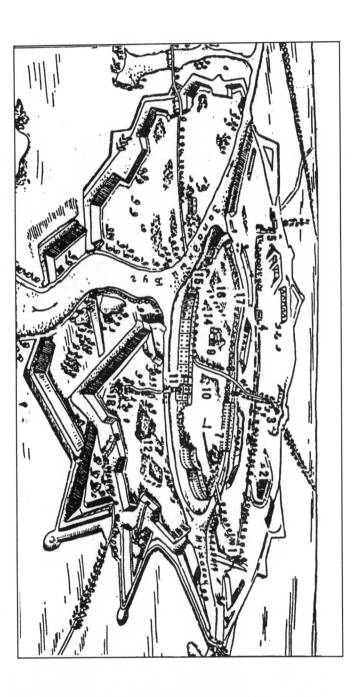

The Fortress at Brest

They had tried on 15 May to have Stalin consider full mobilization by sending him a draft order that could have triggered a preemptive attack on the German forces in Poland (Portugal'skii 1994, 138). Stalin had returned it through his personal secretary, Poskrebyshev, rejecting the idea by saying that the chairman of the People's Commissars had a better idea about the perspectives for Soviet relations with Germany than the chief of the General Staff (Iakovlev 1995, 37).

In June, Stalin reminded them that mobilization was equivalent to a declaration of war. He then asked how many Soviet divisions were located in the western military districts. Zhukov responded that as of 1 June there were 149 divisions and one separate rifle brigade in those districts. Stalin then said that, according to his information, the Germans did not have that number of troops. When Zhukov answered that according to intelligence data the German divisions were 14,000 to 16,000 troops strong and that Soviet divisions were only half that strength, Stalin commented that intelligence could not be trusted in everything. As he walked by Zhukov and Timoshenko, he glanced at their documents, then threw them on the table and said that he had other documents. He showed them a folder of reports, which Timoshenko believed were Golikov's. Knowing Stalin's opinion, Golikov strove to accommodate him and simply questioned the validity of any reporting that was not in accord with Stalin's views (Portugal'skii 1994, 139, 140).

## THE TASS ANNOUNCEMENT OF JUNE 14
After the 13 June meeting, Stalin told Zhukov that the Soviet news service, TASS, would publish a declaration to the effect that rumors of Germany's intention to break the pact with the Soviet Union had no basis. When the declaration was published on 14 June, the article also said that the movements of German troops freed from their operations in the Balkans into the eastern and northeastern regions of Germany had no connection with Soviet-German relations (Sandalov 1970, 65).

Leonid Mikhailovich Sandalov, who was chief of staff of the Fourth Army in the Western *Front* at the time, saw the article as an attempt to sound out the Germans by assuring them that the Soviet Union had no intention of violating the pact and hoping that Hitler would respond in a similar fashion. Others saw the article as confusing the Soviet public and weakening the vigilance of the Soviet people and their armed forces (Pospelov 1961, vol. 1, 404).

## THE GERMANS STRIKE—22 June 1941
When war did come, at three o'clock in the morning of 22 June, Stalin remained a captive of his illusions. Order No. 1, which was sent to the troops early that morning, warned them to turn back the invaders but not to succumb to any provocative German actions that could lead to major complications. Zhukov and Timoshenko had to convince Stalin to remove from the text of the order a sentence directing that in case of an invasion the Soviet commanders of forward units should meet with the German commanders and attempt to settle the conflict (Anfilov 1992, 4).

Zhukov and Vatutin, his first deputy, returned to the Kremlin at 0900 the same day to present to Stalin draft directives creating the Stavka of the high command (the general headquarters of the state's military forces) and the law ordering mobilization and martial law in the European area of the country. On 22 June the special military districts became *fronts.*

## STALIN'S LIEUTENANTS AT THE FRONT
By 1300 on 22 June, Stalin had recovered enough of his aplomb to order Shaposhnikov and Kulik to the Western *Front* and Zhukov to the Southwestern *Front* as representatives of the Stavka of the high command. The draft decision document establishing the Stavka had been approved by the Politburo that morning. By using the term *stavka,* the General Staff had opted for the traditional Russian word for the supreme organ directing the military operations of the Russian state.

Stalin told Zhukov that the *front* commanders did not have sufficient experience and had become somewhat flustered. He said he had already given Marshals Kulik and Shaposhnikov their instructions and sent them to the Western *Front.* He wanted Zhukov to leave for Kiev immediately and proceed to the headquarters of the Southwestern *Front* with Khrushchev, who was now the member of the military council of the *front.* When Zhukov asked who was going to head the General Staff in his absence, Stalin answered, "Leave Vatutin." Stalin then added, somewhat irritatedly, "Don't lose any time, we'll manage somehow" (Zhukov 1990, 2:12, 13). This exchange gives some flavor of the dictator's attitude toward the General Staff at this time. He saw the staff as high-ranking clerks who knew how to put his orders into the proper form and ensure that they were correctly addressed and delivered. He did not seek their advice on how to direct the Soviet forces.

Zhukov arrived at the headquarters of the Southwestern *Front* late at night on 22 June. He immediately contacted Vatutin in Moscow and was informed that there was still no firm information on the situation of the Western and Northwestern *Fronts*. Neither the General Staff nor Timoshenko had been able to contact the *front* commanders, Pavlov and Kuznetsov. Zhukov was also informed that Vatutin had been directed to put Zhukov's name on a directive that ordered Soviet troops to counterattack immediately, and to defeat the enemy on the main axes and drive him out of Soviet territory. Zhukov allowed his name to be used after he protested that the Soviet defenders did not know where and with what forces the enemy was attacking. When Zhukov hesitated, he was told that the matter had already been decided.

Despite his reservations about Stalin's order to counterattack, Zhukov advised Kirponos that night to issue a warning order to the mechanized corps to concentrate prior to attacking the main enemy strike forces and to alert the available frontal aviation and long-range bombers of the high command to prepare to support the counterattacks. During the preparations for the counterattack, Zhukov commented favorably on the organizing capability of the *front* chief of staff, M. A. Purkaev, and the chief of the operations section of the staff, I. Kh. Bagramian, whom Zhukov had recruited for the position when he commanded the Kiev Military District. (Zhukov 1990, 2:15).

The next day Zhukov was in the field conferring with the commander of one of the mechanized corps that was to make the counterattack. The commander convinced him that his corps would not be ready until 24 June. Zhukov approved, even though he knew that the attack would be more effective if it were coordinated with three other mechanized corps of the *front.* The other corps could not be ready on the twenty-fourth, but the situation would not permit further delay.

Zhukov considered the 24 June attack to be a success; it forced the Germans to save the situation by committing all of their air support in order to avoid a catastrophe. Although this and other counterattacks did not halt the enemy's advance, the main strike force that was driving toward Kiev was slowed and weakened. As Zhukov's account indicates, the Southwestern *Front* managed to avoid the destruction of the main centers of its communications with Moscow and with its subordinate armies and corps. This may have been due to a lesser effort by the German Army Group South against the Kiev Special Military District than was made against the Western Special Military District. The Germans also, contrary to Stalin's conviction, sent thirty-three divisions (including nine tank divisions) against the Kiev Special Military District, and fifty divisions, including fifteen tank divisions, against the Western Special Military District.

On 26 June, Stalin asked Zhukov to return to Moscow immediately because of the situation on the western front. The enemy was approaching Minsk, Kulik was missing and Shaposhnikov had become ill (Zhukov 1990, 2:34).

### THE WESTERN *FRONT*

When Zhukov returned to Moscow late at night on 26 June, he went directly to Stalin's office, where he found Timoshenko and Vatutin standing at attention in front of the angry dictator. Stalin told Zhukov to confer with his colleagues and tell him what should be done in this situation. He gave them forty minutes. Their recommendation was to move five armies to defend along the line of Zapadnaia Dvina–Polotzk–Vitebsk–Orsha–Mogilev–Mozyr and to prepare a rear defensive line from Lake Selizharovo–Smolensk–Roslavl–Gomel. They also recommended that two or three additional armies be formed from the Moscow *opolchenie* (militia). The objective was to set two defensive lines to weaken the enemy, stop his advance, and counterattack and defeat him. Stalin approved the recommendation, and the orders were issued immediately to put it into effect (Zhukov 1990, 2:35).

## THE COLLAPSE OF THE WESTERN *FRONT*

To understand the ordeal of the Western *Front,* we turn to the account of the chief of staff of the Fourth Army, Leonid Mikhailovich Sandalov. On 22 June, the Fourth Army was defending a 150-kilometer sector of the Belostok salient opposite the German Fourth Army and Guderian's 2d Tank Group. The Tenth Army was on its right and the Third Army defended the northern portion of the salient. (After the war the Soviet-Polish border was realigned so that Belostok was returned to Poland.) Included in the Fourth Army's area of responsibility was Brest, the main rail and highway crossing of the Bug River from occupied Poland on a direct route to Minsk and Moscow.

Intensive work, employing 10,000 hired workers and 4,000 carts and wagons, was under way to complete the Brest fortified region. The army's supply dumps were refilled to replace the supplies, ammunition, petroleum, oil, and lubricants (POL) used during the Finnish war. Yet, despite the general sense of urgency among the senior leaders of the Western *Front,* the units remained in or near their winter quarters, all of the *front* antiaircraft units were assembled for training purposes near Minsk, field artillery units were assembled near Brest, and signal troops were assembled near Kobrin. The army was on alert in some instances; in others, units were continuing to follow peacetime procedures.

Sandalov and army commander A. A. Korobkov, sensing the tension in the air, decided to spend the late hours of 21 June in the army headquarters building in Kobrin. They were there when the first warning order came in around 0330. By 0400 they had alerted the 42d Division, which was quartered in the Brest Fortress, to deploy, and notified the commandant of the Brest fortified area.

At that time German artillery opened up all along the border. At the same time the German Air Force conducted massive strikes on all Soviet airfields in the area. By 0430 it was decided to evacuate the headquarters building. All the army staff sections were ordered to move with their significant documents to the field headquarters site seven kilometers northeast of Kobrin. Sandalov barely managed to leave the building when it was hit by 500-kilogram bombs. A second wave of bombers soon followed, and the building was destroyed. The army headquarters had no antiaircraft weapons to protect it.

Sandalov's assistant, who had fled the building with him, was carrying a message just received from the military district headquarters in Minsk. It read, "In the course of 22–23.6.41 a surprise attack by the Germans on the fronts [of the border military districts] is possible . . ." (Sandalov 1970, 77).

During the next several days the Fourth Army strove to halt the invading Germans. It achieved some successes despite interruptions to communications both with *front* headquarters and with the headquarters of subordinate units. Contact was maintained to a large extent by liaison officers.

When communications were regained with *front* headquarters at 1600 on 22 June, the army was ordered to counterattack using one of its mechanized corps as a strike force. When the attack was launched the next morning, it surprised the Germans, and they were driven back several kilometers in some places. But within thirty minutes the Soviet troops were met with unopposed dive-bombers, which took their toll on the exposed Soviet troops and vehicles. The counterattack was soon halted, and the survivors took up defensive positions.

The army was visited by Pavlov's deputy for higher education institutions on 23 June. His purpose was to pass on Pavlov's very strict order to shoot any group of troops if necessary but halt the retreat and take firm control of all formations and units (KVS 1991, no. 11, 56).

The army was virtually without air support and soon began experiencing shortages in supplies, fuel, and ammunition as the German air force began locating and destroying depots and dumps. As the Russian Army retreated to the east, Pavlov gave them successive river lines that were to be held "at all costs." It was also learned that the Germans had penetrated through the Third Army on the northern flank of the *front* at least as far as Guderian and his company had penetrated on the Fourth Army's front. As late as 24 June, Pavlov was still ordering counterattacks, to the disgust of the member of the Fourth Army's military council, who was already convinced that counterattacks were too costly in view of the enemy's superiority in tanks and combat aircraft.

By 26 June, the Fourth Army learned that the *front* headquarters had been moved from Minsk to Mogilev on the Dnieper River, 175 kilometers to the east. On 28 June, as the Germans captured Bobruisk and approached the Berezina River, Sandalov was ordered by his commander to substitute for him and report to *front* headquarters in Mogilev. There, for the first time since the war started, Sandalov encountered Pavlov. Sandalov had served under Pavlov as chief of the *front* operations section before joining the Fourth Army. He was struck by the changes in Pavlov's appearance: his face was drawn, he seemed hunched up, and his eyes seemed to gleam with alarm. His voice had become soft. Pavlov ordered the Fourth Army to retake Bobruisk from the Germans and told Sandalov that he was very dissatisfied that the Germans had been able to take the town so easily.

Sandalov also encountered Marshal Shaposhnikov, who, with Pavlov, described the Fourth Army's main mission: to hold the positions it now occupied to allow the concentration of the forces from the internal regions of the country behind the Dnieper. The second mission was to reconstitute the 28th and 47th Rifle Corps. The army headquarters was to move to Rogachev, located on the Dnieper River approximately 125 kilometers south of Mogilev.

The *front* headquarters had just moved east of Mogilev into a forest that had been divided among the staff sections. Wires carrying the internal staff communications were strung on trees; under the trees, maps and folders were lying on field tables. Red Army soldiers were building *zemlianki,* improved dugouts used for field living quarters (Sandalov 1970, 74–128).

## VOROSHILOV ARRIVES AT THE WESTERN *FRONT*

At about this time, Voroshilov arrived at Mogilev in a special train. According to his aide, Khadzhi Mamsurov, he arrived at Mogilev on 26 June but could not locate Western *Front* headquarters until the next day. Mamsurov located it first but could not believe that what he found was a *front* headquarters. He believed that a gypsy encampment would be neater. He saw one of Shaposhnikov's aides and then Shaposhnikov himself lying on the ground, his trench coat under his head and his body covered with another raincoat. At first Mamsurov thought that Shaposhnikov was dead. Mamsurov saw Pavlov sitting alone under a pine tree eating kasha out of a soldier's mess kit. He seemed to be so hungry that he didn't notice the falling rain.

When Mamsurov saw that Shaposhnikov was alive, he introduced himself and told him that Voroshilov was in Mogilev. Shaposhnikov sat up, wincing with pain, and thanked God that Voroshilov had come. When Mamsurov reported to Pavlov, he got up awkwardly, looking pale and confused. When Mamsurov told Pavlov that he was an aide to Marshal Voroshilov, who was waiting in his train in Mogilev, Pavlov sighed and said, "I'm done for" (Mamsurova 1988, 12).

Mamsurov returned to the train and reported that he had found the *front* headquarters. By the time he and Voroshilov returned to the *front* command post, there was a control post established at the entrance to the headquarters area, and Shaposhnikov was on his feet, freshly shaven and ready to give Voroshilov a joyous greeting. When Pavlov appeared and reported to Voroshilov, his hands shook. Voroshilov instructed Pavlov to establish contact with the troops and ordered Mamsurov to send Shaposhnikov to Mogilev once he had seen a doctor. When the member of the military council, A. Ia. Fominykh, appeared with his cap on backward, Voroshilov accused him of having been asleep and launched a tirade at him.

Mamsurov missed the remainder of Voroshilov's dressing down of the *front* leadership because he took the headquarters' liaison plane to make a vain search for Marshal Kulik, who apparently had gone forward to the Tenth Army area and been cut off there along with the bulk of the army.

Voroshilov was discussing Pavlov with Shaposhnikov in the salon car of the train when Mamsurov returned from his unsuccessful flight. Voroshilov said that he had been instructed to remove Pavlov as *front* commander and send him under guard to Moscow. Shaposhnikov agreed that Pavlov was not competent to be a *front* commander but argued against his arrest. Shaposhnikov said that an arrest would cause confusion among commanders who hadn't forgotten the recent disappearance of people and would now fear similar treatment in the event of failure. Voroshilov, after some thought, read aloud the message he was going to send to Stalin. It recommended that Pavlov be removed, demoted, and transferred to a lesser post. Shaposhnikov throughout this exchange remained stretched out on a divan in the salon.

Voroshilov then ordered supper. Three minutes later the cook brought in bread, ham cut in large pieces, and tea. Voroshilov ate a piece of ham and suddenly was in a rage again. He called for the cook by name—Comrade Franz! Franz came in and stood at attention before Voroshilov. Voroshilov asked him how he dared serve such a supper when he, Voroshilov, was a marshal of the Soviet Union and when another marshal of the Soviet Union was lying on a divan; he pointed to Shaposhnikov, who was laid out like a dead man. "What have you cut? Do people cut ham this way? In a goddamn pub they serve better ham!" With the Western *Front* crumbling around him, Voroshilov was worrying about how his ham was cut! Franz shifted from foot to foot and smiled apologetically. Later, Voroshilov told Mamsurov that Franz was a Czech who had worked for Frunze until Frunze died (Mamsurova 1988, 13).

The next day Mamsurov was witness to a scene that he said he would never forget as long as he lived. Pavlov came to the train to report, and Voroshilov started by telling him that he was a failure as *front* commander. Then he recalled that Pavlov had once complained to Stalin that Voroshilov did not allow young cadres (meaning Pavlov) to grow. Voroshilov then asked Pavlov if he knew what his poor performance had cost and said that Pavlov could not be trusted with a division, let alone a *front*. At this point, Pavlov fell on his knees and asked for forgiveness. Then he started kissing Voroshilov's boots. Disgustedly, Voroshilov said, "I thought better of you" (Mamsurova 1988, 13).

On 29 June, according to Mamsurov, Voroshilov announced that Pavlov, his chief of staff (Klimovskikh), the *front* artillery officer (Klych), and others were to be arrested and sent to Moscow. When Klych gave up his weapon to Mamsurov, he said quietly, "That's how it is, and all because of this windbag and peacock." He meant Pavlov (Mamsurova 1988, 13). This account of Pavlov's arrest differs from other sources.

After the arrest of Pavlov and the others, Mamsurov felt that the situation on the Western *Front* grew worse. There was uncertainty, fear of failure, and nervousness. In his opinion the arrests did more harm than good.

## THE ARREST AND TRIAL OF GENERAL PAVLOV

Pavlov was relieved as commander of the Western *Front* on 29 June 1941 by Andrei Ivanovich Eremenko, who had been commanding an army in the far east. Eremenko, under orders, had started his return to Moscow before the war began, so there was no apparent connection between his assignment to the Western *Front* and his return from the far east. He arrived in Moscow on 28 June, reported to Timoshenko, was told of the situation, and was ordered to take command of the Western *Front*. He was accompanied by German Kapitonovich Malandin, who was to replace Klimovskikh as chief of staff.

When Pavlov saw Eremenko, an old acquaintance, he greeted him warmly and asked what he was doing there. In response, Eremenko handed him Timoshenko's written order relieving him and placing Eremenko in command. After reading the order and absorbing it, Pavlov could only ask where he was to go. Eremenko conveyed Timoshenko's message that he was to go to Moscow. But Moscow apparently had not decided his future, nor had it decided who was to command the Western *Front*.

On 4 July Semen Konstantinovich Timoshenko arrived to take command of the *front*, and Eremenko remained as Timoshenko's deputy (Eremenko 1964, 64, 78, 87). At about this time, Pavlov was ordered to go to Moscow, presumably to report to Stalin. On arrival he reported to Zhukov, who barely recognized him because he had changed so much after eight days of command at the front. Stalin decided not to see him, but he did have a short, cool audience with Molotov, who told him that the question of the retreat was being considered by the Politburo. Pavlov was ordered to return to Mogilev by staff car. He was arrested after passing through Smolensk.

While Pavlov was making his futile trip to Moscow, Lev Zaharovich Mekhlis, the chief of the Main Political Administration, had arrived in Mogilev on 2 July. He had convened a Western *Front* military council, which included Timoshenko, Mekhlis, Voroshilov, Budenny, and Shaposhnikov (according to Ivan Stadniuk, he chased the original member of the military council away from the command post), and ordered the arrest of Pavlov, Klimovskikh, Grigor'ev, Klych, and Korobkov, the Fourth Army commander. They were tried and found guilty. Pavlov, Klimovskikh, Grigor'ev, and Korobkov were shot on 22 July 1941.

In the course of Pavlov's interrogation and trial, the prosecutor attempted to have Pavlov admit that he was a plotter and a traitor. He was accused of plotting with Meretskov (who was arrested on 23 June) while they were serving in Spain. He was also accused of maintaining close ties with Uborevich, who had been tried and executed with Tukhachevsky in 1937. Pavlov denied these allegations, although he did admit that he was strongly influenced by Uborevich and Meretskov. Pavlov also admitted his own shortcomings as a commander. Among them were that he had not followed up to ensure that his orders were carried out and that he had interpreted and executed the orders of the General Staff in his own way.

The final indictment against Pavlov and the others did not include mention of treason and plotting against the regime. Instead it seemed to focus on their incompetence as a commander and staff officers. Pavlov was convicted of cowardice, inaction, absence of administrative ability, losing control of his forces, permitting the enemy to seize his weapons without battle, and abandoning his positions without authority. It was later determined that these weaknesses did not make him an "enemy of the people," but they did not prevent his entire family, including his mother-in-law, from being exiled to Krasnoiarsk for five years and being denied the right to vote for the same period (KVS 1991, no. 14, 65).

## THE FATE OF THE KIEV AND BALTIC SPECIAL MILITARY DISTRICTS

As the Western *Front* was being driven steadily to the east, the Southwestern *Front* was being pushed toward Kiev, and the Northwestern *Front*, under F. I. Kuznetsov, was falling back to the northeast. On 4 July, Kuznetsov was relieved. According to Vladimir Karpov, the General Staff did not receive a clear report on the situation on the Northwestern *Front* for the first eighteen days of the war (Karpov 1989, no. 11, 161, 165). This failure to keep the General Staff informed was probably one of the causes for Kuznetsov's relief—thirteen days after the war started. Kuznetsov, however, was not tried. On 24 July he was placed in command of the newly formed Central *Front*, which was given the mission of defending Gomel and Bobruisk. By 24 August the Germans had captured both towns, and the *front* was disbanded. Its units were absorbed by the Briansk *Front.* In late September, Kuznetsov was sent to the Crimea where he took command of the Fifty-first Separate Army (Chernov 1968, 124).

Kirponos and the Southwestern *Front,* after a bitterly contested retreat, were surrounded when Guderian's 2d Tank Group closed the armored ring around Kiev on 15 September. Kirponos refused to be flown out of the encirclement and also would not leave without a written order authorizing him to withdraw. On 18 September, as the *front* headquarters began to make its way through the German ring, it was observed from the air and attacked. Kirponos was wounded in his left leg. The group was then caught under mortar fire, and Kirponos was wounded in the head and chest; he soon died. The tragedy of Kirponos and the Southwestern *Front,* which lost 616,304 troops in the Kiev operation, could have been avoided. On 29 July, Stalin refused to accept the recommendation of his chief of the General Staff, Zhukov, to abandon Kiev and take up the defense of the left bank of the Dnieper. The *front* military council in early September made a similar recommendation and had been rebuffed (Gor'kov 1995, 104).

## THE REMOVAL OF ZHUKOV AS CHIEF OF THE
## GENERAL STAFF

On 29 July, Zhukov briefed Stalin on what the General Staff anticipated would be the next moves of the Wehrmacht. The German Army Group Center had captured Smolensk on 16 July, but the Soviet front remained intact. Army Group Center was not in a position to attempt to drive on to Moscow at that time without reinforcements, both in terms of quantity and quality of troops. There was also the problem of the exposed left flank of Army Group Center. If it were to proceed eastward, it would be vulnerable to a blow from the Central *Front,* possibly reinforced by troops from the Southwestern *Front.*

This was the reasoning that Zhukov, speaking for the General Staff, tried to present to Stalin on 29 July. Zhukov concluded that the Germans would use part of their force to defeat the Central *Front* and the Southwest *Front,* thereby securing their right flank before continuing on to Moscow. To counter this German move, Zhukov recommended that the Southwestern *Front* remove all of its forces to the left bank of the Dnieper and prepare to meet a blow from the north. He also recommended reinforcing the Central *Front,* even at the expense of withdrawing some of the troops before Moscow. When Stalin asked about Kiev, which is on the right bank of the Dnieper, Zhukov replied that it should be abandoned to the invaders. Zhukov also recommended that the El'nia salient should be eliminated by a counterstrike, to which Stalin replied that Zhukov was talking nonsense *(chepukha).* Soviet troops did not know how to attack, and how could anyone come up with the idea of abandoning Kiev? Zhukov lost his temper and said that if Stalin thought that his chief of the General Staff talked nonsense, he should send him to the front. That afternoon Stalin placed Zhukov in command of the Reserve *Front* and replaced him as chief of the General Staff with Shaposhnikov (Zhukov 1990, 2:121, 122). Zhukov had been chief of the General Staff almost exactly six months.

Within a few days Zhukov was at the headquarters of the Twenty-fourth Army, which was defending before the El'nia salient. Here it was decided that the army would need ten to twelve days to prepare to reduce the salient. The time was to be used to reinforce the army with two or three divisions and artillery units. The enemy's defensive system would have to be studied, and supplies and ammunition would have to be stocked. These preparations were to be made as far as possible without the enemy becoming aware of them.

The Twenty-fourth Army attacked on 30 August, striking the town from the northeast. On the next day, Stalin's aide, Poskrebyshev, called and asked whether Zhukov was free to come to Moscow. Because the battle had just started, Zhukov asked to remain, and it was not until 6 September that Soviet troops retook the city. On 7 September, Zhukov was in Stalin's quarters—one hour and five minutes late. The subject under discussion was Leningrad.

At that time there were no overland communications with the city, which placed the city's populace in a difficult situation. A member of the State Committee of Defense remarked that it had just been reported to Stalin that the command of the Leningrad *Front,* then commanded by Klim Voroshilov, was incapable of correcting the situation.

In response to Stalin's question, Zhukov gave as his opinion that the Germans would not resume their attempt to take Moscow soon, nor would they attempt to do so until they had taken Leningrad. He was then asked about the performance of the Twenty-fourth Army. Zhukov gave an encouraging report. Then, without transition, Stalin gave Zhukov a handwritten note to Voroshilov that transferred command of the Leningrad *Front* and the Baltic Fleet to Zhukov. Voroshilov was to return to Moscow immediately (Zhukov 1990, 2:117–43).

In what seemed like an afterthought to their conversation, Stalin mentioned that things were shaping up badly for Budenny, who was commanding the southwestern axis *(napravlenie)*. Axes were headquarters, hastily assembled at the beginning of the war, that controlled two or more *fronts*. The southwestern axis included the Southwestern and Southern *Fronts*. Stalin continued, saying that it had been decided to relieve Budenny and asking Zhukov whom he would recommend for the position. Zhukov recommended that Timoshenko be sent there because he had recently gained a great deal of experience in organizing combat operations, and he knew the Ukraine well. In response to the CINC's next question, Zhukov recommended that Ivan Stepanovich Konev, then commanding the Nineteenth Army of the Western *Front*, take Timoshenko's post as commander of the western axis. As Zhukov describes his exchange with Stalin, these major command changes were decided in a matter of minutes.

Before Zhukov departed, Stalin asked him how he saw the future plans of the enemy. Once more Zhukov warned Stalin that the Germans were planning to envelop Kiev. Stalin promised to discuss the matter with Shaposhnikov, and with Timoshenko when he arrived (Zhukov 1990, 2:143, 45).

Zhukov arrived at the headquarters of the Leningrad *Front* on 10 September as a meeting of the *front* military council was in progress. The council, which had not been forewarned that he was coming, was discussing the destruction of various installations within the city to prevent them from falling into the hands of the enemy. Zhukov was chagrined to hear that one item they were considering was the sequence in which the warships of the Baltic Fleet were to be scuttled. Zhukov immediately ordered the ships to be cleared of demolitions and moved to anchorages closer to the city, from which they could support the city's defenders with their heavy guns and their forty units of fire *(boekomplekty)*. Zhukov told Konstantin Simonov in 1950 that he had rebuked those planning the destruction of the ships.

> How can you prepare those ships for destruction? Yes, it is possible that they will be destroyed. But, if they are, they must only be destroyed in battle, firing (Simonov 1987, no. 7, 48).

Zhukov remained in Leningrad until 7 October, when Stalin called him back to Moscow to deal with the crisis on the Western *Front.* While in Leningrad he had shown great ingenuity in reinforcing the city's defenses. He used a portion of the city's antiaircraft guns on the most favorable tank approaches. He started construction of deeply echeloned engineer defenses, to include mines and electrified wire on all vulnerable approaches. Separate rifle brigades were formed from sailors of the Baltic Fleet, the local military schools, and the NKVD. Soviet marines were used in small amphibious operations behind the German lines. Zhukov believed that these operations convinced the Germans to content themselves with siege operations, using aerial and artillery bombardment to bring the city to its knees.

### THE PERFORMANCE OF VOROSHILOV AND KULIK

On 1 April 1942 the Politburo issued a "strictly secret" resolution entitled "On the performance of com[rade] Voroshilov." After criticizing his leadership of the Commissariat of Defense during the Finnish war, which led to "a dragging out of the war and unnecessary casualties," the resolution devoted a paragraph to his performance in Leningrad.

First, he proved to be incapable of organizing the defense of Leningrad—his main mission as commander of the northwestern axis. He also committed serious errors. He issued an order authorizing the election of battalion commanders in units of the people's militia. This order was canceled by direction of the Stavka. He organized the Military Council of the Defense of Leningrad, but he did not enter the council. This order was also overruled by the

Stavka as incorrect and harmful because the workers of Leningrad might have interpreted that as an indication that Voroshilov did not believe in the defense of Leningrad. He also became engrossed in the establishment of workers' battalions armed with shotguns, pikes, and daggers but overlooked the organization of an artillery defense of the city that had especially favorable possibilities (Sidorov 1995, 41). Voroshilov's thinking in a crisis was always in terms of *partizanshchina*.

Marshal Kulik also failed to perform as might have been expected from a marshal of the Soviet Union. He had walked out with the remnants of the Tenth Army following their encirclement in the Belostok salient early in the war. Kulik had arrived at the headquarters of the Tenth Army on 23 June. At first his arrival was greeted with joy. As a deputy commissar of defense, he was expected to know how Moscow intended to organize the defeat of the invaders. The marshal knew nothing about the war plans. Instead he seemed to have difficulty understanding why the Tenth Army was retreating. It took Kulik twelve days dressed as a peasant to escape through the German ring. He claimed that at one point his feet pained him so that he could hardly walk and he considered suicide. On his return, Stalin ordered him to Moscow, where he was roundly reprimanded by the CINC.

Despite almost causing the major embarrassment of a Soviet marshal being captured during the first week of the war, Kulik was given command of the Fifty-fourth Army in August. The Fifty-fourth Army was formed in the vicinity of Volkhov to reinforce the extended left flank of the Leningrad *Front* and its junction with the Northwestern *Front*. It was Kulik's inability to organize his army for a coordinated offensive with the Leningrad *Front* in early Ocotober that led to his relief and delayed Zhukov's return to Moscow.

Kulik's next assignment was to help the embattled Soviet forces in the Crimea, the locus of the main naval base of the Black Sea Fleet—Sevastopol—and the gateway to the North Caucasus. The German Eleventh Army, commanded by Erich von Manstein, had seized Perekop and, after a ten-day battle, had broken through stubborn Soviet resistance on the Ishun peninsula on 20 October. Since there were no prepared positions (other than at Sevastopol), the Germans rapidly overran the peninsula and drove the defending

Fifty-first Army to Kerch. Kulik arrived in Kerch on 15 November and reported to Moscow the difficult situation of the Soviet troops defending the city. He recommended that they be withdrawn to the Taman peninsula. The answer he received authorized the withdrawal of the artillery and equipment from Kerch and then the withdrawal of the infantry from the city. The infantry then had to firmly hold on the eastern side of the Kerch peninsula. The directive was not a model of clarity. Apparently the Stavka wanted to hold a bridgehead on the peninsula in anticipation of an effort to relieve the besieged naval base at Sevastopol.

During the investigation that followed the retreat from Kerch, Adm. Gordei Ivanovich Levchenko, who had been in overall command in the Crimea, testified that Kulik, as representative of the State Committee of Defense, had arrived in Kerch on 12 November and remained two and a half hours. After Kulik became familiar with the situation, Admiral Levchenko asked him to send the other units of the division that had been given to Levchenko by the Stavka. Kulik replied, "I will not give you any more units. The situation at the front is hopeless; save the equipment" (Bobrenev 1993, no. 9, 45). The admiral went on to say that Kulik, rather than interfering for the sake of restoring order in the forces and eliminating confusion and panic, diverted efforts to organize the defense of the city to plans to evacuate and turn the city over to the enemy. Kulik, however, would not give Levchenko a written order to withdraw from the city. He would tell Levchenko only to withdraw according to the plans he had already drawn up. The Germans occupied the city on 15 November, immediately after the commander of the Fifty-first Army, Lt. Gen. Pavel Ivanovich Batov, gave the order to withdraw to the Taman peninsula.

Kulik was tried on 16 February 1942 before a court chaired by V. V. Ul'rikh and two members—army commissar first rank E. A. Shchadenko and Col. Gen. P. A. Artem'ev. Kulik did not deny that he had authorized the withdrawal from the Kerch peninsula. He claimed that there was nothing in the city to defend it—only a shabby band. Despite hostile questions from the court suggesting that his actions stemmed from cowardice and that he had violated his oath, Kulik stubbornly maintained that withdrawal was the only possible action under the circumstances. When it became obvious that Kulik was not going to admit to anything beyond perhaps exceeding his authority, Ul'rikh declared a recess. When the court reconvened, Kulik was punished by being reduced in rank three grades to the rank of major general (one star), and all of his decorations were taken from him (Bobrenov 1993, no. 9, 47).

During the course of the trial, a question was asked about why it had taken so long for Kulik to arrive at Kerch since he had at his disposal a "Douglas" (a DC-3). Kulik said that the delay was due to the weather. After the trial, Mekhlis raised the question of the misappropriation of 85,898 rubles in which Kulik was somehow involved. Attached to Mekhlis's note were documents describing the peregrinations of Kulik and his aide to Kerch, Krasnodar, Sverdlovsk, and Moscow, and the movements of Kulik and his wife and carloads of food and liquor at a time when the country was enduring its cruelest crisis and people were beginning to starve to death.

On 24 February 1942, the combination of Kulik's performance at Kerch and the knowledge of his personal conduct at the front—systematic drunkenness, living a dissolute way of life, and abusing the rank of marshal of the Soviet Union—caused the Politburo to remove him from the Central Committee and replace him as deputy commissar of defense. We do not know to whose account the 85,898 rubles was debited.

## KONEV AND THE COLLAPSE OF THE WESTERN *FRONT*
In early September Ivan Stepanovich Konev assumed command of the Western *Front* from Timoshenko. Konev, who was one year younger than Zhukov, was conscripted into the Russian Army in 1916 and had served as a noncommissioned officer in an artillery battalion. During the civil war he had served as a commissar. In 1931 he had transferred to the command line and commanded a rifle division, a rifle corps, and the Second Separate Red Banner Far Eastern Army. In 1940 and 1941 he had commanded the Transbaikal and North Caucasus Military Districts. With the outbreak of the war, he had formed and commanded the Ninteenth Army in the North Caucasus Military District. The army initially was placed in the reserve of the Stavka while it completed its mobilization. In July, before mobi-

lization was completed, the army was committed on the Western *Front* and participated in the battles for Smolensk. It was perhaps in these battles that Konev came to Zhukov's attention, although Zhukov's memoirs do not provide any rationale for his recommendation of Konev for command of the Western *Front* to Stalin on 9 September.

By the end of September, the Germans had dealt with Kiev and had decided that at this time Leningrad would be besieged and not taken. It was now time to launch a "general offensive" on Moscow. There were three *fronts* defending the city against Army Group Center: the Western, under Konev, consisting of six armies; the Reserve, under Budenny, consisting of two armies; and the Briansk, under Eremenko, consisting of three armies and an operational group. According to Soviet historians, the Wehrmacht enjoyed overall superiority in manpower, tanks, artillery, and planes. The margin of superiority widened significantly as the Germans concentrated on selected axes of advance.

On 5 October, Stalin called Zhukov and asked him to return immediately to Moscow. A complication had arisen on the left flank of the Reserve *Front* (Budenny), and the Stavka wanted to confer with Zhukov. Zhukov asked for a delay because of problems with the Fifty-fourth Army commander (Kulik) and did not fly to Moscow until 6 October. When he arrived he found Stalin sick with a cold and irritated because a difficult situation had developed on the Western and Reserve *Fronts* and he was not being kept informed. He ordered Zhukov to go to the Western *Front*, find out the situation there, and call him at any time. Zhukov had been given a remarkable assignment and was to accomplish it in a remarkable way.

## ZHUKOV'S PERSONAL RECONNAISSANCE

After a brief stop at the General Staff to learn the latest details of the situation from its chief, Shaposhnikov, to collect the necessary maps, and to receive written instructions from the Stavka for the commanders of the Western and Reserve *Fronts*, Zhukov set out for the headquarters of the Western *Front*. Arriving in the darkness he found Konev and his staff seated in the light of stearin candles, apparently completely worn out.

From his conversations with the staff of the Western *Front*, Zhukov had the impression that the catastrophe that had befallen the Western and Reserve *Fronts* could have been avoided. The Stavka had warned of the approaching German offensive as early as 27 September. The axes of the German main efforts could have been predicted, and defenders could have been concentrated there at the expense of more passive sectors. This was not done, and the powerful attacks of the enemy tore large gaps in the Soviet defenses through which the Wehrmacht's mechanized forces moved to their typical deep envelopment objectives. The encirclement of five armies to the west and southwest of Viazma was one result of this operation.

Zhukov reported the dismal facts to Stalin at 0230 on 8 October and then set off to find Budenny. He found him in the building of the Maloiaroslavets town council, looking at a map and trying to locate his headquarters, which had moved during his absence. Zhukov, who had located the new headquarters of the Reserve *Front,* directed Budenny to return there and report to the Stavka. Zhukov continued on toward Iukhnov to determine how far the enemy had advanced. When he reached Kaluga, a staff officer handed him an order to return to the headquarters of the Western *Front.*

When Zhukov arrived there on 10 October, he received a call from Stalin, who informed him that he was to take command of the Western *Front* and the remnants of the Reserve *Front,* which was to be deactivated. Its commander, Budenny, was ordered back to Moscow. Konev was to become Zhukov's deputy and take charge of the eastern wing of the *front,* which later became the Kalinin *Front.* (Zhukov 1990, 2:202–16). During the same conversation, not reported in Zhukov's memoirs, Stalin told Zhukov three times to send Konev to Moscow, where he intended to have Konev tried by a court-martial. Zhukov protested that a trial would have a negative effect on the army.

The trial and execution of D. G. Pavlov had not helped the situation at the beginning of the war. Everyone knew that Pavlov did not have the ability to command a division, and no one should have been surprised that he could not command a *front.* Konev was more capable than Pavlov, and Zhukov proposed that Konev remain as his deputy. Stalin reluctantly approved (Anfilov 1996, 4). Unfortunately, there is no record of Stalin's reaction to Zhukov's comments about Pavlov's competence and his selection for the important post of Western *Front* commander.

## ROKOSSOVSKY ENTERS THE FRAY

In 1930, Konstantin Konstantinovich Rokossovsky commanded a division in which Zhukov was a regimental and then a brigade commander. By 1941, due to his having spent three years in prison, Rokossovsky was now an army commander in Zhukov's Western *Front*. In August 1937, Rokossovsky was accused of being a Polish spy and was released in August 1940 on the assurances of Timoshenko and Zhukov that he was loyal. On his release, he was given the one-star rank of major general and command of the 5th Cavalry Corps. In November he was given command of the 9th Mechanized Corps, which was just forming. He was commanding that corps in the Southwestern *Front* when the war began.

Rokossovsky knew both Kirponos and Pavlov and considered them weak and not fit for their positions. On 17 July, Rokossovsky was ordered to the Western *Front* to take command of miscellaneous troops who had escaped through German encirclements and of reserve divisions that eventually became the 7th Mechanized Corps. In late July, the 7th Corps aided the Sixteenth Army to escape an enemy encirclement, and in the beginning of August the staff of the 7th Mechanized Corps joined the staff of the Sixteenth Army. Rokossovsky became the Sixteenth Army commander. In September, Rokossovsky was promoted to lieutenant general (Sverdlov 1995, 5–10).

On 5 October, as the German offensive was beginning, Rokossovsky was ordered to transfer the sector that his army was defending and his troops to the neighboring Twentieth Army and, together with his staff, travel to Viazma. There, five rifle divisions with reinforcements were concentrating. Rokossovsky and his staff were to lead this force in a counterattack in the direction of Iukhnov. Rokossovsky was truly puzzled by this unusual order, and he requested a retransmission with the personal signature of the *front* commander. That night he received the order signed by Konev and the member of the military council, N. A. Bulganin. Liaison officers from the Twentieth Army arrived, and the Sixteenth Army staff began moving toward Viazma.

En route to Viazma the staff column encountered vehicles and personnel from various units that had been scattered by an attack by German parachutists and fleeing civilians carrying personal belongings on carts. The evidence of the refugees and the army's own reconnaissance suggested that a large enemy armored column had penetrated deeply north of the Iartsevo-Viazma highway and that it would probably turn south to execute an envelopment. The Sixteenth Army staff did not encounter any sign of the promised five divisions and could not establish communications with the *front* headquarters. One of the army staff encountered V. D. Sokolovskii, chief of staff of the Western *Front,* but Sokolovskii said that he did not know what was going on. When Rokossovsky reached Viazma, the chief of the local garrison assured him that there were no troops in the town or in its suburbs.

Rokossovsky was not in the town too long before there was an alarming cry that German tanks had been seen. Rokossovsky confirmed the sighting with his own eyes, and the army staff was forced to flee—it had no means of defending against the German tanks. It now appeared that the German pincers were to close at Viazma.

On the evening of 6 October, the staff of the Sixteenth Army took cover in a forest north of the Viazma-Mozhaisk highway. By the end of the next day, the army staff had established that it was located between the inner and outer rings of the German encirclement. Rokossovsky decided to break out to the northeast. Stragglers who joined the staff were organized into units with commanders, and the staff was to move in three columns at night. After walking some thirty kilometers and being joined by a Moscow militia division, the column learned that there were Soviet troops some ten kilometers away in Gzhatsk. Even though it was getting light Rokossovsky decided to push on to the town. To do so the column had to cross the river Gzhat, and they encountered German troops. It turned out that Gzhatsk was not in friendly hands.

On 10 October the column managed to contact the *front* headquarters near Mozhaisk. They found Voroshilov, Molotov, Konev, and Bulganin, who were searching for someone to blame for the collapse of the Western *Front.* Their first question to Rokossovsky was how he was there with the Sixteenth Army staff but without troops. When Rokossovsky showed Voroshilov the order signed by Konev, Rokossovsky reported that a "stormy" conversation took place between Voroshilov and Konev supported by Bulganin (Rokossovsky 1988, 49–58). That order alone would seem to have provided sufficient basis to try Konev.

Later Zhukov came into the room and was introduced to Rokossovsky as the new Western *Front* commander. Zhukov ordered the Sixteenth Army, such as it was, to defend the Mozhaisk sector, but by 14 October the army was moved to Volokolamsk. By 16 October, German tanks were attacking the left flank of the army. The army's only assigned rifle division was the 18th Rifle Division, made up of Moscow militiamen. They were soon joined by units such as the 3d Cavalry Corps, which entered the army area through the accident of battle (Rokossovsky 1988, 61).

## THE DEFENSE OF MOSCOW

From October until early December, the Western *Front* stretched in a broad arc from Volokolamsk to Kaluga through Mozhaisk and Maloiaroslavets. Shattered armies were re-formed. In the rear of first-echelon defenders, construction was begun on all the likely tank approaches to Moscow. Troops surrounded in the Viazma and Briansk pockets continued to fight their way out of the encirclements. When they succeeded they were collected and debriefed. Some were arrested, assigned to penal units, and reinserted in the line as riflemen. None were decorated.

As the Germans pressed ever closer to Moscow, the pressure on Zhukov and his commanders from Stalin became intense. The loss of a village became a matter demanding the personal attention of the *front* commander. The relations between him and his subordinate army commanders at times became poisonous. In one episode Rokossovsky recommended that his army be permitted to adjust his position by withdrawing to a more favorable defensive location. Zhukov did not approve. Rokossovsky appealed over Zhukov's head to Shaposhnikov, the chief of the General Staff, who authorized the move. Zhukov, in a rage, overruled the chief of the General Staff. The Sixteenth Army did not change its position. Similar clashes with his senior subordinates, often in the presence of their junior officers, harmed Zhukov's relations with the senior command staff, who in 1946 would acquiesce in his disgrace and exile.

In early November, Stalin became convinced that the situation was ripe for preemptive attacks on the *fronts* of the Sixteenth and Twentieth Armies. Zhukov attempted to convince the CINC that the Western *Front* did not have sufficient reserves to mount such attacks. Stalin refused to accept his objections, and the attacks went forward. The results were as Zhukov had expected. The Germans were still strong enough to contain them, and the Soviet losses were heavy.

In early December it became apparent to Zhukov that the German offensive was weakening. The cumulative effect of heavy combat losses, partisan actions against the long supply lines, and the onset of severe winter weather, for which the Germans had not prepared, brought the Wehrmacht's leaders in the field to urge Hitler to authorize withdrawals. The Soviet forces had suffered heavy casualties as well, but in the first 15 days of November they had received 100,000 reinforcements, 300 tanks, and 2,000 artillery pieces. In these circumstances Zhukov called Stalin on 29 November and asked him to give the order for a counteroffensive. Stalin was doubtful, but after receiving Zhukov's assurance that the enemy was exhausted, he said he would confer with the General Staff. Approval was received that night.

The Western *Front* counteroffensive, which began on 6 December, had the relatively modest objective of driving the invaders back twenty to thirty kilometers. But they began the night that Guderian, the German Second Panzer Army commander, issued an order to withdraw to positions approximately eighty kilometers southwest of Moscow. The other armies in German Army Group Center were also authorized to adjust their positions to the pullbacks of the panzer formations.

By 16 December the left wing of the *front* had driven Guderian back almost 130 kilometers. The Germans had yielded Solnechnegorsk, Klin, and Kalinin. At this point Zhukov believed that the Western *Front* should have been reinforced with two more armies, and the offensive continued with the aim of forcing the Germans back to the positions they had held in October. The supreme high commander, under the influence of the victories before Moscow, had become very optimistic. Stalin decided on a general offensive along the entire front (Zhukov 1990, 2:250–52).

### "HELLO COMRADE MERETSKOV! HOW ARE YOU TODAY?"

With this breezy greeting in September 1941, Stalin welcomed back into the fold Kirill Afanas'evich Meretskov, a man he had not seen in three months, a man who had been a deputy commissar of defense, a man he had designated to be a member of the Stavka on 23 June 1941. Both Stalin and Meretskov knew how Meretskov was feeling after three months in one of Beriia's prisons, being beaten with rubber truncheons, and after confessing to being a participant in the military plot with Kork and Uborevich. The organs had collected testimony from more than forty witnesses as to Meretskov's guilt. It is not known if the testimony of D. G. Pavlov was included (Vaksberg 1988, 13). Meretskov, who had been sent to Leningrad by Timoshenko on 21 June as a representative of the high command and was there when the war began, was ordered back to Moscow, where he was arrested on either 24 or 26 June.

The pattern of arrests in the six months before the war and in its immediate aftermath suggests that a supplementary purge was beginning. In addition to Meretskov, many others spent the summer of 1941 in prison: B. L. Vannikov, the commissar of armaments; Ia. V. Smushkevich, who had flown in support of Zhukov at Halhin Gol and was assistant to the chief of the General Staff for the air force; G. M. Shtern, who was head of the antiaircraft directorate; P. V. Rychagov, the head of the air force; A. D. Loktionov, commander of the Baltic Special Military District; G. K. Savchenko, deputy to the head of the main artillery directorate; and I. Iu. Proskurov, head of the main intelligence directorate. But when the war exploded, Stalin realized that he needed some of these officers. Vannikov and others in weapons design and production were returned to their offices and drafting tables. Meretskov was one of the fortunate military officers who was needed in the area around Leningrad.

In October 1941 the Germans moved toward Moscow, and parts of the government and the General Staff were evacuated to the east. On the night of the fifteenth, the central offices of the NKVD were evacuated to Kuibeshev. On 28 October, all of those officers named above except Vannikov and Meretskov were executed without trial (Vaksberg 1988, 13).

## WHY STALIN NEEDED MERETSKOV

The bitter experience of the war with Finland made Meretskov a specialist in the conduct of operations in boggy forested areas such as those in the northwestern parts of the Soviet Union and in the Soviet far east. These were not the primary axes of advance into the Soviet Union, nor were they the axes along which the great victories were achieved by the Soviet offensives of 1944 and 1945. As commander of the Volkhov, Karelian, and 1st Far Eastern *Fronts* (the latter during the short war against Japan in 1945), Meretskov learned that no matter how great the need at the front, newly arriving reinforcements had to be schooled in the distinctive features of operating in areas of restricted communications and visibility. This training included how to construct defensive positions, shelters, and roads under such conditions. The name of Meretskov was never associated with the achievement of brilliant victories, but it should be associated with names of such combat leaders as Wingate and Eichelberger, who accepted the conditions under which they had to operate, taught their troops what they had to do to accommodate to those conditions, and doggedly pushed forward to the final victory.

Meretskov's first postarrest assignment was to help the Northwestern *Front* stabilize its defenses. It had received a sharp jolt at the end of August that had sent it reeling back to positions stretching from Lake Seliger to Lake Il'men. This Meretskov managed to do by 17 September with the aid of reinforcements and changes in the command of one of the armies of the *front*. He was summoned to Moscow, where Stalin ordered him to the Seventh Army, which he had commanded during the Finnish war, to check on why it was retreating before the Finns and to take command if he thought it necessary. When Meretskov arrived, the army had been split: one group defended the mouth of the Svir River, which joins Lakes Ladoga and Onega; a second group defended Petrozavodsk; and a third group was 120 kilometers to the northeast. After taking command of the army, Meretskov managed to stabilize the defense along the Svir preventing the Germans and the Finns from linking to complete the encirclement of Leningrad.

In November, while Meretskov and the Seventh Army were facing north along the Svir, the Germans launched an attack toward the northwest against the Soviet Fourth Army. They seized Tikhvin, approximately 200 kilometers from the rear areas of the Seventh Army. There were no existing communications between the Seventh and Fourth Armies, and the Stavka provided no information. The sudden German attack scattered the Fourth Army headquarters, disrupting its control over its retreating troops. Meretskov, sensitive to the German desire to link up with the Finns, with the Stavka's approval took command of the Fourth Army, collected its disorganized units around field kitchens, and reestablished its communications. After reorganizing the army staff and using Seventh Army reserves, Meretskov directed a counterattack, which drove the Germans back into Tikhvin, where they were content to assume a defensive posture. In late November, having received some reinforcements, the Fourth Army attacked and by 9 December had driven the Germans out of Tikhvin (Meretskov 1970, 228–49).

## COMMANDING THE VOLKHOV *FRONT*

Meretskov's reward for his leadership around Tikhvin was the command of the Volkhov *Front,* which was in the process of being formed. The *front* derived its name from the Volkhov River, which flows roughly south to north from Lake Il'men to Lake Ladoga. In Stalin's presence, Shaposhnikov briefed Meretskov and M. S. Khozin, the commander of the Leningrad *Front,* and the commanders of two of the armies that were to make up the new *front.* Meretskov's mission was to cooperate with the Leningrad *Front* in halting the German offensive on Leningrad, freeing the city from its land blockade, and destroying the invaders in the process. The new *front* was to consist of the Fourth and Fifty-second Armies, already engaged on the Volkhov, and the Fifty-ninth and Second Shock Armies, which were being formed behind the line of contact. Meretskov argued for including the Fifty-fourth Army in his command since it was on his right and was separated from the Leningrad *Front.* He lost the argument because the Stavka (read Stalin?) reasoned that if the Leningrad *Front* thought that it was better to have command of that army, then so be it (Meretskov 1970, 250–52).

## THE AGONY OF THE SECOND SHOCK ARMY

The immediate mission of the Volkhov *Front* was to cross the Volkhov River and make a deep envelopment of the German forces pressing on Leningrad. At the same time, the Fifty-fourth Army was to attack, surround, and destroy enemy forces in its zone north to Lake Ladoga. For Meretskov, "Everything in the plan was good; the objectives were clear and the plan was simple. Only the forces were inadequate" (Meretskov 1965, no. 1, 53). The Second Shock Army was a case in point. Originally known as the Twenty-sixth Army, it was renamed a "shock" *(udarnaiia)* army in December 1941 in an apparent effort to give the impression that it was somehow different in manning and equipment and therefore more capable than the other ground armies. The terminology had been used to describe the breakthrough armies when the concepts of deep battle were discussed before the war. In this case it may have been used to raise the morale of the troops. The Second Shock Army was not a specially trained and equipped army: its strength—one rifle division and seven rifle brigades—was closer to that of a corps. The army headquarters had no experience in the conduct of combat operations, and the army commander was a general who had been a deputy commissar of internal affairs whose approach to combat leadership was based on "long outlived understandings and dogmas" (Meretskov 1965, no. 1, 55). He was relieved of command the week before the Volkhov *Front* took the offensive on 13 January.

Despite these handicaps, the Second Shock Army achieved initial success breaking through the German positions along the Volkhov. The other armies of the *front,* however, made no progress, and it was decided to seek the more modest objective of cutting the Moscow-Leningrad rail line in this sector of the front. A cavalry corps from the *front* reserve and an infantry division taken from an adjacent army were pushed into the breakthrough, which by 12 February had been widened to thirty-five kilometers along the Volkhov but was only thirteen kilometers wide at its narrowest, near the village of Miasnoi Bor, west of the Volkhov. The operations of the Second Shock Army, which were logistically supported through this gap in the German lines, soon became bogged down before the enemy defensive positions. Meretskov reports that on his visits to the army he found the troops poorly equipped, fatigued, operating under German air superiority, and suffering from the bitter cold of the winter of 1941–42. Nevertheless, the Stavka insisted categorically that the rail line be cut by 1 March.

The rail line was not cut by 1 March, and on 9 March, Georgii Malenkov, a member of the Politburo and the State Defense Committee, arrived at *front* headquarters accompanied by Voroshilov and Lt. Gen. A. A. Vlasov. As the representative of the Stavka, Voroshilov had been overseeing Meretskov's activities since February. He had returned to Moscow briefly, and now he was back at the front with Malenkov. Apparently, command changes were in the offing. The Politburo resolution of 1 April 1942, which criticized Voroshilov's performance as Leningrad *Front* commander, also noted that his presence on the Volkhov *Front* failed to yield the desired results. It also states that Voroshilov was offered command of the Volkhov *Front* and had refused on the grounds that it was a difficult *front* and he did not want to fail in this task. The resolution concluded, "Send comrade Voroshilov to rear services military duty" (Sidorov 1995, 41).

Vlasov was assigned by the Stavka to be Meretskov's deputy, apparently without Meretskov's knowledge. It may have seemed to Meretskov that the Stavka was not satisfied with his performance and that Vlasov was his potential successor. Although Meretskov does not admit it, he must have known Vlasov before the war. Vlasov was a division and corps commander in the Kiev Military District. He wrote articles published in the national press on Meretskov's favorite subject—troop training. And he reportedly shared a platform with him discussing training tasks for 1941. In December 1941, as commander of the Twentieth Army, he had a prominent and well publicized role in the defense of Moscow, for which he was decorated and promoted to lieutenant general (Steenberg 1970, 12–20).

Meretskov's retrospective impression was that Vlasov felt uncomfortable as his assistant and wanted to be more in the limelight. According to Meretskov, he displayed no initiative as deputy commander and fulfilled sluggishly those tasks that were given him. On 21 March, when the commander of the Second Shock Army became ill, Vlasov was flown into the now completely surrounded army to take command by order of the Stavka. The thirteen-kilometer-wide corridor, which was being interdicted by German artillery fire and aerial bombardment, was closed on 19 March. As the spring thaw quickened, movement in and around the trapped army's area became more amd more difficult. Meretskov's solution to these problems was to request the Stavka to give him another army in order to take advantage of the bridgehead over the Volkhov and possibly end the blockade of Leningrad. The Stavka did not object to Meretskov's plan, but reinforcements did not begin arriving until early April. In the meantime, by scraping together various odds and ends from his reserve, Meretskov managed to reopen the line of communication to the Second Shock Army. For Meretskov, who saw a lot of action during the war years, "these weeks were the most difficult for me . . ." (Meretskov 1970, 280).

Using reinforcements furnished by the Stavka and units from his reserve, Meretskov formed a rifle corps with which he planned to reinforce the Second Shock Army and launch a new offensive to cut the rail line. But, to his complete surprise, the Volkhov *Front* was disbanded on 23 April and its units became an operations group under the command of the Leningrad *Front*.

Meretskov first learned of the new command arrangements when M. S. Khozin, the Leningrad *Front* commander, appeared at the Volkhov *Front* headquarters in a very happy frame of mind with the Stavka's directive in his pocket. Meretskov was told later that Khozin had convinced Stalin that if he had command of the Volkhov *Front* forces, he could effect the relief of the blockade at Leningrad. During their meeting, Meretskov tried to convince Khozin that the Second Shock Army was in a perilous position and that it should be reinforced. Khozin did not agree, nor did Stalin when Meretskov reported to him on the situation in Moscow (Meretskov 1970, 281–82).

Meretskov was assigned as deputy to the commander of the western axis, Zhukov, who was then engaged in reorganizing his forces after the counteroffensive, which had driven the Germans from the gates of Moscow. When he reported to Zhukov, Meretskov told him that he could better serve if he were given an army to command. Zhukov promised to raise the issue with the Stavka, and soon Meretskov was given command of the Thirty-third Army. That army had been surrounded south of Viazma and had suffered considerable losses (including that of the army commander, M. G. Efremov) extricating itself from the encirclement. It required complete reorganization.

Meretskov was in the midst of this task on 8 June when he was ordered to report to Stalin in Moscow immediately. There, Meretskov, still in muddy boots, was told by Stalin that combining the Volkhov and Leningrad *Fronts* had been a mistake, that Khozin had handled matters badly, that Meretskov was to reestablish the Volkhov *Front*, and that the Second Shock Army was to be rescued even if it meant abandoning the army's heavy artillery and equipment.

In the two months that Meretskov had served under Zhukov, the condition of the Second Shock Army had become increasingly desperate. Stalin had rejected all requests from the Volkhov *Front* for permission to withdraw the army. One of these requests, according to Vlasov's biographer, was made to Stalin by Vlasov in person (Steenberg 1970, 24).

As supplies diminished and German attacks increased in intensity, casualties mounted. On 14 May, Stalin authorized the army to withdraw, and several divisions were extracted through the "throat." On 20 May, the escape corridor was closed again, internal army communications were disrupted by German attacks, and the army disintegrated into small groups, each seeking its own salvation. When Meretskov returned to reestablish the Volkhov *Front* in June, he was accompanied by the chief of the operations directorate of the General Staff, A. M. Vasilevsky. With whatever reserves they could find, they managed to regain contact with Second Shock Army units on 19 June, but the Germans closed the corridor again on 25 June. It was not to open again for the Second Shock Army.

Vlasov was captured on 12 July—betrayed, according to the Germans, by the Soviet headman of the tiny village where he was hiding (Steenberg 1970, 24–28). Within two months of his capture, Vlasov proposed that a Russian liberation army be created to overthrow the Stalin regime. It was not until 1944 that Vlasov was given authority to take command of the various small units of Russian prisoners of war and Russian émigrées serving with the German Army and to organize them into an army—the Russian Liberation Army. Two divisions were to be established first, but it was not until February 1945 that they were ready for combat. When they were, there was no clear policy within the collapsing German leadership as to how and where they were to be used. In May 1945, Vlasov surrendered to the U.S. Army, which allowed him to be captured by the Soviet Army. On 2 August 1946, it was announced that he and nine other former Soviet officers had been tried and executed by hanging.

The Vlasov movement was a major embarrassment for the Soviet Union, and it could have been avoided. There is no evidence that Vlasov was any more disaffected than other senior officers by the events of 1937 and 1938. He fought well early in the war when, if he were inclined to defect, he could have done so more easily and safely. His attempt in 1945 to lead his "army" against the Soviet Army was either quixotic or desperate. It did, however, provide the world with some dimension of Soviet opposition to Stalin, even though, under the circumstances of 1945, the world had to pretend that what had occurred was a minor aberration.

## THE GENERAL OFFENSIVE OF JANUARY 1942

While the undermanned Volkhov *Front* was struggling to break through and relieve the siege of Leningrad, Stalin was attempting to realize a grand strategic conception. On 5 January 1942, Stalin assembled the *front* commanders to announce his plan to continue the offensive of the Western *Front* all along the entire German-Soviet front. Reasoning that the Germans were bewildered by the defeats they had suffered before Moscow and that they were poorly prepared for winter, Stalin did not want to give them breathing space to restore their losses and resume their offensive on Moscow in the spring. A general offensive would cause them to exhaust their reserves while the Soviet Army at that time would be receiving new reserves.

The main effort would be made against the Army Group Center by the Kalinin, Western, and Briansk *Fronts* and part of the Northwestern *Front*. They would execute a double envelopment designed to surround and destroy the Army Group Center in the area of Briansk, Rzhev, and Smolensk. The Leningrad, Northwestern and the Volkhov *Fronts* would destroy Army Group North and liquidate the blockade around Leningrad. The Southwestern and the Southern *Fronts* would defeat Army Group South and the Caucasus *Front* and the Black Sea Fleet would liberate the Crimea (Zhukov 1990, 2:254).

During the discussion that followed, only Zhukov and N. A. Voznesensky raised any objections. Zhukov said that in order to carry out such an offensive successfully the army would have to be reinforced with troops and equipment, particularly tanks. Voznesensky, who was responsible for wartime economic planning, said the country at that time did not have the material resources to support an offensive on all *fronts*.

Stalin would not accept any objections, and the directive ordering the offensive was received the next day. A few days later, *front* and army commanders received a "directive letter" from the CINC giving practical instructions on the employment of strike groups and the organization of an artillery offensive. These instructions were to be followed unconditionally. However, as Zhukov observed, the Soviet Army in the winter of 1942 did not have the forces and the means of carrying them out. Without the forces, the strike groups could not be assembled. To conduct an artillery offensive, more guns were required; above all, adequate supplies of ammunition were needed (Zhukov 1990, 255–58).

In 1962, Konstantin Rokossovsky recalled that, from his point of view, by 20 December the Germans had recovered sufficiently that it was unwise to continue the offensive without reinforcements. Instead, the Stavka ordered the offensive to continue. He remembered that his army was short of weapons and ammunition. The infantry attacked in the snow under heavy enemy artillery fire without support from its own artillery. The country was not yet strong enough to support the offensives of five *fronts*. The enemy was on the strategic defensive, and the Soviet Army should have done the same.

## GOLIKOV FAILS BEFORE SUKHINICHI

During the Western *Front* counteroffensive Filip Ivanovich Golikov commanded the Tenth Army, which attacked on the left flank of the *front*. Golikov had been on diplomatic missions to the United States and Britain since the war began (Gor'kov 1995, 215, 216). In response to his urgent requests, he was given command of the Tenth Army (this was a completely new army, not to be confused with the

Tenth Army which defended Belostok in June 1941). The new Tenth Army was organized and trained in approximately two weeks.

On 24 November, Golikov was called by Shaposhnikov and told that his army, which included many untrained recruits and had assembled on 8 November in the vicinity of Perm, was to move to Riazan prepared to participate in the Western *Front* offensive. At that time, three of the infantry divisions of the army were not completely armed. The army, which had a strength of approximately 100,000 men, was expected to close in its new areas by 2 December. Due to various problems with the rail net, the army did not close until 5 December. As the divisions prepared to enter combat, the 57th and 75th Cavalry Divisions were completely unarmed, some of the rifle divisions had one third of its weapons, and all units including the army headquarters were short of radios.

The Tenth Army nevertheless attacked as scheduled on 6 December, and by mid-January 1942 it had invested Sukhinichi, a road and rail junction which the Wehrmacht had determined to hold, approximately 175 kilometers from the Riazan area. According to Golikov, during the battles for Sukhinichi from 1 through 24 January, the Tenth Army suffered 5,570 casualties (killed, wounded, and frostbitten) (Golikov 1967, 176).

On 21 January, Zhukov, the *front* commander, ordered Rokossovsky to turn over his troops to the neighboring armies and bring his headquarters and the staff of the Sixteenth Army to the vicinity of Sukhinichi and take the town. While surveying the situation in the vicinity of Sukhinichi, Rokossovsky tried to give the impression that he had come with his entire army. Whether or not he was successful in this is not known. What is known is that the Germans evacuated the town on 29 January as Rokossovsky was preparing to attack (Sverdlov 1995, 15) (Rokossovsky 1988, 105–6). Golikov became Zhukov's deputy and probably the butt of some wry remarks. In 1943, as Zhukov was again preparing to relieve Golikov, this time from his post as commander of the Voronezh *Front,* he was overheard recalling Golikov's performance at Sukhinichi (Mirkina 1988, 168).

## TIMOSHENKO TAKES THE OFFENSIVE

After one more attempt to energize the Western *Front* to further offensive operations on 20 March, the Stavka at the end of March allowed the *front* to go on the defensive. The winter offensive had moved the line of contact 70 to 100 kilometers to the west and, in Zhukov's words, had "somewhat" *(neskol'ko)* improved the operational-strategic situation on the western axis. In the same period, the other *fronts* had not been been able to accomplish the objectives assigned them in January (Zhukov 1990, 266).

At the end of March, Stalin held a meeting of the State Defense Committee to consider Soviet plans for the summer campaign. Voroshilov, Timoshenko, Khrushchev, Bagramian, Shaposhnikov, and Vasilevsky were in attendance. The meeting began with a report by Shaposhnikov on the German situation which concluded that the enemy was still capable of strategic initiatives on two axes: an offensive aimed at capturing Moscow and an offensive in the southern part of the country to capture the lower Volga and the Caucasus. Stalin was most concerned that the Germans would make another effort to capture Moscow.

Stalin favored an active defense with limited offensives in the Crimea, in the area of Kharkov, on the L'gov-Kursk axis and in the area of Leningrad and Demiansk. It was typical of Stalin that he did not seem to realize that these partial offensives spread over a wide area would consume resources without yielding the results that concentrated efforts could bring.

Zhukov, for his part, repeated the recommendation that he had made in January: reinforce the Western, Kalinin, and Briansk *Fronts* and attack the large enemy concentration in the Viazma-Rzhev area. Timoshenko proposed an operation on the southwestern axis using the Southwestern, the Southern, and Briansk *Fronts*. This operation was opposed by Shaposhnikov, speaking for the General Staff, on the grounds that there were not sufficient reserves available and that it would be difficult to organize. Stalin interrupted him saying that he did not want to sit with folded hands waiting for the Germans to strike the first blow. He was opposed to Zhukov's recommendation that only the Western *Front* attack. He wanted to conduct a number of preemptive strikes on a broad front to feel out the enemy's readiness. After some further discussion, he directed the preparation of partial operations in the Crimea, on the Kharkov axis, and in other areas.

Timoshenko supported Stalin and said that his command was in condition to strike preemptively to upset the enemy's plans against the Southern and Southwestern *Fronts*. He was supported by Voroshilov, who was shortly to be the subject of the stinging resolution of the Politburo consigning him to service in the rear areas. Zhukov protested once more the decision to conduct several offensive operations at the same time. He received no support, even from Shaposhnikov, who Zhukov believed was also opposed to the idea of partial offensive operations. Zhukov had not reached his *front* headquarters when he learned that he had been relieved as commander of the western axis and that the Kalinin *Front* was now subordinate directly to the Stavka. The axis was disbanded. This demotion, Zhukov understood, was a result of his opposition to Stalin's plan to conduct a number of preemptive offensive operations (Zhukov 1990, 2:271–78). Timoshenko's original plan for an offensive on the southwestern axis, which would have involved three *fronts*, was scaled back because of the objections of the General Staff to a two-*front* operation designed to retake Kharkov. Stalin squelched further objections from the General Staff and directed that the operation was to be considered an internal matter of the southwestern axis (Vasilevsky 1973, 71).

The Southwestern *Front* began the offensive on 12 May and achieved some initial gains. But by 17 May an enemy strike group of eleven divisions led by Colonel General Kleist began an offensive from the area of Slaviansk and Kramatorsk. It broke through the defenses of the Ninth Army and threatened the Fifty-seventh Army of the Southern *Front*. Timoshenko had not taken the necessary steps to secure his attacking force from a blow from that direction. Vasilevsky, who had now become the chief of the General Staff because of Shaposhnikov's illness, tried to have Stalin call off the Southwestern *Front* offensive. Stalin refused because he said that he had assurances from Timoshenko that the necessary measures had been taken. On 18 May, Khrushchev called and asked Vasilevsky to call Stalin and ask him to abort the offensive. Vasilevsky, having called Stalin on this matter the day before, suggested that Khrushchev call Stalin himself. Khrushchev reached Malenkov and through him learned that the CINC wanted the offensive to continue.

The offensive was finally halted on 19 May when the Germans reached the rear areas of Timoshenko's strike group. It was too late. Three armies of the Southwestern and Southern *Fronts* suffered serious losses, and the way was open to Stalingrad and the Caucasus (Vasilevsky 1973, 193).

While the Wehrmacht was regrouping and preparing to continue its offensive to the south and east, the Stavka was considering who was to answer for the disastrous Kharkov offensive. Bagramian, the axis chief of staff, was removed from his post by direction of the Stavka. "He had in the course of three weeks, thanks to his frivolity, not only lost a half-won operation, but succeeded in giving the enemy 18–20 divisions . . ." (Portugal'skii 1994, 248). Timoshenko remained *front* commander until the early days of Stalingrad, when he was relieved by Eremenko. He did not receive another command until October 1942 when he was given command of the Northwestern *Front*. Khrushchev remained at Stalingrad as the member of the Military Council on the Stalingrad *Front*.

## MEKHLIS AND THE CRIMEA DISASTER

Another consequence of Stalin's decision at the end of March to conduct partial offensives was a crushing defeat in the Crimea. The Crimean *Front* had been formed in late January 1942 with the mission of aiding the forces who had been defending the Sevastopol defensive area since the beginning of the war. The *front*, consisting of three armies, made three attempts from 27 February until 13 April to break through the German positions at Karasubazar, without result. The *front* was then ordered to take up defensive positions to hold Kerch and the peninsula. On 8 May the Germans mounted an offensive and retook Kerch on 14 May. These defeats hastened the final fall of Sevastopol on 4 July 1942.

The defeats and the reaction to them by the Stavka serve to illustrate the conflicts that could and did arise between the military commander, in this case D. T. Kozlov, and the representative of the Stavka, L. Z. Mekhlis.

The name of Mekhlis has been linked closely with several Party investigations of the military that seemed to end in tragedy for their targets. It will be recalled that Mekhlis was somehow involved in the return of Bliukher to Moscow and to his death in 1938, and the trial and execution of D. G. Pavlov in 1941. Ivan Stadniuk, who based his novel *Voina* (war) on his conversations with Molotov, attributes to Mekhlis the policy of blaming the early losses in the war on traitors and saboteurs. Thus, the defeats were not the fault of Stalin or the Party but of those in uniform who betrayed their country. Perhaps the most notable contribution Mekhlis made to military-Party relations came during the Finnish war when he was chief of the Main Political Administration: after a quick and unjust trial, members of the 44th Division who had escaped from an encirclement—including the division commander, the chief of the political section, and the division chief of staff—were shot before a formation of the division (Portugal'skii 1994, 95, 96).

In the Crimean case, Mekhlis complained to Stalin about the performance of Kozlov. Stalin in response sent Mekhlis a stinging reply to the effect that Mekhlis was not just an observer at the *front* but a responsible representative of the Stavka and, as such, should have taken action to correct whatever was wrong. He also reminded Mekhlis that the Stavka did not have a supply of "Hindenburgs" to send to take command of the Soviet forces and that the Soviet Army would have to make do with what it had (Vasilevsky 1973, 186, 187). In his anger it was remarkable that the only military name that Stalin could produce was that of the "Wooden Titan" who would have helped the situation in the Crimea. One senses in the military memoirs that the authors took delight in quoting Stalin's message to the "gloomy demon."

## STALINGRAD—THE TURNING POINT

The attention of most of the free world was focused on Stalingrad in the late summer of 1942. For the Soviet Army the crushing defeat at Kharkov had been followed by a series of defensive battles on the distant approaches to Stalingrad beginning on 17 July. By 23 July the enemy force numbered eighteen divisions and threatened to envelop the Sixty-second and the Sixty-fourth Soviet Armies in the big bend of the River Don. Soviet Reserves in the region were sparse. A counterattack using available forces saved both armies from encirclement. They were to play a critical role in the defense of the city.

It became clear in early August that one *front* would not be able to cope with the breadth of the front that would become involved with Stalingrad, so the Stalingrad *Front* was divided into two with the creation of the Southeastern *Front*. By early August reinforcements began to arrive and by 20 August fifteen rifle divisions and three tank corps had arrived. German attacks on the city began on 19 August, and the Germans reached the Volga north of the city on 23 August.

The drama of the defense of the city continued until 19 November, when the great counteroffensive began and the tables were turned on the German Sixth Army. Then the principal players became Rokossovsky and the Don *Front* which took the surrender of the German Sixth Army on 31 January.

Stalingrad had been a military turning point, but it was also a turning point in the relations between Stalin and the General Staff. Stalin from this time on would heed those who had planned and executed the great victory of Soviet arms. Vasilevsky and Zhukov working in tandem had spent many days and nights in and around the city. They had also logged many hours on flights along the front to and from Moscow. Vasilevsky completed one of the more remarkable of these on 18 November when he was summoned to Moscow to a meeting of the State Defense Committee. There, Stalin showed him a letter he had received from the commander of the Fourth Mechanized Corps, B. T. Vol'skii, a unit designated to play a decisive role in the operations of Eremenko's Stalingrad *Front*.

In his letter, Vol'skii predicted the offensive would fail and urged Stalin to postpone and revise the plans for it. Vasilevsky, asked for his opinion of the letter, expressed surprise, especially since Vol'skii had not expressed the slightest doubt to him that the operation would succeed or that Vol'skii's corps could execute its mission.

Stalin called Vol'skii directly from the meeting, talked with him briefly and then ordered Vasilevsky to leave him in command but to report to him on Vol'skii's performance. On 21 November, Vasilevsky was able to report that the 4th Mechanized Corps had fought well which apparently closed this curious incident.

M. M. Popov, who became Eremenko's deputy in October 1942, replacing Golikov, provides a more complete picture of Vol'skii, the 4th Mechanized Corps, and their performance during the opening phases of the counteroffensive. The corps had been formed in the fall of 1942 on the lower Volga from the 28th Tank Corps. It had officially joined the Stalingrad *Front* on 24 October. It had moved up the Volga by rail, thence cross-country 150 kilometers to assembly areas on the left bank of the Volga. The corps was allotted one crossing over the Volga and the bulk of the corps was forced to wait in relatively open areas to cross the Volga under the continuous threat of German air attack. Because of a shortage of trucks, some of the trucks intended to transport the motorized infantry of the 4th Mechanized Corps were used to haul supplies and by the start of the operation more than 100 trucks had not returned to their units. It is not difficult to understand why Vol'skii had some doubts about the success of the operation.

The morning of the attack was foggy, but the start of the artillery preparation in that area was not delayed. Vol'skii was at a forward command post with Popov; and, when it became time for the 4th Mechanized Corps to move into the battle, he did not move until at last Popov insisted that the corps move forward. About eleven o'-clock Vol'skii gave the signal "forward!" by radio but nothing happened. Vol'skii left the command post to meet his troops. At last, the first two brigades of the corps appeared but then there was a long interval during which the next scheduled units did not appear. Popov himself went to the rear to find the remainder of the corps unhurriedly refueling.

After a sharp exchange between Popov and its commander, the brigade finally moved forward. The Soviet Army was beginning to learn how to win.

When the story of Stalingrad is recounted, the names of the soldiers stand out—Rokossovsky, the Don *Front* commander who took overall command of the liquidation of the German Sixth Army from Eremenko and saw the operation through to its successful conclusion. Malinovsky, the Second Guards Army commander, who had lost command of the Southern *Front*, took a newly formed army and was able to prevent von Manstein, from extricating Paulus from the clutches of the Soviet envelopment. Tolbukhin, the Fifty-seventh Army commander, and Chuikov, the Stalingrader of Stalingraders, commanding the Sixty-second Army in the city itself, taking the desperate German attacks while striving to comply with Eremenko's less than helpful directives from the safety of the east bank of the Volga.

# EPILOGUE

On 9 May 1995 the Russian Federation observed the fiftieth anniversary of the defeat of Germany in World War II. The night before, a gala concert was held in the State Kremlin Palace. The audience included many officers in Soviet uniforms, invited foreign veterans, and various government officials. There were two speakers, President Yeltsin on behalf of the federation and retired general of the army Viktor Kulikov speaking on behalf of the Russian veterans. In the course of his remarks, Yeltsin mentioned the number of Soviet casualties the war had cost—now estimated at 27,000,000 persons. Kulikov did not mention casualties, but he did make one remark that evoked considerable applause, easily more than had responded to the President's remarks. Kulikov called on the Russian people never to forget the system that had brought them this victory.

One of the purposes of this book was to examine the Soviet system as it developed under Stalin into what seemed a mighty nation state. Given its centralized command and control apparatus and its monolithic decision making system, the Soviet state under Stalin seemed to be ideally configured to become the superpower of the next millenium. The system had one fatal flaw. Its operator was a paranoid who was prepared to believe that there were people of many different backgrounds and origins who were constantly plotting to remove him and to destroy what he considered his personal contribution to world development and history—the Soviet Union and its satellites. As we have seen, Stalin arranged to surround his person with individuals who attempted to make him think that he always made the correct decision. If something went badly, it was the fault of incompetents, traitors, or saboteurs. During peacetime, the resilience and the recuperative powers of the Soviet peoples made it possible to commit huge errors and cover them up with famines, concentration camps, and mass trials. Complete control of the press ensured that only the government's version of events would become public. There were escapees, of course, but who really believed them?

War was a different matter. Your opponent would not likely conceal that he had taken 500,000 prisoners at Kiev. The capture of important cities such as Kiev, Leningrad, Minsk, and Odessa could not be hidden. Nor eventually could the enormous numbers of casualties his troops were suffering be hidden from either friend or foe. For the Soviets, a plausible casualty number is unlikely ever to be found, given the primitive personnel accounting system in use during the war, the lack of incentives to report the truth on losses, and the general disorganization of widespread areas of the country caused by the invasion.

But the dead remain, some still unburied more than fifty years after their bodies were cruelly wasted by a megalomaniac and his willing henchmen. They are still mourned, the missing are still sought, and the disabled still cared for. It seems clear that the system that produced these casualties never really concerned itself with them as matters requiring more than a new propaganda slogan.

## AN ARTILLERYMAN REMEMBERS

One who sensed personal responsibility for the enormous losses that the country had suffered was marshal of artillery Nikolai Dmitrievich Iakovlev. Iakovlev served as head of the main artillery directorate from 19 June 1941 until 1948. The reader who has followed the career of Grigorii Kulik, the man whom Iakovlev relieved as head of the GAU, can imagine the state of that institution when Iakovlev took command on the eve of the war. One has only to recall Kulik and Stalin's decision to halt the production of 45mm and 57mm antitank guns in order to concentrate on producing 107mm tank guns to understand the chaos which Iakovlev had to contend with. Iakovlev succeeded in spite of knowing that any slip-up might cost him his head.

Soon after he assumed command of the GAU, Iakovlev clashed with Mekhlis. Mekhlis reported this to Stalin. Iakovlev's relations with Stalin cooled. But it was not until 1952 that Iakovlev was arrested because an accident occurred with an artillery piece that the GAU had certified to be operational. Fortunately for Iakovlev, Stalin died in March 1953 and Iakovlev was released from prison.

Iakovlev's son, Nikolai Nikolaevich, told me that after his father retired he would often take him on drives throughout the countryside. Marshal Iakovlev was born in Staraia Russa, near Leningrad, and he often visited old friends and colleagues there. Each time the car would pass a roadside grave or a monument marking some long forgotten skirmish, the marshal would have the car stopped so that he could pay his respects to any fallen serviceman whose remains might be there. Nikolai Dmitrievich died on 9 May 1972 after he had put on his uniform and was planning to pay his respects at the flame of the unknown soldier. As an artilleryman he had always done his best to save the lives of Soviet soldiers.

## THE FIRST CAVALRY ARMY'S REWARD

Despite Voroshilov's record of failure and the stinging written rebuke he received from the Politburo for his errors in 1941 and 1942, including the directive that his activities be restricted to the rear areas, he nevertheless returned to the front in November 1943 to coordinate an attempt by the Separate Maritime Army, commanded initially by I. E. Petrov and later by A. I. Eremenko, to regain the Crimean Peninsula. "To help the command of the Separate Maritime Army, the Stavka sent K. E.Voroshilov" (Vasilevsky 1973, 392). Stubborn German opposition and a faulty attack plan caused the Stavka acute displeasure, heavy casualties were incurred, and a new plan of action was demanded. The new plan also did not yield the desired results.

The German presence in the Crimea was not liquidated until early April when a combined attack of Tolbukhin's Fourth Ukrainian *Front* and Eremenko's Separate Maritime Army overcame German and Romanian opposition. After the operation, the Maritime Army became part of the Fourth Ukrainian *Front* and its commander, A.I. Eremenko, took command of the Second Baltic *Front*. Vasilevsky, who was representative of the Stavka to Tolbukhin and the Fourth Ukrainian *Front,* had considerable problems convincing Voroshilov of the viability of his plan to attack from the north as Voroshilov remained a prisoner of his civil war impressions of the Crimean theater.

Voroshilov's doubts about the feasibility of the operation infected Tolbukhin. Vasilevsky threatened Tolbukhin that he, Vasilevsky, would take command of the *front* and execute the planned operation. Voroshilov was invited to send his concerns to the Stavka. Threatened with the loss of his command, Tolbukhin immediately overcame his doubts while Voroshilov declined to submit his objections to the Stavka (Kumanev 1995, 4). The operation was a success and the Germans were finally driven out of the Crimea.

Voroshilov retained his high rank throughout the war and into the postwar Soviet governments. He served on the Allied Control Commission in Hungary from 1946 until 1953 and in various positions in the Soviet government until his death in 1969. When he was confronted with the enormity of the arrests and executions during the military purges he could only wonder why so many had signed confessions.

### KULIK IS RESTORED IN RANK

During the de-Stalinization period numerous victims of the purges were publicly cleared of the fantastic crimes for which they had been convicted. Kulik's performance as a senior commander on the Western *Front* and in the Crimea seemed to have warranted fairly his reduction in rank. His misappropriation of government property and failures at Kerch would seem to have merited a prison sentence—if not worse—in 1942. Yet in 1943 Kulik was given the command of another army composed of the best assault divisions and increased in rank to lieutenant general in an attempt to restore his command image, but he was relieved of command in September and eventually assigned to duties with the troop replacement command where he failed again. Kulik had friends such as Zhukov and they tried in vain to keep him afloat. He was arrested in 1946 and executed in 1950. That he was restored in rank to marshal of the Soviet Union in 1957 makes his case a prime example of the capriciousness of Soviet justice.

## MEKHLIS THE GLOOMY DEMON

David Ortenberg, editor of *Krasnaia Zvezda* from 22 June 1941 until 31 July 1943, perhaps was closer to Lev Zakharovich Mekhlis than most and clearly has written about him with the most sympathy. Mekhlis, Ortenberg reports, even after the fiasco at Kerch and his reduction in rank and responsibility, continued to be a member of the military council of various *fronts* throughout the rest of the war. When Ortenberg saw him on the day following the defeat at Kerch, he was tormented and depressed. That very day he received notification that he was a member of an important commission in the Main Political Administration which could only be interpreted to mean that Stalin had not lost confidence in him, that all was not lost, and there was still time to recoup his personal standing with the dictator. This in fact happened. After serving as member of the military council of various *fronts,* he returned to the position of commissar for state control after the war.

Ortenberg also relates that, by the time of the Nineteenth Party Congress in 1952, Mekhlis asked Stalin for permission to attend as an alternate delegate even though he was very ill. Stalin refused, saying that the congress should not become an infirmary. Several days later when the listing of the new Central Committee was published, Mekhlis's name was on it! (Ortenberg 1995, 183, 184.)

## FILIP IVANOVICH GOLIKOV—THE DE-STALINIZED STALINIST

Filip Ivanovich Golikov, after his relief as commander of the Voronezh *Front* in late March 1943 (for which he blamed Zhukov), was immediately given a new assignment by Stalin. He became the head of the main directorate of cadres. In 1944 he was also given the task of supervising the repatriation of Soviet citizens who had been scattered over Europe by German forced labor policies. In this position he earned a reputation as a ruthless pursuer of those Soviet citizens who might have chosen to remain abroad after the war. From 1950 until 1956 he commanded a separate mechanized army and from 1956 until 1958 he headed the armored academy.

It was in his nonmilitary activities that he perhaps achieved his most significant career success. In 1946 he was one of the most vocal of Zhukov's accusers. Golikov heaped dirt on Zhukov's head, according to Marshal Konev. In 1957, when Zhukov was again under siege, Golikov was one of his leading detractors. His animus toward Zhukov was so obvious that Khrushchev chose him to be Zhukov's keeper. Golikov was named head of the Main Political Administration and made a marshal of the Soviet Union—the only occasion in the history of the Soviet Army that the head of that directorate was awarded such a high rank.

In 1962 Golikov was suddenly relieved and replaced by A. A. Epishev who had to be content to head the MPA with the rank of general of the army. There has been speculation that Golikov's relief had something to do with the Cuban Missile Crisis (Shukman 1993, 87). According to Russian academicians, he was relieved because prominent members of the Leningrad party organization could not stand the sight of Golikov on Lenin's mausoleum during the annual May Day and October Revolution parades. Golikov had been prominent in the commission that investigated the Leningrad affair in the late 1940s and which recommended severe sanctions against Leningrad communists. The Stalinist had been exposed. He retained his cheaply earned rank without a position until his death in 1980.

## EFIM AFANAS'EVICH SHCHADENKO—CAREER COMMISSAR

Among Stalin's lieutenants, Efim Afanas'evich Shchadenko, who has been described as a product and a strongpoint of the Stalinist system and, at the same time, a victim of it, did not fight in any of the battles of World War II. He was nevertheless responsible for many of the Red Army's casualties. In 1937 he became a member of the Military Council of the Kiev Military District. In three months one corps commissar, two division commissars, four brigade commissars, four regimental commissars, and one political instructor had been removed from the party and relieved from their duties. Also dismissed from the army were forty-six middle level commanders. Shchadenko's performance apparently impressed Stalin, for in November 1937 he was made a deputy commissar of defense and chief of the directorate which eventually became the main cadres directorate in charge of officer assignments. This directorate had been led by B. M. Fel'dman from 1934 until April 1937. In June 1937 Fel'd-man accompanied Tukhachevsky to the execution chamber.

Shchadenko had served with Stalin and Voroshilov at Tsaritsyn and Trotsky had on one occasion tried to have him censured by the local party organization but the censure did not appear on his record. In 1931 the fact that he had been almost censured by Trotsky was taken as a commendation and Shchadenko proudly brought that fact to the attention of his superiors. As many others of his First Cavalry Army comrades, he was an avid supporter of the cavalry as an arm of the service and after his experience with Trotsky an unreconciled opponent of the military specialists.

In 1936, while Shchadenko was a political officer at the Frunze Military Academy, he clashed with the commander of the academy, Avgust Ivanovich Kork, which resulted in the transfer of Shchadenko to the Kharkov Military District. In June 1937, when Kork was repressed along with Tukhachevsky, Shchadenko became more convinced that his attitude toward the military specialists was the correct one. As chief of the main cadres Directorate, Shchadenko devoted himself to removing all real and potential opponents of Stalin's policies and he helped lead a massive attack on the officer corps of the services.

In 1940 when Stalin apparently began to realize that the coercion pendulum had swung too far, Shchadenko was the scapegoat who was blamed for the massive shortages in officer personnel. Shchadenko attempted to blame the "criminal" activity of the General Staff for the shortages (Shchadenko 1990, 178). This did not save Shchadenko and he was without a position almost a year until the start of the war. At that time he was named chief of the main directorate of forming and staffing the forces of the Red Army where he served throughout the war. He died in 1951 (Khorev 1991, 5).

## THE SYSTEM THAT BROUGHT VICTORY

Under Stalin there was nothing that could be called justice. Stalin's lieutenants seemed to survive or fall on the basis of his whims. Some, like Kulik, seemed to prosper on the basis of service with the dictator in the long forgotten defense of Tsaritsyn, others managed to develop a reputation for reliability during the severe early days of the war. But there were limits for even the most proven of this group—witness Zhukov. And, there was a large group for whom there was zero tolerance for failure. Yes, one would agree that the system that brought victory to the Soviet Union in World War II should not be forgotten. It should not be forgotten in order that it never be repeated—a codicil that could probably find some 27,000,000 supporters. To them we can with deepest respect say—

*Tsarstvo Vam nebesnoe, khrabrim soldatam Rossii!*

# BIBLIOGRAPHY

**Books in English**

Akhmedov, Ismail. *In and Out of Stalin's GRU: A Tatar's Escape from Red Army Intelligence.* Frederick, MD: University Publications of America, 1984

Bidwell, Bruce W. *History of the Military Intelligence Division. Department of the Army General Staff: 1775–1941.* Frederick, MD: University Publications of America, 1986.

Bonch-Bruyevich. *From Tsarist General to Red Army Commander.* Moscow: Progress, 1966.

Conquest, Robert. *The Great Terror: A Reassessment.* New York: Oxford University Press, 1990.

Davies, Norman. *White Eagle, Red Star.* New York: St. Martin's Press, 1972.

Deutscher, Isaac. *Stalin: A Political Biography.* New York: Oxford University Press, 1949.

DeWeerd, Harvey A. *President Wilson Fights His War.* New York: Macmillan, 1968.

Erickson, John. *The Soviet High Command.* New York: St. Martin's Press, 1962.

Feferman, Anita Burdman. *Politics, Logic, and Love.* Wellesley, Mass.: A. K. Peters, 1993.

Fischer, Louis. *The Soviets in World Affairs.* Princeton: Princeton University Press, 1951.

Goerlitz, Walter. *History of the German General Staff 1657–1945.* New York: Praeger 1953.

Hilger, Gustav and Alfred G. Meyer. *The Incompatible Allies.* New York: Macmillan, 1953.

Irving, David. *Hitler's War.* New York: Avon Books, 1990.

Kennan, George F. *Russia Leaves the War.* Vol. 1, *The Decision to Intervene.* Vol. 2. New York: Atheneum, 1967.

Lincoln, W. Bruce. *The Conquest of a Continent: Siberia and the Russians.* New York: Random House, 1994.

Luckett, Richard. *The White Generals.* New York: Routledge and Kegan Paul, 1971.

Manstein, Erich von. *Lost Victories.* Novato, Calif.: Presidio Press, 1982.

Mawdsley, Evan. *The Russian Civil War.* Boston: Allen & Unwin, 1987.

Medvedev, Roy A. *Let History Judge.* New York: Knopf, 1972.

Payne, Robert. *The Life and Death of Trotsky.* New York: McGraw Hill, 1977.

Pershing, John J. *My Experiences in the World War.* 2 vols. New York: Stokes, 1931.

Rapoport, Vitaly and Yury Alexeev. *High Treason.* Durham N. C.: Duke University Press, 1985.

Reese, Roger R. *Stalin's Reluctant Soldiers: A Social History of the Red Army 1925–1941.* Lawrence, Kansas: University Press of Kansas, 1996.

Seaton, Albert. *The Horsemen of the Steppes.* London: The Bodley Head, 1985.

Shukman, Harold, ed. *Stalin's Generals.* New York: Grove Press, 1993.

Steenberg, Sven. *Vlasov.* New York: Knopf, 1970.

Stone, Norman. *The Eastern Front 1914–1917.* New York: Charles Scribner's Sons, 1975.

Tanner, Väinö. *The Winter War.* Stanford, Calif.: Stanford University Press, 1992.

Thomas, Hugh. *The Spanish Civil War.* New York: Harper and Row, 1977.

Trotsky, Leon. *My Life.* New York: Grosset and Dunlap, 1960.

Ulam, Adam B. *Stalin: The Man and His Era.* New York: Viking, 1973.

Wandycz, Piotr S. *Soviet-Polish Relations 1917–1921.* Cambridge: Harvard University Press, 1969.

Wheeler-Bennett, John W. *Brest–Litovsk: The Forgotten Peace, March 1918.* London: Macmillan, 1938.

Wildman, Allan K. *The End of the Russian Imperial Army.* 2 vols. Princeton, N. J.: Princeton University Press, 1980, 1987.

Wolfe, Bertram D. *Three Who Made a Revolution.* New York: Dial, 1948.

**Books in Russian**

Akshinskii, V. S. *Kliment Efremovich Voroshilov: Biograficheskii Ocherk* (Kliment Efremovich Voroshilov: Biographic Outline). 2d ed. Moscow: Politizdat, 1976.

Azovtsev, N. N. *Grazhdanskaia voina v SSSR* (The Civil War in the USSR). 2 vols. Moscow: Voenizdat, Vol. 1, 1980; Vol. 2, 1986.

Berkhin, I. B. *Voennaia reforma v SSSR 1924–1925gg* (Military Reform in the USSR, 1924–1925). Moscow: Voenizdat, 1958.

Buchin, A. N. *170,000 Kilometrov S. G. K. Zhukovym* (170,000 Kilometers With G. K. Zhukov). Moscow: Molodaia Gvardiia, 1994.

Budenny, S. M. *Proidenniy Put'* (The Path Travelled). Bk. 1. Moscow: Voenizdat, 1958.

Dushen'kin, Vasilii Vasilevich. *Ot soldata do marshala* (From a Soldier to a Marshal). 3d ed. Moscow: Politizdat, 1966.

―――. *Proletarskii marshal* (The Proletarian Marshal). Moscow: Politizdat, 1973.

Egorov, A. I. *Razgrom Denikina 1919* (The Defeat of Denikin, 1919). Moscow: Voenizdat, 1931.

Eimansberger, Ludwig von. *Tankovaia voina* (Tank Warfare). Translated from the German, 3d ed. Moscow: Voenizdat, 1937.

*Entsiklopedicheskii slovar'* (The Encyclopedic Dictionary). 41 vols. St. Petersburg: Brokgaus & Efron, 1891.

Eremenko, A. I. *V nachale voiny* (In the Beginning of the War). Moscow: Nauka, 1964.

Frenkin, Mikhail Samuilovich. *Russkaia Armiia i revoliutsiia 1917–1918* (The Russian Army and the Revolution 1917–1918). Munich: Logos, 1978.

Golikov, F. I. *V Moskovskoi bitve* (In the Moscow Battle). Moscow: Nauka, 1967.

Gor'kov, Iurii. *Kreml', stavka, genshtab* (The Kremlin, the Stavka, the General Staff). Tver: Antek, 1995.

Grabin, Vasilii Gavrilovich. *Oruzhie pobedy* (The Weapons of Victory). Moscow: Politizdat, 1989.

Iakovlev, N. N. *Sud'ba polkovodtsa: Zhukov, Makartur, Rommel'* (The fate of a Great Captain: Zhukov, MacArthur, Rommel). Moscow: Prosveshchenie, 1995.

Ivanov, S. P. *Shtab armeiskii shtab frontovoi* (Army Staff Front Staff). Moscow: Voenizdat, 1990.

Ivanov, V. M. *Marshal M. N. Tukhachevsky*. Moscow: Voenizdat, 1990.

Kakurin, N. E. and V. A. Melikov. *Voina s Belopoliakami 1920g* (The War With the White Poles, 1920). Moscow: Voenizdat, 1925.

Kardashov, V. *Voroshilov.* Moscow: Molodaia Gvardiia, 1976.

Khromov, S. S., ch. ed. *Grazhdanskaia voina i voennaia interventsiia v SSSR* (The Civil War and Military Intervention in the USSR). Moscow: Sovetskaia Entsiklopediia, 1983.

Korablev, Iurii Ivanovich. *V. I. Lenin i sozdanie Krasnoi Armii* (V. I. Lenin and the Establishment of the Red Army). Moscow: Nauka, 1970.

Krivosheev, G. F., ed. *Grif sekretnosti sniat* (The Stamp of Secrecy Has Been Removed). Moscow: Voenizdat, 1993.

Kulikov, V. G., ed. *Akademiia General'nogo Shtaba* (Academy of the General Staff). Moscow: Voenizdat, 1976.

Kuznetsov, N. G. *Nakanune* (On the eve). Moscow: Voenizdat, 1966.

Meretskov, Kirill Afanas'evich. *Na sluzhbe narodu* (In Service to the People). Moscow: Politizdat, 1970.

Mirkina, A. D. and V. S. Iarovikov. *Marshal Zhukov: polkovodets i chelovek* (Marshal Zhukov: Great Captain and Man). 2 vols. Moscow: Novosti, 1988.

Mukhoperets, I. "Aleksandr Egorov" in *Polkovodtsi Grazhdanskoi Voiny* (Great Captains of the Civil War). Moscow: Molodaia Gvardiia, 1969.

Naida, S. F. et al, *Istoriia grazhdanskoi voiny v SSSR* (History of the Civil War in the USSR). 5 vols. Moscow: Politizdat, Vol. 3, 1957; Vol. 4, 1959; Vol. 5, 1960.

Nenarokov, A. *Vernost' dolgu* (Faithful to Duty). Moscow: Politizdat, 1973.

Nikulin, Lev. *Tukhachevsky.* Moscow: Voenizdat, 1964.

Ortenberg, David. *Stalin, Shcherbakov, Mekhlis i drugie.* (Stalin, Shcherbakov, Mekhlis and others). Moscow: MP "Kodeks," 1995.

Osipov, I., ed. *XX let raboche-krest'ianskoi Krasnoi Armii i Voenno-morskogo Flota* (20 years of the Workers-Peasants Red Army and Fleet). Leningrad: Lenpolitizdat, 1938.

Petrov, Iurii P. *Stroitel'stvo politorganov partiinykh i Komsomol'skikh organiztsii armii i flota* (The Structuring of Party and Komsomol Organizations of the Army and the Fleet). Moscow: Voenizdat, 1968.

———.*Partiinoe stroitel'stvo v Sovetskoi armii i flote (1918–1961).* (Party Structuring in the Soviet Army and Fleet 1918–1961). Moscow: Voenizdat 1964.

Plotnikov, Ivan Fedorovich. *Deciat' tysiach geroev* (Ten Thousand Heroes). Moscow: Nauka, 1967.

Portugal'skii, R. M., A. S. Domank, A. P. Kovalenko. *Marshal Semen Timoshenko*. Moscow: MOF "Pobeda 1945 god," 1994.

Pospelov, P. N., chmn. ed. comm. *Istoriia Velikoi Otechestvennoi Voiny Sovetskogo Soiuza 1941–1945* (The History of the Great Fatherland War of the Soviet Union 1941–1945). 6 vols. Moscow: Voenizdat, 1961–1965.

Rakovskii, Leontii. *Mikhail Tukhachevsky*. Leningrad: Lenizdat, 1967.

Rokossovsky, K. K. *Soldatskii dolg* (A Soldier's Duty). Moscow: Voenizdat, 1988.

Sandalov, L. M. *Perezhitoe* (Past Experiences). Moscow: Voenizdat, 1966.

———. *Na Moskovskom napravloenii* (On the Moscow Axis). Moscow: Nauka, 1970.

Shaposhnikov, Boris Mikhailovich. *Mozg armii* (The Brain of the Army). Vol. 1, Moscow: Voennyi Vestnik, 1927; Moscow, Leningrad: Gosizdat, Vol. 2 and 3, 1929.

———. *Na Visle* (On the Vistula). Moscow: Voenizdat, 1924.

———. *Vospominaniia—Voenno-nauchnye trudy* (Recollections—Military-scientific works). Moscow: Voenizdat, 1974.

Shchetinov, Iurii A. and Boris A. Starkov, *Krasnyi marshal* (The Red Marshal). Moscow: Molodaia Gvardiia, 1990.

Shtemenko, C. M. *General'nyi shtab v gody voiny* (The General Staff in the War Years). Moscow: Voenizdat, 1968; bk. 2, Moscow: Voenizdat, 1975.

*Sovetskaia voennaia entsiklopediia* (The Soviet Military Encyclopedia). 8 vols. Moscow: Novosti, 1989.

Stadniuk, Ivan. *Voina* (War). Moscow: Voenizdat, 1981.

Sverdlov, F. D. *Neizvestnoe o Sovetskikh polkovodtsakh* (The Unknown About Soviet Great Captains). Moscow: Biograficheskii Club, 1995.

Triandafillov, V. K. *Kharakter operatsii sovremennykh armii* (The Character of the Operations of Contemporary Armies). 3d ed. Moscow: Voenizdat, 1936.

Trotsky, Lev Davidovich. *Materialy i dokumenty po istorii Krasnoi Armii* (Materials and Documents on the History of the Red Army). 3 vols. *Kak vooruzhalas' revoliutsiia* (How the Revolution Was Armed). Vol.

1, 1923; vol. 2, bk.1, 1924; vol. 2, bk. 2, 1924; vol. 3, bk. 1, 1924; vol. 3, bk. 2, 1925. Moscow: The Supreme Military Editorial Commission.

Tukhachevsky, M. N. *Voina klassov* (The War of the Classes). Moscow: State Publishing House, 1921.

———. *Izbrannye Proizvedeniia* 2 vols. Moscow: Voenizdat, 1964.

Vasilevsky, A. M. *Delo vsei zhizni* (The Matter of an Entire Lifetime). Moscow: Politizdat, 1973.

Volkogonov, Dmitri A. *Lenin*. 2 books. Moscow: Novosti, 1994.

———. *Trotskii: Politicheskii portret* (Trotsky: a Political Portrait). 2 books. Moscow: Novosti, 1992.

———. *Triumf i tragediia: Politicheskii portret I. V. Stalina* (Triumph and Tragedy: A Political Portrait of J. V. Stalin). 2 books, 4 parts. Moscow: Novosti, 1989.

Voroshilov, Kliment E. *Rasskazy o zhizni* (Tales of a Life). 1st book. Moscow: Politizdat, 1971.

———. *Stalin i Krasnaia Armiia* (Stalin and the Red Army). Moscow: Partizdat, 1937.

Zakharov, M. V. *Uchenyi i voin* (Savant and Warrior). 2d ed., Moscow: Politizdat, 1978.

———. *General'nyi shtab v predvoennye gody* (The General Staff in the Prewar Years). Moscow: Voenizdat, 1989.

———. *50 let vooruzhennykh sil SSSR* (50 Years of the Armed Forces of the USSR). Moscow: Voenizdat 1968.

Zhukov, Georgii Konstantinovich, *Vospominaniia i razmyshleniia* (Reminiscences and Reflections). 10th ed. 3 vols. 1990.

Zhukovy, Era i Ella. *Marshal Pobedy* (Marshal of Victory). Moscow: Voenizdat, 1996.

### Book in French
Pilsudski, Jozef. *L'Année 1920* (The Year 1920). Translated from the Polish by Lt. Col. C. Jezc and Commandant J.-A.Teslar. Paris: La Renaissance du Livre, 1929.

### Book in German
Teske, Hermann. *Profile bedeutender Soldaten-Band 1-General Ernst Kostring,* (Profiles of Important Soldiers-volume 1-Ernst Kostring). Frankfurt am Main: E. S. Mittler, n.d.

**Articles in English**

Mamsurova, Lida. "The First Days of the War." *Moscow News*, no. 29, 17 July 1988.

Roberts, Cynthia A. "Planning for War: The Red Army and the Catastrophe of 1941." *Europe-Asia Studies*, vol. 47, no. 8, 1995.

Tarleton, Robert E. "The Life and Fate of the Stalin Line 1926–1941." Unpublished seminar paper submitted to Professor Donald W. Treadgold, University of Washington, June 1991.

Van Dyke, Carl. "The Timoshenko Reforms: March–July 1940." *The Journal of Slavic Military Studies*, vol. 9, no. 1, March 1996.

**Articles in Russian**

Anonymous. "Delo no. R-24000 generala Pavlova Dmitriia Grigorievicha" (Case no. R-24000 of General Pavlov Dmitrii Grigorievich) *Kommunist Vooruzhennykh Sil* nos. 8, 9, 11, 13, 14, 1991.

"AKT o prieme Narkomata Oborony Soiuza SSR tov. Timoshenko, S. K., ot tov. Voroshilova, K. E." (An Act on the Assumption of the Commissariat of Defense of the Union of the SSR com[rade] Timoshenko from com[rade] Voroshilov). *Izvestiia Tsk KPSS*, no. 1, 1990.

Anfilov, V. "U Zhukova v Sosnovke" (With Zhukov at Sosnovka). *Krasnaia Zvezda*, 24 April 1992.

———. "My uchilis' v khode voiny" (We Learned in the Course of the War). *Krasnaia Zvezda*, 6 April 1996.

Bliukher, Glafira. "S Vasiliem Konstantinovichem Bliukherom-shest' let" (With Vasily Konstantinovich Bliukher Six Years). *Voenno-istoricheskii Zhurnal*, nos. 3, 4, 5, 6, 1989.

Bobrenev, V., and V. Riazantsev. "Marshal protiv marshala" (Marshal Against Marshal). *Armiia*, nos. 8, 9, 10, 1993.

Chernov, Iu. "General-polkovnik F. I. Kuznetsov" (General Colonel F. I. Kuznetsov). *Voenno-istoricheskii Zhurnal*, no. 9, 1968.

Daines, V. "Pervye marshaly: Vasilii Konstantinovich Bliukher" (The First Marshals: Vasily KonstantinovichBliukher). *Sovetskii Voin*, no. 1, 1985.

———. "'Taina gibeli marshala Bliukhera" (The "Secret" of the Death of Marshal Bliukher). *Argumenty i Fakty*, nos. 46, 47, November 1992.

Danilov, V. D. "Klim Voroshilov: Portret pri svete pravdy" (Klim

Voroshilov: A Portrait in the Light of Truth). *Komsomol'skaia Pravda,* 12 February 1989.

———. "Ot shtaba RKKA k General'nomy shtaby Raboche-Krest'ianskoi Krasnoi Armii (1924–1935)" (From the Staff of the RKKA to the General Staff of the Workers-Peasants Red Army [1924–1935]). *Voenno-istoricheskii Zhurnal,* no. 8, 1978.

Golikov, F. I. "My raspolagaem samymi luchimi kadrami" (We Have the Very Best Cadres). *Istochnik* no. 2, 1996.

Golubev, A. "Pervaia Konnaia na Pol'skom fronte" (The First Cavalry on the Polish Front). *Voenno-istoricheskii Zhurnal,* no. 8, 1966.

Gorokhov A. "'Zagovor' v Krasnoi armii" (A "Plot" in the Red Army). *Pravda,* 29 April 1988.

Isserson, G. "Razvitie theorii sovetskogo operativnogo iskustva v 30-e gody" (The Development of Soviet Operational Art in the 30s). *Voenno-istoricheskii Zhurnal,* no. 1, and no. 3, 1965.

Kabakov, M. "Kliment Voroshilov: fenomen slavy" (Kliment Voroshilov: Phenomenon of Glory). *Soviet Patriot,* 17 May 1989.

Kalinovskii, P. "Iz istorii voenno-ekonomicheskii rabotii shtaba RKKA" (From the History of Military-Economic Work of the Staff RKKA). *Voenno-istoricheskii Zhurnal,* no. 5, 1972.

Karpov, Vladimir. "Marshal Zhukov, ego soratniki i protivniki v gody voiny i mira" (Marshal Zhukov, His Comrades in Arms and Opponents in the Years of War and Peace). *Znamia,* nos. 9, 10, and 11, 1989.

Khorev, Aleksei. "Marshal Tukhachevsky". *Krasnaia Zvezda,* 4 June 1988.

———. "Boites' ravnodushnykh" (Fear the Indifferent Ones). *Krasnaia Zvezda,* 4 September 1991.

———. "Kak sudili Tukhachevskogo" (How They Tried Tukhachevsky). *Krasnaia Zvezda,* 17 April 1991.

———. "Sud'ia Ul'rikh" (Judge Ul'rikh). *Krasnaia Zvezda,* 8 April 1989.

———. "Kar'era komissara" (The Career of the Commissar) *Krasnaia Zvezda,* 16 November 1991).

———. "General Kirponos" *Krasnaia Zvezda,* 8 July 1995.

Khor'kov, Antolii. "Ten' na Marshala Zhukova" (A Shadow Is Cast on Marshal Zhukov). *Pravda,* 16 January 1992.

————. "Ukreplennye raiony na zapadnykh granitsakh SSSR" (Fortified Areas on the Western Borders of the USSR). *Voenno-istoricheskii Zhurnal*, no 12. 1987.

Komitet partinogo kontrolia. "Delo o tak nazyvaemoi 'antisovetskoi Trotskistka voennoi organizatsii' v Krasnoi Armii" (The Case of the So-called "Antisoviet Trotskyite Military Organization" in the Red Army). *Izvestiia Tsk KPSS*, no. 4, 1989.

Kopylov, N. Ia. "K biografii Marshala Sovetskogo Soiuza A. I. Egorova" (To a Biography of Marshal of the Soviet Union A. I. Egorov). *Istoricheskii Arkhiv*, no. 1, 1962.

Kumanev, G. A. "Voina glazami nachal'nika Genshtaba" (War in the Eyes of the Chief of the Gen[eral] Staff). *Pravda*, 28 September 1995.

Kuz'min, N. "Ob odnoi nevypolnnoi direktiva Glavkoma" (On one unexecuted directive of the CINC). *Voenno-istoricheskii Zhurnal*, no. 9, September 1962.

Kvartadze, A. "Iunskoe nastuplenie Russkoi Armii v 1917g" (The June Offensive of the Russian Army in 1917). *Voenno-istoricheskii Zhurnal*, no. 5, 1967.

Meretskov, Kirill Afanas'evich. "Na Volkovskikh rubezhax" (On the Volkhov Firing Line). *Voenno-istoricheskii Zhurnal*, no. 1, 1965.

Moiseev, M. "Smena rukovodstva Narkomata oborony SSSR v svazi s yrokami covetsko-finlandskoi voiny 1939–1940 gg" (The Change in the Leadership on the Comissariat of Defense in Connection With the Lessons of the Soviet-Finnish War 1939–1940). *Izvestiia TsK KPSS*, no 1, 1990.

Murav'eva, Inna. "Voina s sobstvennym narodom" (War With Your Own People). *Rossiiskaia Gazeta*, 22 October 1992.

Nikiforov, N. I. "Voroshilov-Tukhachevsky". *Voennaia istoriia i konfliktologia* in *Geopolitika i Bezopastnost'*, June 1993.

Pal'chikov, P. and A. Goncharov. "Izmeny ia ne sovershil" (I Did Not Commit Treason). *Voennoe Znanie*, no. 11, 1991.

Popov, A. "Iz istorii sozdaniia Revvoensoveta Respubliki" (From the History of the Formation of the Revolutionary Military Council of the Republic). *Voenno-istoricheskii Zhurnal*, no. 2, 1967.

Ramanichev, N. "Shaposhnikov". *Kommunist Voorvzhennykh Sil*, no. 16, August 1990.

Ryzhakov, A. Col. "K voprosu o stroitel'stve bronetankovykh voisk Krasnoi Armii v 30-gody" (On the Question of the Structuring of Armored Troops of the Red Army in the 1930's). *Voenno-istoricheskii Zhurnal*, no. 8, 1968.

Sharov, A. and L. Vlodavets, "I eshche paz o Bliukhere" (And Once Again About Bliukher). *Voennoe Znanie*, no. 8, 1993.

Siderov, Nikolai. "I pervyi Marshal v Boi Nas Povedet" (And the First Marshal Will Lead Us Into Battle). *Istochnik*, no. 5, 1995.

Simonov, Konstantin. "Besedy s Admiralom Flota Sovetskogo Soiuza I. S. Isakovym" (Conversations With Admiral of the Fleet of the Soviet Union I. S. Isakov). *Znamia*, no. 5, 1988.

————. "Zametki k biografii G. K. Zhukova" (Notes to a Biography of G. K. Zhukov). *Voenno-istoricheskii Zhurnal*, no. 6, 1987.

Skuratov, A. "Zagovor voennykh" (The Plot of the Military).*Situatsiia*, no.3 (11) 1991.

Smetanin, A. "Nachgenshtab Egorov" (Chief of the General Staff Egorov). *Krasnaia Zvezda*, 7 October 1989.

Todorskii, A. "Razmyshleniia nad prochitannymi memuarami" (Thoughts Over Perused Memoirs). *Voenno-istoricheskii Zhurnal*, no. 12, 1962.

Vaksberg, Arkadii. "Taina Oktiabria 1941-go" (The Secret of October 1941). *Literaturnaia Gazeta*, 20 April 1988.

Vannikov, Boris L'vovich. "Iz zapisok Narkoma voorvzheniia" (From the Notes of the People's Commissar of Armaments). *Voenno-istoricheskii Zhurnal*, no. 2, 1962.

Viktorov, Boris. "Zagovor v Krasnoi Armii" (A Plot in the Red Army). *Pravda*, 29 April 1988.

Zavalishin, N. "Vstrechi s Marshalom Egorovym" (Meetings with Marshal Egorov). *Voenno-istoricheskii Zhurnal*, no. 11, 1963.

Zakharov, M. V. "Nakanune vtoroi mirovoi voiny"(On the Eve of the Second World War). *Novaia i noveishaia istoriia*, no. 5, 1970.

————. "Kommunisticheskaia partiia i tekhnicheskoe perevooryzhenie armii i flota v gody predvoennikh piatiletok"(The Communist Party and the Technical Rearmament of the Army and the Fleet in the Years of the Prewar Five Year Plans). *Voenno-istoricheskii Zhurnal*, no. 2 1971.

**Public Documents in English**

Faymonville, Philip R. Report no. D 43 1934 to the War Department
in the National Archives, Washington T1249 Roll 23.

U. S. Embassy, Moscow telegrams nos. 113 and 114, June 11, 1937,
National Archives, Washington T1249 Roll 23.

# Index

# Index